BRIDGES 2

Englisch für die Erwachsenenbildung

Classroom Book

von
Bruce Pye und Geoff Tranter

in Zusammenarbeit mit
Linda Gallasch

Ernst Klett Verlag für Wissen und Bildung
Stuttgart · Dresden

BRIDGES 2
Classroom Book

von

BRUCE PYE, Fachbereichsleiter Englisch an der Volkshochschule Nürnberg

GEOFF TRANTER, Abteilungsleiter für abschluß-bezogene Bildung an der Volkshochschule Dortmund, Landesbeauftragter für das ICC-VHS English Certificate in Nordrhein-Westfalen

in Zusammenarbeit mit

DR. LINDA GALLASCH, Fachbereichsleiterin Fremdsprachen an der Volkshochschule Norderstedt

Phonetikübungen:

Jonathan Marks, Gdańsk, Polen

Wortschatz:

Axel Ruland und Peter Bereza, Aachen

Illustrationen:

Ulrike Müller, Heidelberg

Einbandgestaltung:

Hanjo Schmidt, Stuttgart

Gedruckt auf Papier aus chlorfrei gebleichtem Zellstoff, säurefrei und ohne optische Aufheller.

1. Auflage   1 4 3 2 1 | 1997 96 95 94

Alle Drucke dieser Auflage können im Unterricht nebeneinander benutzt werden. Die letzte Zahl bezeichnet das Jahr dieses Druckes.

Druck: Repro-Druck, Fellbach.
Printed in Germany.
ISBN 3-12-501420-4

© Ernst Klett Verlag für Wissen und Bildung GmbH, Stuttgart 1994.
Alle Rechte vorbehalten.

REDAKTION:
Heinke Behal-Thomsen (Projektleitung),
David Shallis, Edda Vorrath-Wiesenthal
LAYOUT:
Luise Vollnhals

INHALT

UNIT CONTENTS		5
UNIT 0		9
UNIT 1	Meeting people	11
UNIT 2	Appearances	18
UNIT 3	Be my guest	25
PREVIEW A		33
UNIT 4	Around the house	35
UNIT 5	Body and soul	43
UNIT 6	Holidays	50
PREVIEW B		58
UNIT 7	Jobs	60
UNIT 8	Eat, drink and be merry	68
UNIT 9	Clothes	76
PREVIEW C		83
UNIT 10	Home and health	84
UNIT 11	Families	91
UNIT 12	On the road again	98
PREVIEW D		106
UNIT 13	Shopping	108
UNIT 14	Information and entertainment	118
UNIT 15	English and me	124
PREVIEW E		131
FILES		134
LANGUAGE SUMMARIES		140
LANGUAGE FUNCTIONS		157
GRAMMAR		162
	Irregular verbs	182
VOCABULARY		184
	Phonetic alphabet	184
	Unit vocabulary	184
	Personal and place names	224
	Alphabetical word list	226
TAPESCRIPTS		235

Symbole

- Cassette/CD
- Überprüfen Sie mit Hilfe der Cassette/CD
- Musik/Lied
- Partnerarbeit
- Gruppenarbeit
- Notieren Sie
- Rollenspiel

Vorwort

Liebe Kursteilnehmer/innen!

BRIDGES 2 ist der zweite Band eines dreibändigen Lehrwerks für Erwachsene aller Altersstufen, die wie Sie gemeinsam mit anderen die englische Sprache systematisch und zielgerichtet erlernen möchten und dabei auch auf Abwechslung, Spaß und persönliche Horizonterweiterung Wert legen.

BRIDGES 2 hilft Ihnen durch seine sorgfältig abgestufte Folge von Aktivitäten, Texten und Übungen, Ihre Grundkenntnisse des Englischen als internationaler Verkehrssprache – und zwar unabhängig davon, ob Sie vorher mit **BRIDGES 1** oder einem anderen Lehrwerk gearbeitet haben – Schritt für Schritt auszubauen, zu vertiefen und abzurunden.

Am Ende von **BRIDGES 2** können Sie eine große Zahl unterschiedlicher Kommunikationssituationen sicher auf englisch bewältigen und haben einen Kenntnisstand erreicht, der den Richtlinien für den Grundbaustein Englisch voll entspricht.

Grundlage des Kursunterrichts mit **BRIDGES 2** ist das vorliegende **Classroom Book**. Es beginnt mit einem kurzen Einstiegs- und Wiederholungskapitel (UNIT 0) und gliedert sich im folgenden in fünf Blöcke von je drei regulären UNITS und einem kürzeren Zwischenkapitel, PREVIEW genannt, weil es neben einer Wiederholung der vorangegangenen UNITS immer auch eine Vorschau auf den nächsten Block enthält.

Die 15 regulären UNITS präsentieren und üben den Lernstoff in einer auf das jeweilige Thema abgestimmten Folge von 10 – 13 Schritten, die durchnumeriert sind und im Unterricht in der Regel der Reihe nach behandelt werden. Arbeitsanweisungen, Symbole und zum Teil auch Zeichnungen zeigen Ihnen an, was jeweils gemacht werden soll. Die Aussprache- und Intonationsübungen sind immer am Ende einer UNIT zu finden.

Alle UNITS sind einsprachig englisch gehalten. Deutsche Übersetzungen aller Wörter und Wendungen, die zum Verständnis und zur Durchführung der Aufgaben in **BRIDGES 2** nötig sind, finden Sie im Kapitel-Wörterverzeichnis im Anhang dieses Buchs.

Für Ihren Lernerfolg ist es wichtig, daß Sie sich auch mit allen anderen Bestandteilen vom **Classroom Book** vertraut machen, die im Inhaltsverzeichnis auf Seite 3 aufgeführt sind.

Darüber hinaus können Ihnen das **Practice Book** und die **Tonmaterialien** zu **BRIDGES 2** (siehe Werkübersicht auf Seite 253) dabei helfen, Ihr Ziel zu erreichen:

Building BRIDGES of understanding!

Viel Erfolg wünscht Ihnen

Ihr **BRIDGES**-Team

Unit Contents
Hauptinhalte der Kapitel

Unit 0

Einstiegskapitel; gegenseitiges Kennenlernen und Kurzwiederholung ausgewählter Inhalte von BRIDGES 1

Unit 1 · Meeting people

Themen/Situationen/Texte
Begrüßungsformen, z.B. Händeschütteln; Small Talk; Gesprächsthemen; Regeln für Parties

Sprechabsichten
auf Vorstellung reagieren; jmdn. grüßen; sich verabschieden; gute Wünsche äußern; sich bedanken; auf Entschuldigung reagieren; ein Gespräch einleiten; ein Beispiel geben; benennen/definieren; etwas anbieten; Nichtzustimmung ausdrücken; einen Rat geben, von etwas abraten; sagen, daß etwas (nicht) erlaubt/notwendig ist

Grammatik
Modalverben: *can/can't, should/shouldn't, have to/don't have to*
Sätze ohne bezügliche Fürwörter
Unbestimmte Fürwörter: *some, someone/somebody, something – any, anyone/anybody, anything*

Aussprache/Intonation
Satzbetonung; steigende und fallende Satzmelodien

Unit 2 · Appearances

Themen/Situationen/Texte
Aussehen; Familienähnlichkeiten; Personenbeschreibungen; persönliche Eigenschaften; Kontaktanzeigen; Veränderungen; Witz und Weisheit

Sprechabsichten
benennen/definieren; zustimmen

Grammatik
Bezügliche Fürwörter: *who/that, which/that*
Unbestimmte Fürwörter: *both/all*
Eigenschaftswörter: Steigerungsform *-er*
Vergleiche: *-er than, (not) as ... as, the same as*
Verstärkende bzw. abschwächende Umstandswörter: *a bit, too, (not) really, average, quite*
Umstandswörter: *not ... either; too*

Aussprache/Intonation
Lautdiskriminierung; Satzbetonung

Unit 3 · Be my guest

Themen/Situationen/Texte
Gäste: ideale, schwierige etc.; Gastgeberprobleme; Pläne; Gedichte: Haikus; (un)gewöhnliche Besichtigungen und Besuchsprogramme

Sprechabsichten
eine ausweichende Antwort geben; etwas/Hilfe anbieten; Wichtigkeit ausdrücken; zustimmen; einen Vorschlag machen/annehmen/ablehnen; um Erlaubnis bitten; sagen, daß etwas notwendig ist

Grammatik
Zukunftsformen: *going to*
Modalverben: *shall ...?, had to, should, couldn't*
Rückbezügliche Fürwörter: *myself, himself, herself, ourselves, themselves*
Mengenangaben: *all/not many/none/neither of them*

Aussprache/Intonation
starke und schwache Formen; stumme Buchstaben

Preview A

Wiederholung von Block 1 und Vorschau auf Block 2

Unit 4 · Around the house

Themen/Situationen/Texte
In der Küche; Schaufenster; Elektrogeräte; Lebensstile in Europa; Erfindungen und ihre Ergebnisse; Alltagsgeschichte aus dem Waschsalon; Einbrecher; Kriminalgeschichten

Sprechabsichten
eine ausweichende Antwort geben; benennen/definieren; (nicht) zustimmen; Überraschung ausdrücken

Grammatik
Zeitformen: Present Perfect Simple
Kurzantworten: *So have/do I. – Nor have/would/do I.*
Eigenschaftswörter: Steigerung (Superlativ): *the most/least*
Umstandsbestimmungen des Ortes: *at the back/front, on the left/right, in the middle*

Aussprache/Intonation
Wortbetonung; Satzbetonung; fallende und fallend-steigende Satzmelodien

Unit 5 · Body and soul

Themen/Situationen/Texte
Gefühle; gute und schlechte Nachrichten; interkulturell unterschiedliche Gefühlsreaktionen; Körperteile; Gymnastikübung; persönliche Gesundheits- bzw. Krankengeschichten

Sprechabsichten
Glückwünsche aussprechen; Sorgen/Hoffnung/Freude/Traurigkeit/Mitleid/Ärger ausdrücken

Grammatik
Aufforderungssätze: *Be happy. – Don't worry.*
Zeitformen: Present Perfect Simple + *for – since*
Die „*-ing*"-Form als Hauptwort
Indirekte Rede: Aussagen

Aussprache/Intonation
Silbenbetonung; Aussprache des Buchstaben ‚g'; fallende und fallend-steigende Satzmelodien

Unit 6 · Holidays

Themen/Situationen/Texte
Europäische Ferienziele im Vergleich; persönliche Reiseziele und Aufenthaltsorte; Ferienarten, Ferienwünsche; im Fremdenverkehrsbüro: Zimmersuche; Hotelbeschwerden; Reiseprobleme; Bericht über einen Katastrophenkongreß; Reisen: Pro und Kontra

Sprechabsichten
Äußerungen einleiten/strukturieren; versprechen, etwas zu tun; sagen, was einem nicht/besser gefällt; reklamieren/sich beschweren; Gelassenheit ausdrücken; eine Bitte äußern

Grammatik
Zeitformen: Present Perfect Simple vs. Past Simple
Die „*ing*"-Form: nach Zeitwörtern/Verhältniswörtern; als Hauptwort
Unbestimmte Fürwörter: *some/something/etc.* in Fragesätzen
Umstandswörter: *only* (Stellung im Satz)

Aussprache/Intonation
Lautdiskriminierung; Betonung in Wörtern und Wortgruppen

Preview B

Wiederholung von Block 2 und Vorschau auf Block 3

Unit 7 · Jobs

Themen/Situationen/Texte
Arbeit und Beruf; Berufserfahrungen, Berufsbilder, Berufswege; berufliche Aktivitäten; geschäftliche Telefongespräche; Telefonnotizen; Was ist Arbeit?; Zufriedenheit im Beruf

Sprechabsichten
eine ausweichende Antwort geben; Wünsche äußern; Telefonkonventionen

Grammatik
Gegenwartsformen: Present Continuous: aktuelle Handlungen; Present Simple vs. Continuous
Zukunftsformen: *will* und Kurzform *I'll*: Versprechungen
Umstandsbestimmungen der Zeit: *at one time, for a while, just now, at the moment*
Indirekte Rede
If-Sätze: Present Simple/Present Simple

Aussprache/Intonation
Intonation

Unit 8 · Eat, drink and be merry

Themen/Situationen/Texte
Essen und Trinken; Kochbücher und Rezepte; Zutaten und Zubereitung lokaler/regionaler Spezialitäten; Wochenendpläne, -verabredungen; Feste und Feiern; Glückwunschkarten; öffentliche und private Fest-, Feier- und Gedenktage

Sprechabsichten
gute Wünsche äußern; Komplimente machen; eine Einladung aussprechen/annehmen/ablehnen; ein Beispiel geben; benennen/definieren; sagen, daß etwas (nicht) erlaubt ist

Grammatik
Present Continuous: Verabredungen; nahe Zukunft
Bezügliche Fürwörter: *when*
Mengenangaben: *a pinch/tin of*
Grundzahlen: *a half, half a, one and a half*
Datum (schriftlich und gesprochen)
Umstandsbestimmungen der Zeit: *on Saturday, in the evening, on this day*
If-Sätze: Past Simple/Conditional

Aussprache/Intonation
Wortbetonungsmuster

Unit 9 · Clothes

Themen/Texte/Situationen
Kleidungsstücke; Farben; Mode für junge Leute; Geschichte der Jeans; Mode und Verschwendung; Wertgegenstände; Komplimente; Stoffe und andere Materialien

Sprechabsichten
Komplimente machen; auf Komplimente reagieren; benennen/definieren; zustimmen; vergleichen

Grammatik
Passivform: Vergangenheitsform
Hauptwörter: Mehrzahl/Einzahlformen: *a pair of, a piece of clothing, clothes*
Besitzanzeigende Fürwörter: *mine, yours, his, hers, theirs*
Bezügliche Fürwörter: *where*
Eigenschaftswörter: Steigerung: *the better ..., the happier .../the more ..., the more ...*

Aussprache/Intonation
Assimilation

Preview C

Wiederholung von Block 3 und Vorschau auf Block 4

Unit 10 · Home and health

Themen/Situationen/Texte
Zu Hause: Räume und Aktivitäten; Wasser- und Energieverbrauch in Privathaushalten früher und heute; Badezimmerutensilien und Toilettenartikel; Haushaltsgegenstände; Luxus; Katastrophen im Haushalt; Schmerzen, körperliche Beschwerden und Hausmittel, Tips dagegen

Sprechabsichten
Wünsche äußern; Überraschung ausdrücken; einen Rat geben; vergleichen

Grammatik
Vergangenheitsformen: Past Simple bei Wunschvorstellungen
Vergangenheitsformen: Past Continuous: unterbrochene Handlungen/Vorgänge
Unbestimmter Artikel: *I've got a headache*, aber: *I've got backache/toothache/etc.*
Eigenschaftswörter: Steigerung: *more/less*

Aussprache/Intonation
fallend-steigende Satzmelodien

Unit 11 · Families

Themen/Situationen/Texte
Persönliche Beziehungen; Zwillinge; Generationen; Familiengeschichte(n); Lebensphasen; Familienformen früher und heute; Familienmodelle in Europa; die Zukunft der Familie; Zukunftsaussichten/wünsche für ein Baby; Eltern und Kinder; Erziehung; Familienprobleme

Sprechabsichten
Hoffnung ausdrücken; Ratschläge geben

Grammatik
Bejahte und verneinte Aufforderungssätze
Zukunftsformen: *will/won't*: Hoffnungen, Vorhersagen
Modalverben: *will be able to*
Unbestimmte Fürwörter: *each, each other*
Mengenangaben: *more – fewer*

Aussprache/Intonation
Intonationsmuster

UNIT 12 · On the road again

Themen/Situationen/Texte
Transportmittel in Gegenwart und Vergangenheit; Was man beim Zugfahren alles tun kann; Verkehrsansagen; Fahrt- und Wegbeschreibungen; Geschichte des Reiseagenten Thomas Cook; Versicherungsmeldungen nach Verkehrsunfällen; Reiseerfahrungen

Sprechabsichten
eine Aussage strukturieren; Gewißheit/Ungewißheit ausdrücken; nach dem Weg fragen u. darauf reagieren

Grammatik
Vergangenheitsformen: Past Continuous vs. Past Simple
Modalverben: *might, will have to, was unable to*
Passiv/Modalverben: *will/won't/might be ...-ed*
Indirekte Fragen

Aussprache/Intonation
fallend-steigende und fallende Satzmelodien

PREVIEW D

Wiederholung von Block 4 und Vorschau auf Block 5

UNIT 13 · Shopping

Themen/Situationen/Texte
Einkaufsmöglichkeiten und Dienstleistungen; Kundenanliegen in Geschäften; Einkaufsumfrage; Einkaufsspiel; Gedächtnisspiel: Großeinkauf im Supermarkt; Gedicht über das Massen- bzw. Überangebot in Supermärkten; Kaufhäuser; Kundenservice im internationalen Vergleich

Sprechabsichten
Verkäufer/innen ansprechen; nach einer Meinung fragen; zustimmen; fragen, was einem gefällt; Unzufriedenheit ausdrücken/reklamieren; eine Bitte äußern; einen Rat erfragen

Grammatik
Passiv mit *get*: etwas machen lassen
Kurzantworten: *Neither have I.*
Hauptwörter, die nur in der Einzahl oder Mehrzahl vorkommen
If-Sätze: Conditional/Past Simple

Aussprache/Intonation
Satzbetonung

UNIT 14 · Information and entertainment

Themen/Situationen/Texte
Medien: Fernsehen und Zeitungen; Fernsehprogrammarten; Fernsehvorlieben in Europa; Planung eines eigenen Fernsehprogramms; Gefahren des Fernsehens für Kinder; Phantasiereise mit Musik; Musik: Arten, Aktivitäten, Instrumente, Spieler/innen, Vorlieben; BRIDGES Talentshow

Sprechabsichten
Gewißheit ausdrücken; fragen, was einem besser gefällt; sagen, was einem nicht gefällt; etwas vorschlagen; einen Gegenvorschlag machen; eine Handlung nach der Art und Weise einordnen

Grammatik
Modalverben: *may*
Bildung von Umstandswörtern: *-ly, in a ... way, fast*

Aussprache/Intonation
Schwa-Laut

UNIT 15 · English and me

Themen/Situationen/Texte
Englisch: Assoziationen, Meinungen, literarische Texte, Wortbilder, Wortspiele; Strategien bei Verständigungsschwierigkeiten am Telefon; Lieblingswörter; Geschichte der englischen Sprache; Sprachstrategien; Rätsel; Englisch überall, z.B. in der deutschen Sprache

Sprechabsichten
um eine Wiederholung bitten; Zeit gewinnen; umschreiben; widersprechen

Grammatik
Verneinte Fragen: *Don't/Wouldn't ...?*

Aussprache/Intonation
Diskussion über Fragen zur englischen Aussprache und Intonation

PREVIEW E

Wiederholung und Zusammenfassung des gesamten Lernstoffs von BRIDGES 2: Spiel, Kursprojekt, Diplom

UNIT 0

1 Getting to know each other

A Write three or four questions to ask your teacher.

"Have you got …?"   "Are you …?"   "Did you …?"   "Do you …?"   "Can you …?"

"What …?"   "When …?"   "Where …?"   "How …?"

B Compare questions and choose five. Ask your teacher.

C Now ask other people. Try to find something in common.

D Report to the class.

"We've both got two children."

"Brigitte and I (both) live in the same street."

"We both like Chinese food."

"Robert and I (both) get up at half past six."

2 A question of English

A Ask your partner some of these questions. Take notes.

Did you learn | English at school? Did you like it?
Are there any | English words you specially like?
Are there any | English words you don't like?
Do you need | English for holidays and travel? Where do you go?
Do you need | English for your job?
Have you got any | English-speaking friends or relatives? Where?
Do you watch any | English language TV programmes? Which ones?
Can you get | English books and magazines here? Which ones?
What's the easiest thing about | English?
What's the most difficult thing about | English?
Do you listen to | English songs?

B Report one or two things about your partner.

3 A to Z

Look at File 1 and play the game.

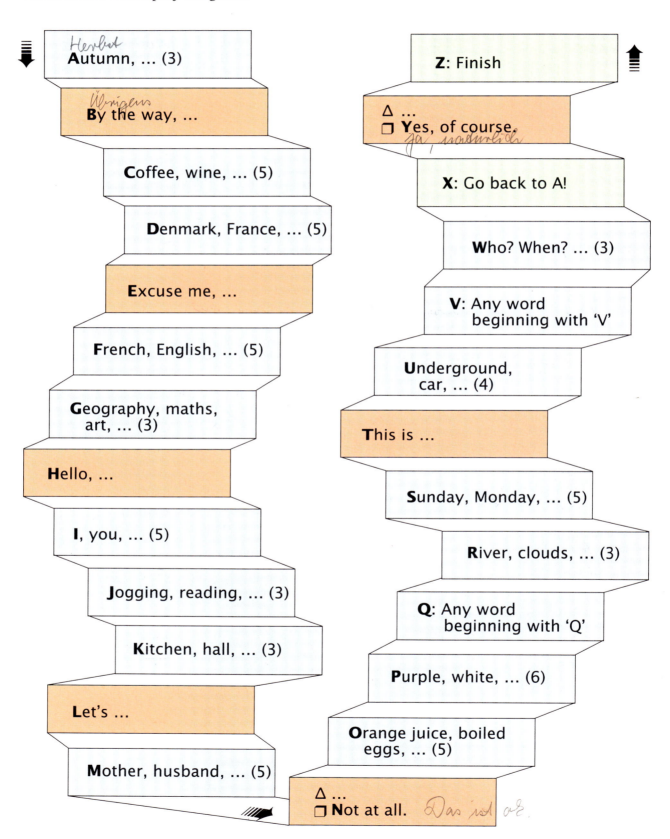

UNIT 1

Meeting people

1 Hello, goodbye

A Write down any 'hellos' and 'goodbyes' you know.

Hellos: *How any you, Welcome to, Hallo,*
Goodbyes: *By, By, See you later, see you next week*

B When do people use these phrases in conversations?

	At the beginning	At the end	Can't say
Did you have a good trip? *Reise*	X		
Don't forget to send a postcard!		X	
Don't worry! No problem. *Keine Sorgen*			X
Enjoy the rest of your trip!		X	
How are you? *Wie geht es Dir?*	X		
It's a lovely day, isn't it?	X		
It was great to be here. *Es war toll hier zu sein*		X	
It was nice to meet you.		X	
It was fine.		X	
Pleased to meet you. *Es hat mich gefreut, dich zu sehen.*	X		
Sorry I'm late.	X		
Thanks for everything.		X	

C Make two or three short dialogues including these phrases.

"*Goodbye.*"   "*It was nice to meet you.*"   "*It's a lovely day, isn't it?*"

"*Pleased to meet you.*"   "*Sorry I'm late.*"

D Act out your dialogues.

1

2 Who says what?

Who are the people in the five dialogues? Listen and match.

Dialogue 1 ☐   a) boyfriend and girlfriend
Dialogue 2 ☐   b) business people meeting for the first time
Dialogue 3 ☐   c) friends or neighbours
Dialogue 4 ☐   d) mother and daughter
Dialogue 5 ☐   e) people who first met a short time ago

3 Shaking hands

Hände schütteln

A Who do you usually shake hands with? Who do you use first names with?

gebraucht

> my boss   other people at work
> people I meet for the first time   neighbours
> friends   close friends   family

nahe Freunde

Handshake: _____

First name: _____

B Compare results.

C Listen to an Englishwoman's answers and tick the boxes.

	Handshake	First name
her boss	✗	
other people at work	✗	
people she meets for the first time	✗	
neighbours	✗	
friends		✗
close friends		✗
family		✗

D According to the speaker, which of these statements are true, which are false?

	True	False
1. The British don't usually shake hands with people they know.	☐	☐
2. British women kiss more than men.	☐	☐
3. Most neighbours call each other 'Mr' or 'Mrs'.	☐	☐
4. 'Mr' and 'Mrs' are used more often with older people.	☐	☐
5. It is unusual for people at work to use first names.	☐	☐

E Are there any differences in the way you and the Englishwoman do things?

4 Small talk

A What do you think? ✔ = That's right! ✘ = I disagree!

___ 1. A lot of women talk about how horrible their husbands are.

✓ 2. Some subjects are just very boring, like illnesses and children.

✓ 3. People talk about the weather just to say something, not because they're really interested in it.

✓ 4. You can ask somebody how much rent they pay, but asking about salaries is taboo.
Verdienst

✓ 5. Most people like talking about other people.

✓ 6. A lot of men talk about sport, cars or politics. Most women aren't interested in that.

B Interview your partner.

1. What do you like talking about? _____
   Themen
2. Which topics do you usually find boring? _____
3. What can you talk about with someone you don't know very well?
   Was kannst Du mit jemand besprechen, den Du nicht so gut kennst.
   _____
   gefährlich
4. Which topics do you think are dangerous? _____
5. Which questions would you like to ask your boss,
   fühlen
   a colleague or a neighbour but feel you can't?
   Welche Fragen würdest Du gern Deinem
   Chef stellen, aber *euren* *Kollegen oder Nachbarn*
   vielleicht nicht?

MEMO PAD

Haustiere = pets

1

C Read this text. What about people in your country?

America Talking

What do people in America talk about?
We went out and asked some Americans
and this is what they said.

Favourite topics include music, children, dogs and other pets, hobbies and politics. A lot of Americans like to talk about their jobs, especially current plans and projects, and families are another popular topic. Indeed, some Americans give strangers a complete family history within an hour of meeting them. The state of the economy is also something people often talk about – the worse it is, the more they talk about it.

Topics named as boring included music, children, dogs and other pets, hobbies, politics, other people's jobs, especially their current plans and projects, families, and – surprise, surprise – the state of the economy.

Our informants all agreed, however, that religion and politics can be dangerous subjects. Americans do not like foreigners to criticize American politics and you would not normally ask anyone how they voted at the last election.

Our favourite unaskable questions included (for the boss) "Did you know that your wife has a lover?" and (for the neighbours) "What are those strange noises I hear through the wall at about 11 o'clock every Tuesday night?"

5 Everything's relative

A Match the beginnings and ends of the sentences.

1. Children are a topic *a*
2. My weight is something *e*
3. The English normally shake hands with people *d*
4. The state of the economy is something *c*
5. Think of a question *b*

a) Americans often talk about.
b) you would like to ask your boss.
c) many people find boring.
d) they meet for the first time.
e) I don't tell anybody.

B Complete each of these sentences in two different ways.

Friends are people you … _____

Home is the place I *allways come back.* _____

Holidays are something most people *relase* _____

6 Keep talking

How long can you keep a conversation going?
Here are some starters.

7 A welcome party

Welcome!

International Party & Disco
For all our students

Meet your fellow students and teachers.

- Lounge / Bar
- Monday, 8 o'clock till midnight
- Disco from 9.30

A You are on an intensive course at an English language school.
The course starts with a welcome party. Give yourself a different identity.
Write the details on a card.

```
Name: _____
Nationality: _____
Profession: _____
Hobbies & Interests: _____
Reason(s) for taking the course: _____
Things you could talk about: _____
```

B Act out the party. Talk to other guests.

1

8 Party etiquette

A Some new neighbours send you an invitation to a housewarming party. *Hauseinweihungsfeier*
You decide to go. Complete the questionnaire.

1. In reply to the invitation ..... *Als Antwort auf*	☒ I phone to say I can go. ☐ I write to say I can go. ☒ I just go.
2. The party starts at 8 o'clock. I arrive at	☐ a few minutes to 8. ☐ 8 o'clock. ☒ any time before 8.30. ☐ _____
3. I wear .... *Frage (Kleidungsstück)*	☐ ordinary clothes. ☒ something I particularly like. ☐ something more formal, like a suit or dress.
4. As a present I take	☐ nothing. ☒ a bottle of wine. ☐ flowers. ☐ _____
5. Before I go I eat	☐ nothing. ☒ something light. ☐ my usual evening meal.

MEMO PAD

Wiederholung am 16.03.99

B Some English friends in your town have got a similar invitation from their neighbours. Give them some advice.

You	can can't have to don't have to should shouldn't	arrive … eat … phone … take … wear … write … …

C Compare your advice with other groups.

1

9 Some and any

> Do you need anybody? – I need somebody to love.
> Could it be anybody? – I want somebody to love.
>
> The Beatles

A Look back through Unit 0 and this unit and find phrases with these words:

some, somebody/someone, something

Some subjects are just very boring.
You can ask somebody how much rent they pay. u.4.3 S.13
What can you talk about with someone you don't know very well.

any, anybody/anyone

B Can you give a rule for *some* and *any*? Compare your ideas with the Grammar section at the back of the book.

PRONUNCIATION

10 A Match the words and the rhythms.

1. Enjoy the rest of your trip!
2. It was fine.
3. Sorry I'm late.
4. Did you have a good trip?
5. Don't forget to send a postcard!
6. No problem.

a) 0oo0
b) 0o0o0o0o
c) o0o0oo0
d) 00o
e) oo0
f) oo0oo0

B Listen, check and practise.

11 A Which of these sentences go up (↗) and which go down (↘)?

1. Are you here on business? ↗
2. Are you here on holiday? ↗
3. It's a lovely day, isn't it? ↗
4. Did you have a good trip? ↗
5. No problem. ↘
6. It was great to be here. ↘
7. Sorry I'm late. ↘
8. It was nice to meet you. ↘
9. It was fine. ↘

B Listen, check and practise.

UNIT 2

Appearances

short
tall
slim
fat
fair hair
dark hair
long hair
short hair
bald
a moustache
a beard
glasses

1 What do they look like?

A Look at this picture of a class reunion. Describe the people.

"He's got dark hair."   "She's tall."

B Listen. Who is who?

Iris Clark	= Number ___	Jenny Robinson	= Number ___
Ann Holden	= Number ___	George Small	= Number ___
Tony Nicholls	= Number ___	Kevin Wall	= Number ___

2 Family likeness

A Read the way the Pyes describe themselves. Underline all the phrases with *very, quite, a bit* and *really*.

Bruce:
I'm quite tall. I've got fair, curly hair, a reddish beard, and I wear glasses. My eyes are blueish grey. When I was young I was very thin and my legs still are. Now I'd like to lose a few kilos, but I'm not really fat.

Martin:
I'm not very tall, but I'm not really short, either. I've got short, straight, fair hair. My eyes are blueish grey.

Caroline:
I'm quite tall with long legs. The others say I've got a nice figure, but I think I'm a bit too fat. I've got dark brown hair, it's straight and quite long, and my eyes are green.

Peggy:
I'm average height, although the others always say I'm short. I've got shortish, straight hair which is dark brown and my eyes are green.

18 eighteen

B What have the members of the Pye family got in common?
How many things can you find in three minutes? Make notes and report.

"Caroline and Bruce are both …"   quite tall, a bit too fat
beide

"Bruce and Martin have both got …"   bluish grey eyes, fair hair
haben beide

C What about you and your family?

"My father and I have both got …"

"We're all …"

"We've all got …"

"My sister and I are both …"

Puzzle

The two Smith boys often play with the Jones twins – a boy and a girl – who live next door. Diane and Peter have both got blonde hair, but are not related. David has not got a sister and is the same age as George. What are the children's full names?

_____ Smith
_____ Smith
_____ Jones
_____ Jones

3 Portraits

A Close your eyes and describe the person next to you.

B Write a description of yourself on a card. Do not write your name on the card.
Put it in a hat. Now take out a card and read the description to the rest of the class.
Who is it?

4 Fitter than he was

A Find someone who:

"Are you fitter than you were ten years ago?"

"Are you taller than your mother?"

is slimmer than he/she was ten years ago.   _____
is fitter than he/she was ten years ago.   _____
is taller than his/her father or mother.   _____
is shorter than his/her children.   _____
is the tallest person in his/her family.   _____
is the shortest person in his/her family.   _____
has got the longest hair in his/her family.   _____

B Report.

2

5 Good or bad?

A Look at this cartoon. Now complete the third picture with words from B.

 B All of these words can describe people. Put them in the columns and compare.

attractive   beautiful   boring   clever   famous   generous
good-looking   hard-working   happy   honest   intelligent
interesting   lazy   nasty   nice   poor   quiet   rich   shy
strong   stupid   ugly   unhappy   weak

Positive	Negative	It depends
_____	_____	_____
_____	_____	_____
_____	_____	_____
_____	_____	_____
_____	_____	_____
_____	_____	_____

HE WAS
SHY
HONEST
QUIET

TO THE UNKNOWN
POLITICIAN.

C Look at these people. Which words from B do you think describe them best?

D Compare with your partner.

6 Lonely hearts

These personal ads are from an American newspaper. Read them quickly and choose a person. Say why.

"I chose ... because ..."

THIS WEEK'S PERSONAL ADS

Widow
61, attractive, educated. Enjoys skiing, movies, dancing, eating out, the arts. Wants to meet gentleman for conversation and friendship. Box 1307

Active man
38, 5'5", non-smoker, non-drinker, enjoys running, aerobics, camping. Seeks lady with similar interests. Box 8733

Athletic male
30, attractive, quiet, self-employed, non-smoker. Enjoys travel. Looking for quiet, small female with similar interests. Box 3217

Must love children
Divorced lady, 33, good sense of humor, good cook, enjoys picnics, boxing, country music. Seeks nice man with good job. Box 6756

Find a new romance with The Fresno Bee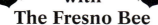

Green eyes
35, attractive divorced lady, enjoys dancing and social events. Wants to meet professional man 25–35. Box 4579

Widowed male
60's, active, seeks lady who likes the good things in life, especially golf. Box 7777

Good-looking
professional musician, 31, seeks attractive female, 25–35, slim, honest, for serious relationship. Box 3505

Romantic lady
23, 5'7", blonde hair, blue eyes. Enjoys long walks, music. Dreaming of romantic single man 20–30. Box 8403

```
1" = 1 inch    =    2.54 cm
1' = 1 foot    =   30.48 cm
```

7 "Consequences"

Listen and play the game.

*Tall Napoleon **met** clever Snow White
in a supermarket **at** midnight.
He **said**, "Let's go to a disco."
She **said**, "I don't like grapefruit."
So they got married.*

8 Those were the days

So war es damals

A Read the three quotes on the right. Which topic are they about?

- [ ] Leaving school *verlassen*
- [ ] A new job
- [ ] Retirement *Ruhestand*

"I've got more time to do the things that I want to now and I enjoy that. Perhaps I'm lazier than I used to be." *ich*

"I'm the sort of person that likes hard work and I find things a bit boring now. I'm not really as happy as I used to be." *war damals*

"I travel quite a lot now and do all sorts of other things, so I'm just as active as I used to be."

B Underline the phrases with *as … as*.

C Compare yourself now with how you used to be. Tick.

	active	clever	fit	happy	strong	nice	shy	slim	____	____
+										
−										
=										

MEMO PAD _____

D Now write sentences like these:

I'm not as _____ as I used to be.
_____

I'm just as _____ as I used to be.
_____

I'm _____ than I used to be.
_____
_____

> "Ah, but I was so much older then, I'm younger than that now."
> — Bob Dylan

E Compare and comment.

"I'm fitter than I used to be."   "I'm not as slim as I used to be."

"Me too."   "I'm not."   "Nor me."   "I am."

22 twenty-two

F Report one thing you have in common with another person.

> "Robert and I are both happier than we used to be."

> "Maria and I aren't as shy as we used to be."

9 Wit and wisdom

A Look at this saying. What do you think it means?

"The grass is always greener on the other side of the hill."

B Fill in.

long
red
wooden
hard
merry

*There was a naughty boy,
And a naughty boy was he,
He ran away to Scotland
The people for to see —
There he found
That the ground
Was as _____,
That a yard
Was as _____,
That a song
Was as _____,
That a cherry
Was as _____,
That a door
Was as _____
As in England —
So he stood in his shoes
And he wondered,
He wondered,
He stood in his shoes
And he wondered.*

John Keats

C Fill in.

as beautiful as   as intelligent as

The writer GEORGE BERNARD SHAW was one of the most intelligent men of his time. A beautiful actress once wrote to him and suggested that they should have children together. With her beauty and his intelligence, she said, their children would be perfect.
Shaw replied that if the children were _as beautiful as_ her and _so intelligent_ him, that would be fine, but what if they were _as beautiful as_ him and _as intelligence as_ her?

2

 D Listen and check.

E First fill in *who* or *which*, then say who or what it is.

1. Someone _____ ran away to Scotland: _____
2. Something _____ people wear on their feet: _____
3. Someone _____ wanted to have children with a famous writer: _____
4. Something _____ is the entrance to a room: _____
5. Someone _____ was famous for his intelligence: _____
6. Something _____ grows on trees: _____
7. Someone _____ wrote poetry: _____
8. Something _____ equals 0.3048 metres: _____

10 Some you like, some you don't …

A Think of a person you like. Find at least six words in this unit which describe the person. Do the same for someone you do not like.

B Tell your partner about the two people.

PRONUNCIATION

 11 A Match the underlined sounds with sounds in the column on the right, for example

George – bald

1. M<u>ar</u>tin
2. B<u>er</u>nard
3. M<u>a</u>ry
4. J<u>oh</u>n
5. D<u>a</u>vid

a) f<u>ai</u>r
b) bl<u>o</u>nde
c) gr<u>ey</u>
d) c<u>ur</u>ly
e) m<u>ou</u>stache

 B Listen, check and practise.

12 A Listen and underline the stressed syllables.

1. I'm quite tall. I've got fair, curly hair, a reddish beard and I wear glasses. My eyes are blueish grey.
2. When I was young I was very thin and my legs still are. Now I'd like to lose a few kilos, but I'm not really fat.
3. I'm not very tall, but I'm not really short, either. I've got short, straight, fair hair. My eyes are blueish grey.

 B Listen, check and practise.

UNIT 3

Be my guest

1 Guests

A What do you think of when you hear the word *guests*?

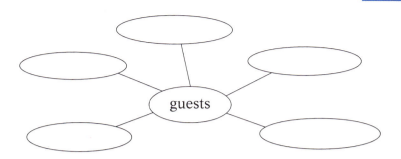

B What is important to you when guests stay with you for a week or longer? Write the sentence numbers in the appropriate circles.

Guests should:

1. offer to do the washing-up.
2. help with the cooking.
3. help with the shopping.
4. go to bed at the same time as you.
5. bring you a present.
6. take you out for a meal.
7. buy wine to go with the food.
8. entertain themselves.
9. not come home late.
10. do what you want to do.
11. not smoke in the house.
12. write a thankyou letter.

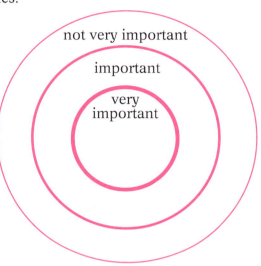

C Compare results.

"I think number 3 is the most important."

"So do I!"

"I think number 5 is more important than number 2. What do you think?"

"Well, it's not as important as 4."

"I don't think 6 is important at all."

"Nor do I!"

2 When you last had guests

A Complete the questionnaire.

1. When you last had guests, who were they?
2. How long did he/she/they stay?
3. Did she (he/they) entertain herself (himself/themselves)?
4. _____
5. _____
6. _____
7. _____
8. Did you enjoy the visit?

twenty-five 25

3

 B Now interview your partner and write down the answers.

> "I had to do all the shopping myself."

> "She entertained herself."

> "It was hard work – we had to do everything ourselves."

C Report something interesting about your partner's guests.

3 Difficult guests

A Look at the picture story, read the letter and say who is who.

Trials of a Troubled Host and Hostess

In the first picture, from left to right, the people are:

Eric, _____

26 | twenty-six

Dear Bridget,

I hope you are all well. We are fine – now! Jim's brother Graham and his family went back home last Wednesday! They are nice people but difficult guests, to say the least. Graham just _sat in front of the TV_ and smoked his pipe all day while Sue _did her aerobics_. Neither of them _helped with the cooking_ or the washing-up or anything. And the children just did what they wanted: they _helped themselves to food_ any time and dropped half of it on the floor. David – the younger one – _used the phone_ without asking permission and Eric _played music_ in his room every night so loud that I couldn't sleep. I had to go outside for some peace and quiet. All that and their enormous, noisy, smelly dog, too! Do you know, they even let it sleep on the sofa! Of course, I didn't like to say anything …

Well, that's all for now.
Love, Shirley

used the phone   did her aerobics ✓
helped with the cooking ✓   helped themselves to food
played music ✓   sat in front of the TV ✓

B Complete the letter.

C Read the letter again. Are these sentences true or false?

Shirley thinks it is all right if guests:

	True	False
1. do not help with the washing-up.		
2. help themselves to food.		✗
3. let their dog sleep on the sofa.		✗
4. use the phone without asking permission.		✗

D Look at the pictures and tell Shirley's story. Do not look at the letter!

"Shirley and Jim had guests a few days ago …"

E Do you have any memories of particularly good or bad guests? Tell the group.

"One of the nicest evenings I've ever spent at the Wilson's … and then you had to go and do that on the rug!"

3

4 Be my guest

A Which three pictures go with each situation?

1 2 3 4 5 6 *present* 7 8 9

Situation 1 An English course and a stay in Scotland. Pictures ___, ___, ___
Situation 2 An invitation to a housewarming party. Pictures ___, ___, ___
Situation 3 A day-trip to York. Pictures ___, ___, ___

B Listen and check.

C Listen to Situation 1 again and answer these questions.

1. Where is the person going to stay during the course? _____
2. How much time is she going to spend in Scotland? _____
3. Who is she going to stay with after the course? _____

D Listen to Situations 2 and 3 again and complete the dialogues.

How long are we going to be there?

What are we actually going to do?

What are we going to give her?

What are you going to wear?

◻ _____
△ Do we have to give her a present?
◻ _____
△ What do you mean, what am I going to wear?

○ _____
▽ I don't know.
▽ _____
○ That depends what time we get started.

28 | twenty-eight

E Write this part of Situation 3 in the correct order. Then listen and check.

▽ And I'm not going to sit down all day.   ▽ I'd like to walk round the walls.
▷ I'm not going to walk around all day.

___

5 What are you going to do?

A Write two or three sentences about yourself.

On my next birthday	
On my next holiday	
The next time we move house	I'm going to …
The next time I stay with anybody	we're going to …
The next time we go to a party	
The next time we have guests	
When I retire	

B Compare results.

6 Haikus

 A haiku is a three-line poem. The first and third lines should each have five syllables, the second line should have seven. Complete the haikus and compare results.

Invitation
Spring has returned here.
___
Come and share the day!

Thankyou Note
___
You gave me food and kindness,
Please accept these words.

Silent Guests
We did not talk much.
What is silence between friends?
___

3

7 Unusual visits

A Sort these words into two groups.

> power stations   restaurants   schools
> museums   offices   old buildings
> castles   factories   hospitals

Things tourists often visit:

_____
_____
_____
_____

Things tourists do not usually visit:

_____
_____
_____
_____

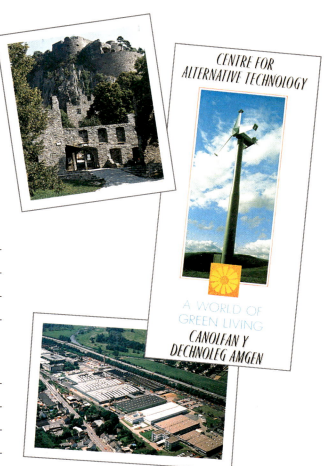

 B Listen to the interview with Sophie Bernstein and tick the things she is interested in.

You are going to hear about an unusual programme for student visitors to the USA. Students on this programme stay with families and visit things which tourists do not usually see. Before they go to the States they have to fill in a form to say what things they are interested in.

••••••• **Visit the USA** •••••••

Areas of interest

Please indicate your areas of interest by checking (✔) the appropriate box.

☐ Community Organisations & Social Events
☐ Culture (Music, Arts, etc.)
☐ Education
☐ Environment & Technology
☐ Health
☐ History
☐ Industry & Commerce
☐ Legal System
☐ Politics & Government
☐ Religion

8 Sightseeing

 A What do you think visitors to your town or area are usually (not) interested in? Complete these sentences.

All of them		
Most of them	visit	
A lot of them	go to	
Some of them	want to see	
Not many of them		
None of them		

MEMO PAD

B Read out your sentences and compare with other groups.

9 A programme for visitors

A Your class is going to have English-speaking visitors. Make suggestions for a programme.
Choose: 1. something cultural,
2. something historical,
3. something ecological,
4. something unusual and
5. a social activity.

Let's	take them to
Shall we	show them
Why don't we	go to
I think it would be nice to	visit
We could	look at
	…

B Read out your suggestions. React to other people's suggestions.

"Good idea!"   *"Let's … instead."*   *"I'd rather …"*

"I'd prefer to …"   *"Why not?"*

C You are going to show some visitors around your town or area.
Plan a programme for a day or a week.
Include something from the five categories in A and two different meals.

D Report.   *"We're going to …"*

3

10 Good questions for a guest

A Write five questions for guests. Use these beginnings.

Can I _____?
Is it all right if I _____?
Shall I _____?
Can you _____ , please?

B Compare results.

PRONUNCIATION ....

11 A First listen and say the words in the box.
Then listen and say the sentences. What is the difference?

are, we, to, be	How long are we going to be there?
there, are	There are lessons most mornings.
do, you	What do you mean?
can, you, a	Can I get you a drink?
and, are	My sister and I are both tall.

B Look at the underlined sounds in these sentences and listen.
Mark them *w* if they are weak and *s* if they are strong.

1. <u>Are</u> <u>you</u> here on business? (w w)
2. <u>Are</u> <u>you</u> here on business? (w s)
3. What <u>are</u> <u>you</u> going <u>to</u> wear?
4. How long <u>are</u> <u>we</u> going <u>to</u> <u>be</u> <u>there</u>?
5. You phone <u>to</u> say <u>you</u> <u>can</u> go.
6. Guests should take <u>you</u> out <u>for</u> <u>a</u> meal.
7. It <u>was</u> great <u>to</u> <u>be</u> here.
8. I'm happier <u>than</u> I used <u>to</u> <u>be</u>.

C Listen again, check and practise.

12 A Each of these words or phrases includes a letter or letters which are not normally pronounced. Underline the silent letters.

- cas<u>t</u>le
- tourists
- next time
- next birthday
- I ju<u>s</u>t thought
- old buildings
- they helped themselves
- the tallest person

B Listen, check and practise.

PREVIEW A

1 Card games

Write these sentence beginnings on cards. Now look at File 2.

Let's …	I'm going to …	A lot of people …
Is it all right if I …?	You shouldn't …	Did you …?
I'd prefer to …	You don't have to …	Have you got …?
Shall we …?	We've all got …	Are you here …?
We could …	I'm not as …	Perhaps I'm …
I'm not going to …	I'm as …	I'd rather …
I think …	I think it would be nice to …	

2 Act it out

A Write down two sentences or phrases from each of Units 1, 2 and 3. Give them to another group.

B Write a dialogue which includes at least four of the six sentences and act it out.

3 "In the Midnight Hour"

Listen. How many times do you hear *going to* in the whole song?

4 Crazy comparisons

Find ten adjectives from Units 1 to 3 to make comparisons like these:

as lazy as lunchtime
as fit as fifteen fish
as shy as a shop-assistant

_____
_____
_____

thirty-three 33

PREVIEW A

5 Winners

A You and your partner have won a free weekend with a famous person.

Decide …
- who you are going to spend the weekend with.
- where you are going to spend it.
- what you are going to see and do.

Think of …
- a present you are going to take.
- something you are going to bring back as a souvenir.

B Report.

"We're going to spend the weekend with …"

6 Look ahead

Choose one of these topics from the next three units. Using words you know, make a wordmap for the topic and show it to the class.

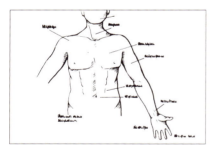
The human body

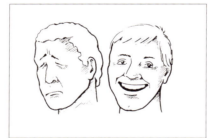
Feelings

Burglars

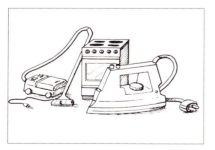
Electrical equipment

Holidays

Hotels

UNIT 4

Around the house

1 In the kitchen

A Write in the names of the things.

- clock
- cooker
- freezer
- fridge
- toaster
- dishwasher
- washing machine
- food processor
- coffee machine
- microwave
- hoover
- iron
- kettle
- radio

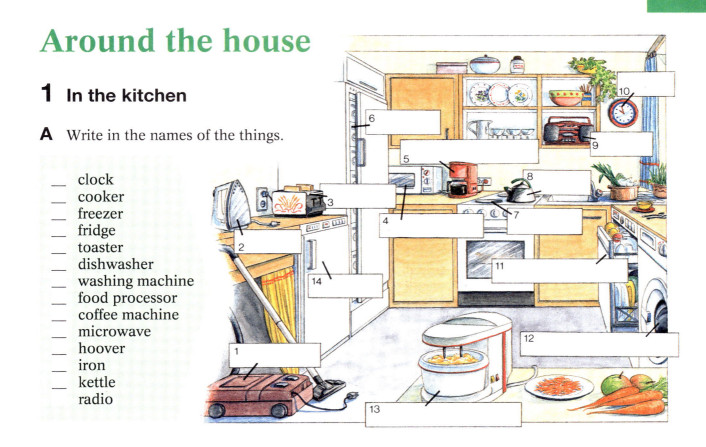

B Tick the things you have got in your kitchen at home.

 C Compare. What has everyone got?

"I've got a …"   "I haven't got a …"

"So have I."   "I haven't."   "Nor have I."   "I have."

2 Shop window

A Look at the shop window. Where are the items?

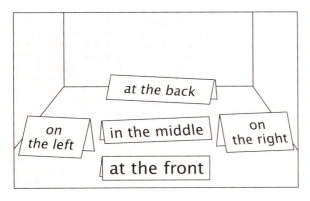

"The fridge is at the back on the left."

thirty-five **35**

4

B Write five sentences about the picture. Some sentences should be true, others false. Read the sentences out. The others say 'True' or 'False'.

The hoover is in the middle on the right.
_____
_____
_____
_____
_____

C Student A: Look at File 3. – Student B: Look at File 5.

3 Electrical equipment

A We interviewed Carole McKendrick about the equipment in her house. Listen and note her answers.

Of all the things in her house:

1. which is the oldest?
2. which is the newest?
3. which is the most useful?
4. which is the least useful?
5. which is the most frustrating?
6. which is/are particularly annoying?

Are there any things which:

7. she is going to buy soon?
8. she would really like to have?

colour printer
electric guitar
food processor
freezer
gameboy
hoover
microwave
video recorder
walkman
washing machine

B Ask your partner and report.

"Which is the oldest thing you've got?"

"And the newest?"

"What do you think is the most useful thing in your house?"

MEMO PAD
_____
_____
_____
_____

C Look at these statistics and talk about them with your partner.

"Look at this!"   *"That's interesting, isn't it?"*   *"That's surprising!"*

LIFESTYLE IN EUROPE 1991

% of population that have/use	GB	D*	I	F	E	NL	B	P	GR	DK	IRE	
Microwave oven	48	32	6	24	9	19	22	4	2	13	17	*West Germany only
TV set (one)	98	97	98	94	98	98	97	92	94	98	98	
Two TV sets	36	25	36	23	35	31	19	20	16	23	26	
Video recorder	58	42	25	35	40	48	42	22	37	39	38	
Credit card	41	10	6	39	13	19	18	7	8	15	14	

Professor Schnabel's cleaning lady mistakes his time machine for a new dryer.

4 Inventions and their results

A Complete the sentences.

has made washing clothes easier   has changed millions of jobs
has made cooking a lot easier   has spoiled family life
has made listening to music more enjoyable
has not improved the taste of coffee

1. The CD player _____.
2. The coffee machine _____.
3. The computer _____.
4. The microwave _____.
5. Television _____.
6. The washing machine _____.

 B Listen and check.

4

 C Complete these sentences. Compare results.

1. The _____
   _____ changed _____.
2. The _____
   _____ improved _____.
3. The _____
   _____ spoiled _____.
4. The _____
   _____ made _____.
5. The _____
   _____.

5 Agreeing and disagreeing

 A Listen to the statements. Do you agree (+) or disagree (–)?

1	2	3	4	5	6	7	8	9	10

 B Listen again and say what you think.

"That's true."   "I agree."   "I wouldn't say that."

"I think so, too."   "So do I."   "Nor would I."

"I don't think so."

"Nor do I."

"It depends what you mean by …"

6 Everyday stories

Complete the minisaga.

♥♥♥♥♥♥♥♥♥♥ **Love among the laundry** ♥♥♥♥♥♥♥♥♥♥

When Sally found a man's striped sock curled among her clothes at the launderette she returned it to the tall dark young man with a shy smile.

They met there once a week for several months, then were seen no more. One of their wedding presents was a _____.

Molly Burnett

7 Burglars!

A What have the burglars done? Make notes.

"They've taken …"

B Report.   "They've broken …"   "They've damaged …"   "They've drunk …"

4

8 A burglary

A Last summer there was a burglary at Geoff's house. Read the questions. What do you think happened?

1. Where was Geoff when the burglary happened?
   - [ ] at work
   - [ ] on holiday
   - [ ] out shopping

2. How did the burglars get in?
   - [ ] through the back door
   - [ ] through the front door
   - [ ] through the kitchen window

3. What did they damage?
   - [ ] the doors
   - [ ] the furniture
   - [ ] the windows

4. Which of these things did they take?
   - [ ] cash and cheques
   - [ ] CDs
   - [ ] the computer
   - [ ] some foreign coins
   - [ ] jewellery
   - [ ] a watch

5. Which of these things did Geoff have to do?
   - [ ] go to the police
   - [ ] identify the burglars
   - [ ] make a list of stolen items
   - [ ] send details to the insurance company

6. Which of these things happened in the end?
   - [ ] The burglars were caught.
   - [ ] Geoff got a cheque from the insurance company.
   - [ ] Geoff's family felt unsafe for quite a long time.

B Listen to the story of Geoff's burglary. Compare your answers.

9 Mystery crimes

A Read the story and fill in the missing sentences.

There was a young couple who lived in a nice new house and had a nice new car. Every morning they took the same train to work and left the car outside their house. One morning they opened the front door and were shocked because _____.

They went to the police station and reported the theft. They were very unhappy all day, but of course they went to work, came back home, ate dinner and went to bed as usual. And the next morning they left the house at their usual time. They were amazed – _____.

On the seat was a bottle of champagne and a letter. The letter said, "I am sorry that I borrowed your car. I am a doctor and it was an emergency. Please accept this bottle of champagne and these two theatre tickets." The happy couple phoned the police and told them that their car was back. That night they went to the theatre and enjoyed themselves.

On their way home they suddenly began to worry. They ran up to the house, opened the front door and went in.

_____.

forty

4

 B Listen and compare. Find a title for the story and explain the crime.

C Read the story again and collect the past tense forms.

_____

_____

D Now look at these pictures and tell this story.

"A retired couple won a free weekend in Amsterdam …"

E Do you know any other stories about burglars or burglaries?

10 What have we taken?

 A Choose six things from this unit and write them in the sack.

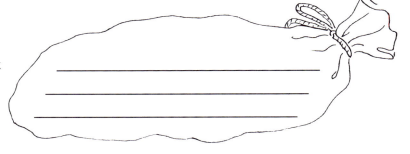

B Write descriptions for two of the things and read them out.
The other pairs try to guess what they are.

It's _____
It's a kind of _____
You use it for _____
It's something _____

"You use it for cooking."

"It's something people have on special occasions."

4

PRONUNCIATION

 11 A Listen and mark the stress in these words and phrases.

postcard	boyfriend	dishwasher
welcome party	thankyou letter	power station
video recorder	coffee machine	wedding present
police station	insurance company	credit card

B Listen again and practise.

 12 Practise saying these sentences to the rhythm on the cassette.

The clock's at the back on the left.
 The clock's in the middle on the right.
  The fridge is at the front on the left.
   The fridge is in the middle on the left.
    The freezer's at the front on the right.
     The microwave's at the back on the left.
      The dishwasher's in the middle on the right.
       The coffee machine's in the middle on the left.

 13 A Listen and practise these two intonation patterns.

1. (↘) OK, equipment, yes, course, ahead, right, oldest, freezer, down, new, old, hoover

2. (↘↗) questions, first question is, months ago, now

B Now listen to the same patterns in the dialogue.

☐ OK, Carole. I'd like to ask you some questions about the equipment you've got in your house.
○ Yes, of course. Go ahead.
☐ Right, well, the first question is: what's the oldest thing you've got?
○ Well, until six months ago, it was the freezer, but then it broke down so I had to get a new one. It was about fifteen years old, the old one. Now the oldest thing is probably the hoover.

C Listen again and read aloud with the cassette.

 D Now read the dialogue in pairs.

Unit 5

Body and soul

1 Don't worry, be happy!

A What makes you happy? Collect ideas and compare with other pairs.

getting up late on Sunday
a cold beer on a hot day
walking in the woods

B Read these texts and collect the words that describe feelings.

happy, worry

When you're bored with yourself, marry and be bored with someone else.
— David Pryce-Jones

MANICdepressant
SOMETIMES I'M HAPPY
sometimes i'm sad
SoMeTiMeS i'm HsAaPdPY
— Kim Dammers

I worry about you.
I can't sleep at night.
Are you sad? Are you lonely?
Or are you all right?
They say that men suffer,
As badly, as long.
I worry, I worry,
In case they are wrong.
— Wendy Cope

A hungry man is an angry man.
— Bob Marley

It takes a worried man to sing a worried song.

Laughter is the best medicine.

Too tired to yawn, too tired to sleep:
Poor tired Tim! It's sad for him.
— Walter de la Mare

Here comes your nineteenth nervous breakdown.
— Rolling Stones

"Don't worry. He's in a good mood."

5

C Listen. How do the speakers feel?

1. _____   4. _____
2. _____   5. _____
3. _____   6. _____

D Mime a mood or feeling. The others guess what it is.

2 Feelings

A Complete the sentences.

1. The place I can relax best is _____
2. I get annoyed when _____
3. I worry about _____
4. My favourite time of day is _____ because _____
5. On Friday afternoons I feel _____ because _____
6. _____ makes me laugh.

B Choose one of the questions and ask other people. Make notes.

1. Where do you relax?
2. When do you get annoyed?
3. What do you worry about?
4. What's your favourite time of day? Why?
5. How do you feel on Friday afternoons?
6. What makes you laugh?

C Report.

"A lot of people said they get annoyed when ..."

"Three people told me they feel ..."

"Petra told me she likes to relax ..."

3 What do you say?

A Good news (+) or bad news (–)?

☐ Congratulations!
☐ How disappointing!
☐ That's terrible!
☐ I'm sorry to hear that.
☐ You must be really pleased.
☐ You must be very upset.

☐ Oh, dear!
☐ Oh, no!
☐ That's great!
☐ Well done!
☐ What a pity!

B What can these people say?

C Listen and complete the dialogues.

1. △ I've just found out I'm going to have a baby!
   ○ That's great! _____
   _____.

2. △ How was your holiday?
   ○ Don't ask! It rained all week and the food was awful.
   △ Oh, dear! _____
   _____.
   And it all looked so good in the brochure, didn't it?

3. △ Somebody's stolen my bike!
   ○ _____. Was it insured?

4. △ I've passed my driving test!
   ○ That's great! _____
   _____.
   You must be really pleased.

5. △ Well, did you pass?
   ○ I'm afraid not.
   △ Oh, dear! _____
   _____.
   You must be very disappointed!

6. △ What's the matter?
   ○ We've had burglars!
   △ Oh, no! That's terrible! _____
   _____.
   When did it happen?

D Play this game.

1. Write two phrases from A on cards.
2. Collect all the cards, shuffle them and hand them out again.
3. Work in pairs. Write a dialogue including three of the four phrases on your cards.
4. Act out the dialogues.

4 How would you feel?

A Think about these situations. How would you feel?

1. You meet an English person. You try to shake hands, but he does not respond.

   ☐ I think he is not very polite.
   ☐ I think he does not like me.
   ☐ I am embarrassed.
   ☐ I do not worry about it.

2. You have arranged to meet a foreign friend. You are on time, but she does not come.

   ☐ I am worried.
   ☐ I am annoyed.
   ☐ I do not mind.
   ☐ I think she probably has something more important to do.
   ☐ I decide she must be an unreliable sort of person.

3. An American friend rings you up at 6 o'clock in the morning.

   ☐ I am annoyed because I was still asleep.
   ☐ I ask her to call back later.
   ☐ I am pleased to hear from her.
   ☐ I think it is perfectly normal.
   ☐ I am worried and think it must be an emergency.

B Compare results. Read File 7.

5 The body

A Label the parts and say what is missing.

chin   ear
eye   hand
finger foot
arm   toe   face
head   knee
leg   mouth
nose   hair
shoulder

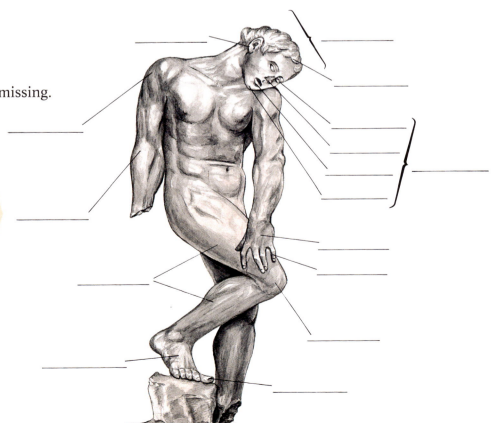

B Which of the words in A are the same in your language?

Same (or similar):

Different:

6 Keep fit

A Complete the instructions.

> bend   press   put   lift
> relax   stand   touch

1. _____ with your feet about 30 cm apart.

2. _____ your arms above your head.

3. _____ forward and _____ the floor between your feet.

4. _____ a bit.

5. _____ your hands on the floor again and _____.

6. Return to your starting position.

Aerobics in Hell

 B Listen and check.

5

7 "Simon says"

A You are going to play a game called "Simon says".

There is only one rule: you have to do all the things which begin with "Simon says …". If you do any of the other things, you are out of the game.

Now listen and play.

B Now play "Simon Says" with the other people in your group.

8 Count your blessings

A Write some true sentences.

I've never been in hospital. Touch wood!

| I haven't | been | seriously ill
in hospital
to the doctor's | for | a long time.
several years. |
| | had | a cold
flu
a hangover | since | I was a child.
I left school.
last Christmas. |

I haven't had a cold for a long time.
_____
_____
_____
_____

🎵🎵🎵🎵🎵🎵🎵🎵🎵🎵🎵🎵🎵

MEMO PAD

operiert werden =
_____
have an operation
_____
_____

B Compare.

C Report.

I've never been seriously ill.

Maria's never been seriously ill. I haven't had a cold for two years.

Maria's never been seriously ill. Robert hasn't had a cold for two years. I haven't had a hangover since last Christmas.

9 Body and soul ABC

 Make as many lines as you can.

A is for arm, which people sometimes break.
B is for body, we've all got one.
C is for cold, a very common thing.
D is for …
E is …
F …

PRONUNCIATION

10 How many two-syllable words can you find in this unit which have the stress on the second syllable?

 11 A Listen to the way the letter 'g' is pronounced in these words.

hangover – angry   What is the difference?

B Which of these words have a 'g' sound in the pronunciation?

missing   finger   language
things   English   long   longer

 C Listen and check.

12 Look at this dialogue.

 The underlined words have one of the following intonation patterns: (↘) or (↘↗).
Listen and mark the patterns.

△ How was your holiday?
○ Don't ask! It rained all week and the food was awful.
△ Oh, dear! I'm sorry to hear that. And it all looked so good in the brochure, didn't it?

UNIT 6

Holidays

1 Who goes where?

A Where do you think most Germans go on holiday?
Name the top three countries.

1. _____   2. _____   3. _____

Where do you think most tourists in Germany come from?
Name the top three countries.

1. _____   2. _____   3. _____

B Read the text and check.

Who goes where in Europe

55% of all West Germans have spent a holiday in Austria, 45% in Italy, 39% in Spain and 35% in France. 52% of Germans from the eastern *Länder* have spent holidays in what used to be Czechoslovakia, 31% in Poland, 29% in Hungary and 26% in Russia. Nearly all Germans have also spent holidays in Germany.

Altogether, Germans are the No. 1 tourists in the Netherlands, Turkey, Greece, Austria, Italy, Switzerland and France, and the second largest group in Norway, Sweden, Britain, Spain and Portugal.
The No. 1 tourists in Germany are - apart from the Germans themselves - the Dutch and the Americans: both 14%.   (1990/1991)

---

2 Which European countries have you been to?

A Which European countries have you:

spent (a) holiday(s) in?
only driven through?
been to on business?
only flown over?
never been to?
lived in?

I've spent several holidays in Italy.
I've only driven through Belgium.
_____
_____
_____
_____

B Compare.

6

3 Has anybody ever been to Australia?

A Guess which countries people have (not) been to.

I think	all of us a lot of us several of us only one or two of us none of us	have been to	_____ _____ _____ _____ _____

B Now check with the rest of the class.

"Has anybody ever been to Australia?" "Who's been to Hungary?"

4 Where and when?

A Which countries has Bruce been to? Listen and tick the correct boxes.

		Austria	Czech Republic	England	France	Germany	Hungary	Ireland	Italy	Scotland	Switzerland	Wales
Bruce has	lived in											
	spent holidays in											
	never been to											
	taken trips to											
	been on business to											
	travelled through											

B Listen again. Match the places and the information.

1. Mannheim *b*
2. Glasgow
3. Normandy
4. Zurich
5. Prague
6. Venice

a) He went there with friends a few years ago.
b) He lived there from 1975 to 1979.
c) He visited some friends there last year.
d) He spent a few days there last Easter.
e) He spent a weekend there last September.
f) He was there on business a few months ago.

C Ask your partner about three countries she or he has been to.

"When did you …?"   "Where exactly …?"   "How long …?"   "How …?"

"What …?"

D Report.

fifty-one 51

6

5 What sort of holidays do you like?

1

Africa!
Camping Safaris and Adventure Holidays

EGYPT · MOROCCO
EAST AFRICAN WILDLIFE
BOTSWANA · ZIMBABWE

Choose from over 50 different tours. Write or phone for FREE colour brochure.

Africa Alive
Dept. ST, 101 Amberley Road,
Westbury BA13 3OX

☎ 0373-703258 – 24hrs

5

600 Miles up the Nile

Leisurely days on a slow cruise from Cairo to Aswan accompanied by Guest Lecturer and Cruise Director.

- 21 Days
- Full board
- From £1,395
- By Egypt Air

Wallace / Dorking / Surrey
Tel. 0306 883529

2

VACANZE IN ITALIA

Traditional farmhouses, villas and apartments in Italy's prettiest regions. Some with pool.
FREE colour brochure
RING (07987) 792
Quote Ref 1202 or write:
Italia Holidays
Dept 1898,
Bignor, Pulborough,
Sussex RH12 1RT

6

WALES
Self-catering holidays on the Pembrokeshire coast
400 of the highest quality cottages available. All peacefully located close to safe sandy beaches. Excellent discounts available.
0348-346614

7

Ski Adventure

- Exciting alpine/nordic skiing choices in unspoilt France, Norway, and Quebec/Canada.
- Excellent hotels & food.
- Options for beginners, experts, families.
- No crowds or lift queues.

Phone (24hrs):
Headwater 0606 48114

8

St. Lucia on British Airways

Enjoy a relaxing week on a tropical island paradise.

The St. Lucian   £499
Royal St. Lucian £699

Call 081 - 741 3131/3851

9

French Chateaux

Explore France staying at the best chateaux and character hotels. Tailor-made holidays with your own car or fly-drive
0462 47 44 23
Embassy Holidays Ltd

3

2 Weeks Holiday in Australia for just £699!

Discover Perth and Western Australia with our special holiday package at a price much less than the normal air fare!
Phone 071-291 3475

10

Walking Holidays

The Himalayas
Morocco • Turkey
Greenland • Iceland
East Africa • South Africa

Call or write for colour brochure.
Trekker Tours Ltd.
101 Amberley Road
Westbury, Wiltshire BA13 3OX
☎ (0373) 827352 – 24 hrs

4

Sun Club Holidays

August bargains save £175

Our fully inclusive holidays provide an unforgettable break, whether you come as a couple, group of friends or family. From the watersports facilities to the chef-prepared food, it's first class all the way. Call now for details of our August holiday discounts.

Bookings and Information:
071-938 2603
24hr brochure line: 071-938 2199

What's included:
+ Flight and transportation.
+ Secluded beachside hotel.
+ 3 superb meals a day.
+ Barbecues.
+ Unlimited wine.
+ Windsurfing & sailing.
+ Waterskiing.
+ Friendly expert tuition.
+ Tennis & aerobics.
+ Children's creche.

All included in the holiday price from around £400 in August with late booking discounts.

Greece • Italy • Sardinia • Corsica • Turkey

11

Summer Holidays in the Heart of London

3star hotels £80 per person incl. continental breakfast and VAT.
Close to Hyde Park, Oxford Street & Bayswater tube station.
For reservations please call
Highgrove Hotels
Tel: 071-449 3400

A Read the holiday ads and find holidays for people who:

a) enjoy lying in the sun   _____
b) enjoy active holidays   _____
c) enjoy travelling around   _____
d) enjoy peace and quiet   _____
e) are interested in history and culture _____
f) are interested in meeting people   _____
g) prefer self-catering to hotels   _____
h) prefer an English-speaking country _____

B What about you? Talk about your holiday preferences.

"*I like / enjoy …*"   "*I prefer … to …*"   "*I'm interested in …*"

"*I don't mind …*"   "*I can't stand …*"   "*I hate …*"

C One of you is a travel agent, the other is a customer.
Look at the ads and find a suitable holiday.
Then change roles.

6 Finding a room

A You are in a Tourist Information Centre and you would like a room.

What do you want to know?

_____
_____
_____
_____

What will the Information Centre want to know?

_____
_____
_____
_____

6

B Listen. Add any questions you did not think of.

_____

_____

C Listen again and note the answers to your questions.

7 Heartbreak Hotel

A What do the guests say to the hotel manager?

> dirty   furniture   an enormous insect
> in my bed   in my room   in the swimming pool
> outside my window   playing cards   water
> workmen

1. Excuse me, there's no _____
   _____. When are you going to fill it up?

2. Excuse me, there are some _____
   _____.
   Would you please do something about it?

3. Excuse me, there's no _____
   _____. Can you do something about it?

4. There's _____
   _____. Will you please do something about it?

5. Excuse me, my bathwater's _____
   _____. Could you do something about it?

B Listen and check.

C Listen again. What does the manager say? Complete the sentences.

1. ___*I'll*___ speak to them immediately.
2. _____ very sorry, madam.
3. _____ deal with it immediately.
4. _____ worry about it.
5. _____ send someone immediately.

8 Problems, problems

A Talk about problems you have had in hotels.

*"I once stayed in a hotel in …
and there was …"*

MEMO PAD

_____
_____

B Think of a hotel problem.
One of you plays the hotel guest and the other is the manager.
Sort out the problem and then change roles.

C Complete this letter of complaint to a travel company.

```
Dear Sir or Madam,

We have just spent two weeks at the _____ Hotel
and are writing to complain.
Although your brochure says the hotel is _____
it was in fact _____
In addition to this, there _____
and _____
After five days we could not stand it any more and moved to
another hotel. We would therefore like our money back.

Yours faithfully,
```

9 Getting tired

A Read the poem.
Fill in the missing word.

Railway stations,
bus terminals,
airports.
Hotels
and
waiting rooms.
Forms
to fill in.
Museums
and
art galleries
to see.
And
empty
churches.

Guide books
and
menus
to read.
Struggles with
words.
Timetables
to study.
Haste.
Must _____
be
so
tiring?

L. L. Szkutnik

6

B What does the writer have to:

1. see? _____
2. fill in? _____
3. read? _____
4. study? _____

 C Now listen to the poem.

10 Roses on Mount Vesuvius

A Read this report of a travel agents' conference.
Put the pictures in the correct order.

The British Association of Travel Agents held their annual conference in Sorrento in 1985. Most of the delegates missed the first day – the conference train was late and the flight was delayed because of fog at Gatwick Airport. A large number of delegates got food-poisoning, two delegates fell down stairs and the marketing director of Kuoni Travel was bitten by a snake and developed blood-poisoning.

When the organizers of the annual golf competition arrived they found that there was no golf course in Sorrento, so they moved the competition to Dublin.

At the high point of the conference the Italian Minister of Development addressed the delegates in the Forum at Pompeii and a local travel agent decided to fly over the delegates and drop 3,500 roses. The ceremony had just started when a low-flying plane appeared. Its noise completely drowned the minister's speech. It dropped its flowers but unfortunately missed the Forum. A few minutes later the plane appeared again, flying just over the delegates' heads. Five times the plane flew over and not a single flower landed near the delegates, but there were roses all over Mount Vesuvius.

 B Write some questions about this story on a piece of paper. Ask another group.

- Who …?
- What …?
- Where …?
- When …?
- Why …?
- How many …?

11 Away or at home

A Think of some arguments for going away on holiday and staying at home.

Holidays away

You don't have to _____

You can _____

Going away is _____ than staying at home.

At home you can't _____

At home you have to _____

Holidays at home

At home you can _____

At home you don't have to _____

Staying at home is _____ than going away.

When you're away you can't _____

When you're away you have to _____

B Discuss.

PRONUNCIATION

12 A Match each of the underlined sounds with a sound in the box below.

G<u>e</u>rmany A<u>u</u>stria R<u>u</u>ssia Sw<u>e</u>den <u>I</u>taly P<u>o</u>land

holiday country Turkey flown Easter driven

 B Listen and check.

13 A Two of these words or phrases have a different stress from the others. Mark them.

holiday ads   swimming pool   food-poisoning   travel agent
self-catering   workmen   power station   art galleries
bus terminals   airports   waiting rooms   railway stations
guide books   timetables   an English-speaking country

 B Listen and check.

PREVIEW B

1 Race round Europe

Play with a partner against other pairs. Each pair chooses a different country and starts and finishes there. The first pair back to their starting point wins. Move by throwing a dice.

- ● Talk about the country.
- 1 Task! Look at File 4.

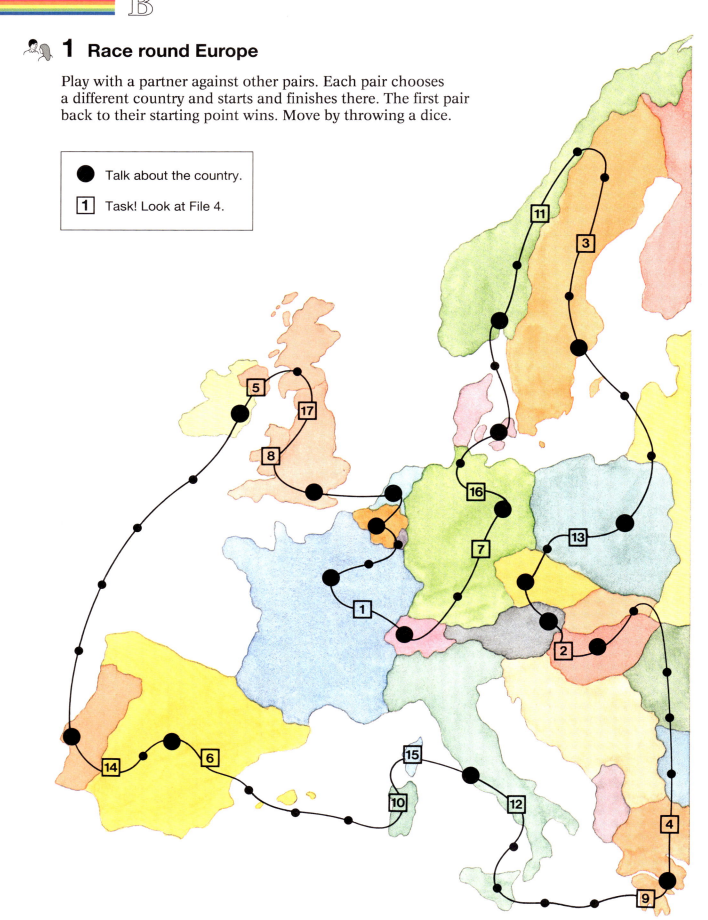

PREVIEW B

2 Find someone who

A Find someone who:
- has lived abroad.
- has had burglars.
- has laughed today.
- has had a cold recently.
- has never used a computer.
- has been to an English-speaking country.
- has been to more than six European countries.
- has bought a piece of electrical equipment recently.

Ask for details. Try to get a different person for each question.

"Have you ever lived abroad?"

"No, I'm afraid not."

"Have you bought any electrical equipment in the last year?"

"Yes, we bought a new cooker a few weeks ago."

B Report something interesting.

3 Write a minisaga

Complete this minisaga. You can change as much as you like, but your finished story should be exactly 50 words long.

When the doorbell rang in the middle of the night, Mrs Smith _____
_____.

At the door was _____ who _____.
Mrs Smith _____. Now when the bell rings, _____.

4 Look ahead

These questions are related to the topics of the next three units.
Choose one of these people and answer the questions for that person.
The others have to guess who it is.

A B C D

1. What do you think her/his present job is?
2. What other jobs do you think she/he has had?
3. What do you think her/his favourite food is?
4. What do you think she/he is going to do this weekend?
5. What three things do you think she/he always carries with her/him?

MEMO PAD

UNIT 7

Jobs

1 What job?

A Read these sentences. Someone hears things like this every day in her job.

- My canary's escaped.
- Help!
- What do I do with this?
- What happens, if it's full?
- Where's the Gents?
- I didn't hear that.
- I need to send a fax.
- What time is it?
- What do I do now?
- Just how wide are the seats?
- Can I get a coffee around here?
- Is it sunny in Los Angeles?
- I have to phone my wife.

B Now listen to some other things she hears. Where does she work, and what is her job? _____

2 A job I've had

A Think of a job you have had. Write down three words or phrases you associate with it.

B Show each other your notes and talk about the job.

"Do/Did you hear that or say it?"   *"Why do/did you say that?"*

3 Jobs, jobs, jobs

A Listen to an interview with Mark Scott. How many jobs has he had? ____

B Listen again. Match the comments and the jobs.

1. waiter
2. librarian
3. working in a vineyard
4. working for a builder
5. making batteries
6. sales assistant
7. tourist guide/disc jockey

a) the pay wasn't very good
b) could be dangerous
c) long hours, good fun
d) hard work
e) I learned a lot
f) OK
g) dirty, unhealthy

60   sixty

C Listen again and complete the text.

> he decided to train as a   he became a
> he got a job as a   he worked as a / for / in

When Mark left school _____ (1) librarian for four years.
In the next few years he had a lot of different jobs.
At one time _____ (2) an antique dealer, and for a while
_____ (3) a factory which made batteries.
At that point he thought it was time to get a proper job so _____
_____ (4) qualified librarian.
But that did not work out and _____ (5) sales assistant
instead. After a while _____ (6) department manager.

D What jobs have you had?
What is/was good or bad about them?
Talk to your partner.

MEMO PAD

E Report something interesting.

*"Doris trained as a …
when she left school."*

*"Robert worked as a …
for a while."*

*"Maria said the best job
she ever had was …"*

Warren Hagstrom:
Professional Western movie
background street crosser

7

4 What's happening?

A Complete the texts.

> he's learning to cook
> I'm brushing up my English
> we're applying for jobs
> he's looking for a new job now
> we're taking a computer course
> ~~I'm getting a bit bored~~

1. "I've been here for two years and I'm thinking about a new job because *I'm getting a bit bored.* I'd like to work with children."

2. "I was really pleased when young John got a job here last year. I've worked here for 20 years and it's a good company, but _____ _____ because they're getting rid of staff, and of course it's last in, first out."

3. "We're finishing our studies this year so _____ _____. We'd prefer to stay in this area, but we're prepared to go anywhere."

4. "Our children have left home now and _____ _____ because we'd like to go out to work again soon. We don't want to spend all day at home on our own."

5. "_____ _____ because my company's doing more and more export business, and I might need it. I've forgotten nearly everything I learned at school."

62   sixty-two

6. "My husband retired last month and _____

   _____

   at last!
   When I stop work next year, we want to do an advanced cookery course together in France. He's looking forward to it, and so am I."

B Listen and check.

C Find more examples of the Present Continuous in the texts. Underline them.

> "I've been here for two years and I'm thinking about a new job ..."

D Write sentences about yourself or other members of your family.

I am looking for a more interesting job. My daughter is learning Italian.
My parents are looking forward to retiring.

_____

_____

_____

5 Present Simple or Present Continuous?

A Write in the correct form of the verb.

1. "Our company _____ (make) professional kitchen equipment. At the moment we _____ (expand) into Eastern Europe."

2. "My job's in the sales department. Just now I _____ (prepare) information material for our agents."

3. "I usually _____ (work) in another department, but I _____ (help out) here for a few weeks."

4. "This machine normally _____ (work) perfectly, but it _____ (give) us some trouble today."

5. "I'm a trainee. I've been here for six months and I _____ (learn) about the different departments in the company. It's all very interesting."

B What is the difference between Present Simple and Present Continuous? Discuss with your partner and then check in the Grammar Section.

7

6 Can I take a message?

A Put the two dialogues in the correct order.

Fine, Mr Taylor. I'll tell her you called.

Good morning, my name's Roger Taylor. I'd like to speak to Jenny Faber.

Hello, this is Liz May. I'm calling about an order. Can I speak to Mr Cosby, please?

Hold on, Mr Taylor, I'll put you through. Oh dear, I'm afraid the line's busy. Would you like to leave a message?

I'm sorry, he's not in this morning. Can I take a message?

~~Mr Cosby's office.~~

Right, thank you, Ms May. I'll tell him.

~~Truman plc. Good morning.~~

Yes, please. Could you ask her to phone me back as soon as possible?

Yes, please. Could you tell him I called and that I'll phone back tomorrow?

△ Truman plc. Good morning.

○ _____

△ _____

○ _____

△ _____

▢ Mr Cosby's office.

▽ _____

▢ _____

▽ _____

▢ _____

Telephone Message

To: _____
From: _____
About: _____
Date: _____

B Listen and check.

7 On the phone

A Complete these sentences in as many ways as you can. Compare.

Caller

Can / Could _____?
I'd _____.
I'm _____.
I'll _____.

Receptionist

Can _____?
I'll _____.
I'm _____.
Would _____?

B Student A: Look at File 8 – Student B: Look at File 13.

8 What is work?

A Is it work?   ✓ = yes   ✗ = no   ? = it depends

1. An evening school teacher goes to the pub with her students after class.
2. A driver waits in the car for his boss.
3. Somebody hides in the office toilet and smokes a cigarette.
4. A woman irons the family washing.
5. A secretary does her English homework in the office.
6. A man digs a hole in the ground and fills it up again.
7. A dog barks at the post(wo)man.
8. A woman dresses up for her husband when he comes home in the evening.
9. A father changes his baby's nappy.
10. A bird builds a nest.

B Choose three of the situations in A and say why you think they are (not) work.

"It's work if ..."   *"It depends. If ..."*   *"If he has to ..."*   *"It is and it isn't. It depends how you look at it."*

"If it's in the office, it's ..."   *"It's not work if ..."*

sixty-five 65

7

9 Job satisfaction

A Match the pictures and the jobs.

nature warden
hospital helper
traffic warden

A

B

C

B Now match the pictures and the texts.

1. = Picture ☐

Linda Goodison has been a sales assistant, worked in an accountant's office and had a number of other jobs, but has never stayed in one job for so long. "A traffic warden's pay is nothing special and I could earn a lot more money than I do, but all the other jobs were so boring. I need to be with people. I like the confrontations. People get so angry and talk such rubbish. It's good fun."

2. = Picture ☐

Vicky Seager's day begins at about 7 a.m., sometimes even at 5, woken by fantastic sunrises. "Every day is different," she says.

As the warden of Hilbre Island nature reserve, she spends most of her time working with people, especially children, and makes sure that they enjoy themselves and keep out of danger. She also does a lot of practical work, for example she builds walls to stop erosion caused by walkers and wave action. "I try not to do too much paperwork, but I have to answer a lot of public enquiries," she says. She also has to write reports.

Vicky has always been interested in nature and studied zoology at Bangor University, Wales. "I just wanted a mixed recipe with wild life and children and being outdoors," she says.

3. = Picture ☐

"My work, I like it. You know that you're helping people. You learn about people. You understand people better. Many people would have no inner problems if they worked here. Sometimes people outside this place have problems for nothing, they fight for a parking space and other things. If they worked here, they would see that life is so short; then they would understand each other better and talk to each other more.

I think this work gives you important experience with life. If you work in a factory, you don't see these things – you see your machine or the cheese you are making. Here we see humanity. I'm married and we have a little girl, and being a hospital helper gives me a chance to better appreciate life, to reflect on it."

C Which person:
1. appreciates life more because of the job? ___
2. does not mind low pay, if the job is interesting? ___
3. enjoys helping people? ___
4. enjoys working outdoors? ___
5. finds angry people amusing? ___
6. likes working with children? ___
7. thinks people too often fight about nothing? ___
8. wanted a job with plenty of variety? ___

D Which of these jobs would you like to have? Why? Why not?

"I'd like to be a nature warden because I enjoy being outdoors."

"I wouldn't like to be a traffic warden because I don't like angry people."

"I wouldn't mind being a traffic warden. It could be interesting."

10 Words at work

A Collect 20 words or phrases from this unit which have something to do with work. Exchange lists with another group.

B Make a word map, including all the words on the list. Add more words as necessary.

C Compare.

11 PRONUNCIATION

A Listen. Note the intonation on the underlined syllables.

I <u>need</u> to send a fax.
Is it <u>sunny</u> in Los Angeles?
My <u>canary's</u> escaped.
I'm <u>calling</u> about an order.
I'd <u>like</u> to speak to Jenny Faber.

B Listen again and practise.

C Practise reading these sentences in the same way.

Good <u>morning</u>.
I <u>have</u> to phone my wife.
The <u>pay</u> wasn't very good.
I <u>trained</u> as a teacher.
Would you <u>like</u> to leave a message?
He's <u>looking</u> forward to it.
I'm <u>getting</u> a bit bored.

D Listen and check.

Unit 8

Eat, drink and be merry

1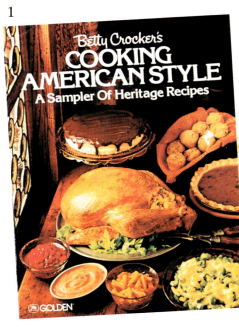

2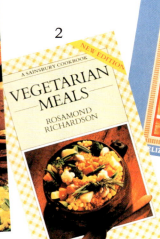

3

4

1 Food, glorious food

 A Match the dishes and the books. 1 ☐ 2 ☐ 3 ☐ 4 ☐

B How many ingredients of these dishes can you name in five minutes? Use a dictionary.

Memo Pad

68 sixty-eight

2 What's cooking?

Vegetable Curry

Serves 4

1 kg mixed vegetables such as aubergines, peppers, potatoes, courgettes, leeks, cauliflowers, carrots
1 tin of tomatoes
1 tablespoon lemon juice
1 piece of fresh ginger (2 cm)
3 – 4 cloves of garlic
2 tablespoons oil
2 teaspoons ground coriander
1 teaspoon ground cinnamon
1/2 teaspoon turmeric
1 teaspoon ground cumin
1/2 teaspoon chili powder
     salt to taste

A Match the instructions and the pictures.

- [ ] Bring to the boil and cook gently for 30 – 40 minutes. Stir occasionally.
- [ ] Heat the oil in a heavy saucepan, add the chopped ginger and garlic and the dry spices and fry for a minute or two.
- [ ] Peel the ginger and garlic and chop finely together using a sharp knife.
- [ ] Prepare the vegetables and cut into pieces (1 – 2 cms).
- [ ] Serve with boiled rice.
- [ ] Add salt.
- [ ] Add the vegetables, the lemon juice and the tinned tomatoes.

 B Listen and check.

8

3 Favourite recipes

A Write the recipe of a local speciality or one of your favourite dishes for English-speaking visitors.

Mm, this tastes great! You must let us have the recipe!

Ingredients:

_____
_____
_____
_____
_____
_____
_____
_____

teaspoon	= tsp/t
tablespoon	= tbsp/T
kilo	= kg
half a kilo	= ½ kg
one and a half kilos	= 1 ½ kg
2 litres	= 2 l
50 millilitres	= 50 ml

MEMO PAD

eine Prise Salz = a pinch of salt
Gabel = fork
_____

Procedure:

_____
_____
_____
_____
_____
_____
_____
_____

add, arrange, bake, boil, chop, cook, cover, cut, fry, grate, heat, mix, peel, pour, roast, season, serve, slice, spread, stir

B Compile a class recipe book.

4 Getting together

A Listen and answer the questions.

1. Where are the people going? _____
2. When are they meeting? _____
3. Where are they meeting? _____

B Student A: Look at File 6.
Student B: Look at File 14.

Would you like to …?

Oh, that would be nice! But I'm afraid …

5 Wild weekend

A Think of some things you could do with other people at the weekend.

_____
_____
_____

B Go around the class and invite people to do things with you.
When you have made an arrangement with somebody, put it in the diary.
Try to fill your weekend.

FRIDAY	Morning *Work!*	Afternoon *Work!*	Evening
SATURDAY	Morning	Afternoon	Evening
SUNDAY	Morning	Afternoon	Evening

C Report on your arrangements for one day.

"On Saturday I'm meeting Susan for lunch and after that we're going to the cinema. In the evening we're going to the disco with Paul."

8

6 Celebrations

A Match the occasions and the cards.

1. Birthday
2. Christmas
3. Easter
4. Retirement
5. Mother's Day
6. New Year
7. Valentine's Day
8. Wedding anniversary

Men, who needs them?
Now I go to films alone
watch a silent telephone
send myself a valentine
whisper softly "I am mine"

Louise Hudson

B Listen. Note the occasion and an appropriate phrase.

	Occasion	Phrase
1.		
2.		
3.		
4.		
5.		

C Write an occasion on a card. Show your card to other people in the class. They react to your card, you react to theirs.

8

7 The Born Loser

A Look at the cartoon.
What do you think the Born Loser forgot last year?

B Do this puzzle to find the answer.

1. Month of the babysitter's birthday
2. Person whose birthday is on May 3
3. Occasion celebrated on June 10
4. Person whose birthday is on September 23
5. Person whose birthday is on January 31
6. Person whose birthday is on June 4
7. Person whose birthday is on July 29
8. People who don't think much of the Born Loser's memory
9. Person whose birthday is on March 18

8 Celebrating

We wish you a Merry Christmas,
We wish you a Merry Christmas,
We wish you a Merry Christmas,
And a Happy New Year.

Another Christmas Poem

Bloody Christmas, here again.
Let us raise a loving cup:
Peace on earth, goodwill to men,
And make them do the washing-up.

Wendy Cope

A Make a list of occasions you celebrate or have celebrated.
Include family traditions, national traditions and personal occasions.

_____
_____
_____

 B Choose one occasion and note how you celebrate(d) it. Report.

Special food or drink: _____
Special activities: _____
Other rituals: _____
Occasion: _____
Presents: _____
Card: _____

"In our family we celebrate
the seventeenth of March
with a family party.
It's a big day for us because …"

9 Special days

Red Nose Day.
A day when people all over Britain
do unusual and amusing things
to raise money for charity.
Many people wear something like
these red noses to show their support.

A What do you think happens on these occasions?

National Stay In Bed Day Yellow Day Carrot Day No Solid Food Day Leave Your Car At Home Day Let Yourself Go Day	is a day when people	are (only) allowed to aren't allowed to don't have to have to	…

B Invent your own public holiday. Decide what you are going to celebrate, and how.

C Make a poster and present your results.

"What we suggest is …"   "On this day people …"   "Every fifth of March …"

"Another thing is that people …"   "This is a design for a card."

10 The "If" game

 A On a card, write five things you would like to be.

| If I were a | place
dish
piece of music
present
public holiday
day of the week
drink | I'd be … |

B Put the card in a hat.
Take one, read it out and guess who wrote it.
Ask the writer to explain one of the things on the card.

"Why did you choose Malta?"

"Because I like islands."

"Why Tuesday?"

"It's just my favourite day."

11 Associations

1. Write down six words or phrases from this unit.
2. Read them to a partner, one at a time. Your partner says what she or he associates with each word or phrase, and why.
3. When you have finished both lists, swop them and work with a new partner.

12 PRONUNCIATION

Find other examples of words connected with food with these stress patterns in Units 1 – 8.

Oo	saucepan	
oO	courgettes	
Ooo	cinnamon	
oOo	tomatoes	
Oooo	cauliflower	
oOoo	ingredients	
ooOo	oregano	

UNIT 9

Clothes

1 Something to wear

A   Write in the names of the clothes.

pair of trousers
hat   pair of tights
shirt   pair of shoes
skirt   dress   blouse
pair of socks   coat
pair of shorts   tie
underwear   suit
pullover   jacket

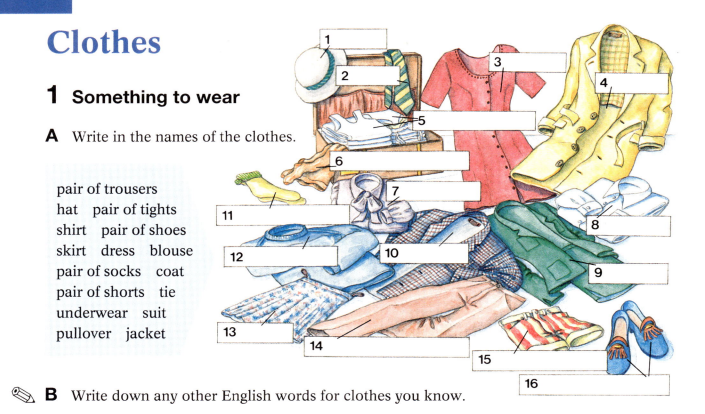

B   Write down any other English words for clothes you know.

C   Put the clothes in the wardrobes. Compare.

His	Hers	Theirs

2 Coat

A   Finish the poem. Compare.

B   Now listen to the original poem.

> **Coat**   Sometimes I have wanted
> to throw you off
> like a heavy coat.
>
> Sometimes I have said
> you would not let me
> breathe or move.
>
> But now that I am free
> to choose light clothes
> or none at all …
>
> Vicki Feaver

3 Colourful clothes

A Listen and answer the questions about your group.

	white	brown	red	black	pink	yellow	green	blue
shirts								
shoes								
socks								
trousers								
blouses								
dresses								
pullovers								

B Listen and follow the instructions. Sit down between instructions.

4 A question of clothes

A Choose one of these questions and ask other people in the class. Note the answers and ask for details.

1. What is your favourite piece of clothing?
2. What is your most comfortable or most elegant piece of clothing?
3. Is there a very expensive piece of clothing you would like? What is it?
4. Have you got a piece of clothing that holds special memories for you?
5. What is your oldest piece of clothing?

MEMO PAD

B Report.

"Tim says his most comfortable piece of clothing is an old pullover he wears in the garden."

"Jane's favourite piece of clothing is a pair of trousers she bought in Italy. It reminds her of holidays."

"Angela's got a hat which she's had for about 30 years. She's only worn it once."

5 Young fashions

A Who says what? Match the statements and the people in the pictures.

"I'm about the same size as my daughter and she just helps herself to my clothes any time she feels like it."

"Children today are into clothes. I think that's a big difference between my generation and my children's generation."

"The fashions didn't change every six months like they do today, and we kept the same clothes for years."

1

2

3

___ a) "My brother and I, we only had one of most things – one pair of shoes, one coat, one pullover, one pair of trousers for school and so on – but it didn't worry us."

___ b) "Her motto seems to be 'What's mine is mine, and what's yours is mine, too.'"

___ c) "We couldn't afford to throw away perfectly good skirts or blouses just because we got bored with them."

___ d) "Clothes weren't very important to us. Certainly not as important as they are to today's young people. And fashion – we didn't know what it meant."

___ e) "She's got more clothes than the rest of us, anyway."

___ f) "We mended them to make them last longer, or we made the dresses a bit longer or a bit shorter."

B Listen and check.

C Have you had similar experiences? Do you agree or disagree with the speakers? Discuss and report.

"When we were children we …"

"So did we."

"That sounds familiar!"

"That's just like my daughter!"

"That reminds me of …"

6 The story of jeans

A Which of these words would you expect to find in the story of jeans? Tick them and compare.

Bavaria	cotton	gold	Nîmes	soldiers
California	cowboys	material	popular	tents
canvas	Genoa	miners	rock 'n' roll	tough

9

B Now read the text and check.

Levi Strauss, who gave his name to Levi's jeans, was born in a small town in Bavaria in 1830. In 1847 he emigrated to the USA and worked at first as a travelling salesman for his two brothers in New York City, selling household goods around the New York area and in Kentucky.

In 1849 gold was discovered in California and the Gold Rush started. Levi Strauss also decided to try his luck in California and sailed for San Francisco, where he planned to start a shop. It was opened in 1851, but before that Strauss travelled around, selling goods from a wagon.

One of the things he sold was canvas for tents, but this did not make much money. However, California was full of farmers, railroad workers, cowboys, lumberjacks and miners, and they all needed tough working trousers, so Levi Strauss decided to use the canvas for trousers instead.

The canvas trousers sold very well, but Levi Strauss was also interested in other materials, especially a new, hard-wearing cotton produced in the French town of Nîmes. This material was called denim, from "serge de Nîmes". He wrote to his brothers in New York, asking them to get some for him. The denim proved very successful and he soon stopped using canvas altogether.

When he died in 1902 at the age of 72, Levi Strauss was a wealthy businessman, and the demand for jeans was still growing. In the 1930s mass production started, and the first jeans were introduced to Europe by American soldiers during World War II. With the rise of rock 'n' roll in the late 50s and early 60s, they became really popular in Europe, too – which was appropriate for an item of clothing whose name comes from the Italian port of Genoa, from where a cotton material known as "jean" was exported.

C Make true sentences.

| In 1849 gold
Levi Strauss' shop
The new French cotton
Jeans
"Jean" | was
were | called denim.
discovered in California.
exported from Genoa.
introduced to Europe by American soldiers.
opened in 1851. |

D What can you remember about these places and dates? Try to answer without looking at the text.

Bavaria	1830	1847
New York	1849	California
San Francisco	1851	Nîmes
1902	the late 50s	Genoa

"Bavaria's the place where …"

"1830's the year when …"

E When are jeans acceptable? Discuss.

seventy-nine

7 The price of fashion

A Read the text.
Put the lines in the correct places.

> the more you waste, the happier you are
> the more money you spend on clothes, the happier you are
> the quicker fashions change, the happier you are

Happiness is waste

The better you look, the happier you are.
To look good, you need fashionable clothes.
Fashionable clothes are expensive.
Therefore _____
_____.

The quicker fashions change, the more clothes you buy
And the more money you spend.
Therefore _____
_____.

The more clothes you buy, the more clothes you throw away.
Therefore _____
_____.

Therefore happiness is waste.

B Listen and check.

C What do you think? Discuss.

8 Valuables

A Tick the objects you are wearing or have got with you now.

- door keys
- car keys
- wallet
- purse
- money
- cheque card
- credit card
- ID card
- driving licence
- handbag
- glasses
- sunglasses
- watch
- ring
- brooch
- necklace
- earrings

B What has everybody got? What has nobody got?

C Play the game.

1. Clear a table. Each person puts at least one small object on the table. You need about 20 objects. Arrange the objects and study them for a minute or two.
2. One pair now goes away while the others change the position of some of the objects and/or take some of them away.
3. The first pair returns and says what has changed.

"You've moved the watch."

"You've taken the wallet away."

"The cheque card was under the ring."

9 Compliments

A Fill in.

1. ❐ _____ new glasses.
   ○ Oh, thank you!

2. ❐ That pullover _____.
   ○ Oh, _____?
   I'm glad you like it.

3. ❐ Those jeans _____.
   ○ _____!

4. ❐ _____ ring.
   ○ Thank you. It was my grandmother's.

5. ❐ _____ blouse, isn't it?
   ○ Yes, I got it last week.
   _____?
   ❐ It's very nice.

Do you like it
That's a new
do you think so
That's a beautiful
look really great
really suits you
Thank you
I like your

 B Listen and check.

C Pay each other compliments and respond.

"Oh, Ginger – you look absolutely stunning ... and whatever you rolled in sure does stink."

9

10 Materials

Write down the names of clothes and other things in the room which are made (mainly) of the following materials. How many can you find in five minutes?

Cotton _____
Leather _____
Metal _____
Paper _____
Plastic _____
Wood _____
Wool _____

11 "Odd one out"

 Write five or six groups of words, each containing something which does not fit. Give the lists to the other groups. They have to say which word is the odd one out, and why.

> *T-shirt, blouse, shoes, jeans*

"The odd one out is 'blouse' because only women wear blouses."

"But it could also be 'shoes', couldn't it?"

12 PRONUNCIATION

 A Listen. Note what happens to the underlined letters.

green blouses	red blouses	white blouses
green pullovers	red pullovers	white pullovers
green coats	red coats	white coats
		white trousers
		white dresses

 B Listen again and practise.

C Now practise these words and phrases.

favourite clothes   we got bored
sit down   a bit longer
favourite piece of clothing   credit card
one pair   handbag
one coat   sunglasses

 D Listen and check.

PREVIEW C

1 In the picture

A Discuss the pictures.

Who are the people?
What is happening?
What has just happened?
What is going to happen next?

B Report and compare.

2 Find the person who …

A Write three sentences about yourself on a card. They should have something to do with the last three units and be things which the other people in your class may not know about. Do not write your name on the card.

1. *I once worked as a cook.*
2. *My wife and I were born on the same day.*
3. *I never wear jeans.*

B Give your card to your teacher.
Write down the sentences your teacher dictates.

C Find the people who wrote the sentences.

"Are you the person who was born on the same day as his wife?"

3 Unusual recipes

A What makes: a nice boss?
a happy Christmas?
a good English lesson?
a good party?
a good weekend?
…?

nice boss — fair

B Write a recipe like this:

Recipe for an ideal job

Take some long holidays and several spoons of good pay. Add some nice colleagues and a pinch of work. Mix the ingredients and put the job in a warm, sunny place. Leave it for a few years until it is time to retire.

4 Listen ahead ➩ ➩ ➩ ➩ ➩ ➩ ➩ ➩ ➩ ➩ ➩ ➩ ➩ ➩

Listen. Which units are these extracts from?

- UNIT 10 Home and health
- UNIT 11 Families
- UNIT 12 On the road again

1. Unit ____
2. Unit ____
3. Unit ____
4. Unit ____
5. Unit ____
6. Unit ____

eighty-three 83

UNIT 10

Home and health

1 At home

A Match the activities and the places, then add as many other activities as you can. Compare.

> cleaning   cooking   eating
> gardening   having a shower   listening to music
> relaxing   shaving   sleeping

Kitchen: _____
Living room: _____
Bedroom: _____
Bathroom: _____
Other places inside: _____
Outside: _____

B Choose about ten activities and write them in the diagram.

enjoyable

listening to music

sleeping

essential ← → **not essential**

cleaning

not enjoyable

C Compare.

2 Where the water goes

A Where do you use water in your home? _____

 B Match the noises and the activities.

___ drinking   ___ washing clothes   ___ washing up
___ flushing the toilet   ___ cleaning teeth   ___ watering the
___ having a shower   ___ washing the car   garden

84 eighty-four

C Which of these activities uses the most water (on average)?
Put them in order.

1. _____
2. _____
3. _____
4. _____
5. _____
6. _____
7. _____
8. _____

D Compare and then check in File 15.

3 The energy price

A Fill in *less* or *more*.

Compared to 30 years ago:
1. heating systems are ___more___ efficient.
2. we use _____ energy for heating.
3. there are _____ one-person households.
4. washing machines use _____ electricity.
5. we do _____ washing.
6. household machines are _____ efficient.
7. we have a lot _____ electrical equipment.
8. we use _____ electricity.
9. _____ people prefer showers to baths.
10. we use _____ water.

B Read the text and check your answers.

Use of Energy

Houses are better insulated and heating systems are more efficient than they used to be. So do we use less energy? No, we don't; we heat our homes for longer, and we heat a greater area. Between 1960 and 1990 the average West German's living space doubled. The number of energy-intensive one-person households is increasing all the time. The result: a 70% increase in the amount of energy used for heating.

Washing machines now use 40% less electricity than 30 years ago. However, the amount of washing per household has almost tripled since then. Other household machines are also more efficient, but people have more of them. An increasing number of households now have a second fridge or freezer, not to mention televisions, hifis, etc. In 30 years the consumption of electricity per household per year in Germany has risen from 870 to 3500 kilowatt hours.

More and more people prefer showers to baths, and of course a shower uses less water. Have we saved water? No; we just shower more frequently. All in all, Germans now use three times as much water as they did 40 years ago.

C Read the text again. Underline any information you find surprising and report.

"I didn't realize that ..."   "I'm surprised that ..."   "I find it difficult to believe that ..."

10

4 In the bathroom

A Label the objects in the picture.

> aspirin   comb   soap   hairbrush   hairdryer
> make-up   mirror   perfume   razor   shampoo
> toothbrush   toothpaste   towels   aftershave
> nail file   scissors   electric shaver

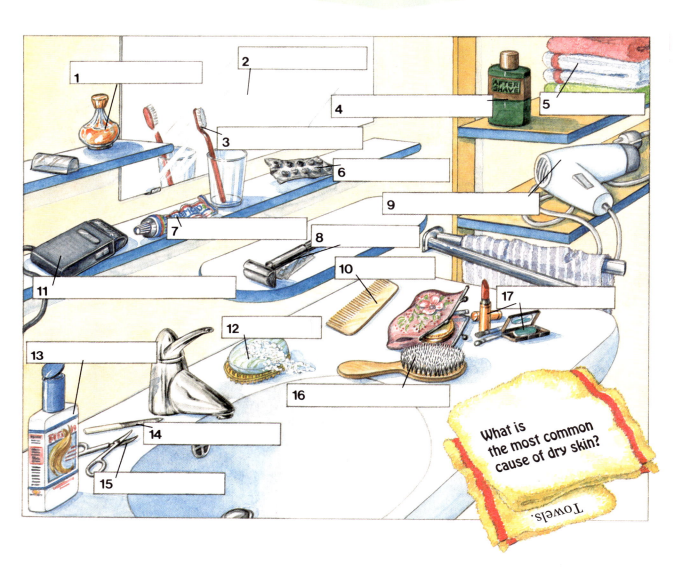

What is the most common cause of dry skin?

Towels.

B How often do you use these items? Put them in one of the boxes.

every day	sometimes	hardly ever	never

10

5 Luxuries and essentials

A What are the most essential things in your house or flat?

B Read the text. Which of the things mentioned are luxuries, in your opinion?

Household Equipment in GB and USA

No British kitchen is complete without an electric kettle. These are even found in hotel rooms, so that guests can make themselves a cup of tea or instant coffee at night or first thing in the morning.

On the other hand, many British houses do not have showers, because people traditionally prefer baths.

On the other side of the Atlantic, most Americans seem to need coffee machines and enormous fridges. Essential equipment in the average American bathroom includes dental floss and electric toothbrushes.

C Read these definitions of luxury, then write one or two of your own.

- Luxury is living on your own in a large flat or house.
- Luxury is when you turn up the heating instead of putting on a pullover.
- Luxury is having more than one toilet.
- Luxury is anything more than food, drink and shelter.

Luxury is _____

Luxury is when _____

Luxury is having _____

D Compare. Which do you like best?

6 Wishful thinking

What would make life in your house or flat easier or more enjoyable?

- I wish my flat was on the ground floor.
- I wish I had one more room.
- If I could afford it, I'd have my own sauna.

10

7 Domestic disasters

A Match the sentences and the pictures.

1. My father-in-law was painting his front door when it started to rain.
2. I was ironing a shirt when the phone rang.
3. My sister was boiling some milk when her son started to cry.
4. My neighbour was running a bath when someone knocked at the door.

B Complete these sentences any way you like and compare.

1. I was _____ one day when I heard a strange noise.
2. I was _____ recently when the phone rang.
3. I was _____ and all of a sudden something moved.
4. I was _____ when I realized it wasn't working properly.
5. I was _____ when I thought, "Why am I doing this?"

C One of you chooses a sentence from B.
Each person adds a sentence to make a story.

8 Aches and pains

 A Mime or draw two or three of these complaints for your partner.

backache   a hangover   a headache   insomnia
a stiff neck   stomachache   a sore throat   toothache

B Which of the complaints could these be remedies for?

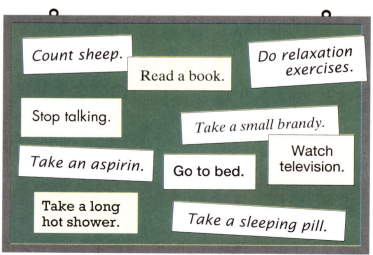

10

"Counting sheep's good for insomnia."   *"Opening the window could be good for quite a lot of things."*   *"Keep moving is good advice if you've got backache."*

 C Choose three of the complaints and write them down. Listen and note the remedies you hear.

Complaints	Remedies
1. _____	_____
2. _____	_____
3. _____	_____

 D Give advice.

1. Write a health complaint on a card.
2. Tell your partner the complaint and ask for advice.
3. Give your partner advice.
4. Swap cards and find a new partner.

"Try …ing"   *"Why don't you …"*

"You'll feel much better."

"It'll really help."   *"Ignore it!"*

> **WORDS OF WISDOM**
>
> If you want to feel happy, just laugh. It really works!

9 "Remember Aspirin"

A Fill in.

_____
when you have a headache.

it'll help
Take sleeping tablets
Think what a fool I've been
take a tranquilizer
Remember aspirin

_____
if you wake at night.

And if you feel lonely
– _____.

But in case this should let you down
– think of me.
_____.

And you'll smile
and
_____.

L. L. Szkutnik

 B Listen and check.

eighty-nine **89**

10

10 Word pairs

How many verb-noun pairs can you find in this unit using these verbs?

do: *do relaxation exercises, do the washing up,* _____
have: _____
take: _____
use: _____
wash: _____

11 PRONUNCIATION

 A Listen. Notice the (⌄) intonation pattern on the underlined sections.

1. If I could <u>afford it</u>, I'd have my own sauna.
2. <u>Luxury</u> is living on your own in a big flat.
3. Opening the <u>window</u> could be good for quite a lot of things.
4. Is it <u>sunny in Los Angeles</u>?
5. My <u>father-in-law</u> was painting his front <u>door</u> when it started to rain.
6. At <u>one point</u> …
7. Can I get a <u>coffee round here</u>?
8. If you want to feel <u>happy</u>, just laugh.

 B Listen again and practise.

C Practise reading these sentences in the same way.

1. I never use a <u>razor</u>; I always use an electric shaver.
2. On the <u>other hand</u>, …
3. Can I speak to Mr <u>Cosby, please</u>?
4. I wouldn't like to be a <u>traffic warden</u>.
5. Counting sheep's good for <u>insomnia</u>.
6. <u>Speaking</u>.
7. Can I take a <u>message</u>?
8. After a <u>while</u>, …

 D Listen and check.

UNIT 11

Families

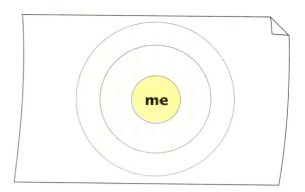

1 Around me

 A Write the names of people or pets that are important to you on a piece of paper.

 B Ask about your partner's people or pets.

 C Change partners. Give your new partner one of the names on your chart. Your partner has three minutes to find out as much information about this person as possible. Take turns.

"How did you …?"   *"What's she like?"*

"How long have you …?"

"What were you doing when you met?"

2 Twins

 A Put the story in the right order.

| 1 | **Twins reunited after 40 years.** Identical twins Carole Wood and Sylvia Scicluna were adopted because their mother was not married when they were born in December 1944. |

| | As a result of this, the sisters wrote to each other and were finally reunited in Perth in August 1985. |

| | Each was adopted by a different family and, although the two families lived less than two miles apart, the twins never met. |

| | In 1967 Sylvia moved to Perth, Australia. |

| | Later, they both trained as nurses in Portsmouth and even worked in the same hospital, although at different times. |

| | Nearly 20 years later, Valerie White saw a woman in a street in Portsmouth who looked just like her friend Sylvia. |

| | One of the friends she left behind was Valerie White. |

| | She stopped the woman and explained the situation. |

| 9 | Carole Wood says, "It's wonderful. Strangely, we have found that we like the same music, we both hate tea and drink coffee without sugar." |

B Read the text in File 16 and check.

 C How many similarities between the twins can you find?

_____
_____
_____
_____

 D What do you have in common with other members of your family? Discuss and report.

ninety-one

11

3 Grandparents

 A Draw your "roots map". First mark your birthplace and the town or area where you are now. Then add the birthplaces of your parents and grandparents. Talk about your maps.

"My mother's parents were from …"   *"My parents met in …"*

"My mother was working in …"   *"They've been in this area for …"*

 B Note five things about your grandparents.

MEMO PAD

C Compare.

D How have families changed since your grandparents' days?

4 Families today

A Read the minisaga and tell the person's story.

"At first there was one person, a baby. The baby …"

Life And Numbers

Once upon a time
there was
just Me.
I soon realised there were
three of us, then gradually
four. At last there were just
the two of us. All at once four
of us. Suddenly just the two
of us again. Now there is
only Me
as in the beginning.

Frances Politzer

11

B Listen to the five people talking about their families. What types of families are they examples of?

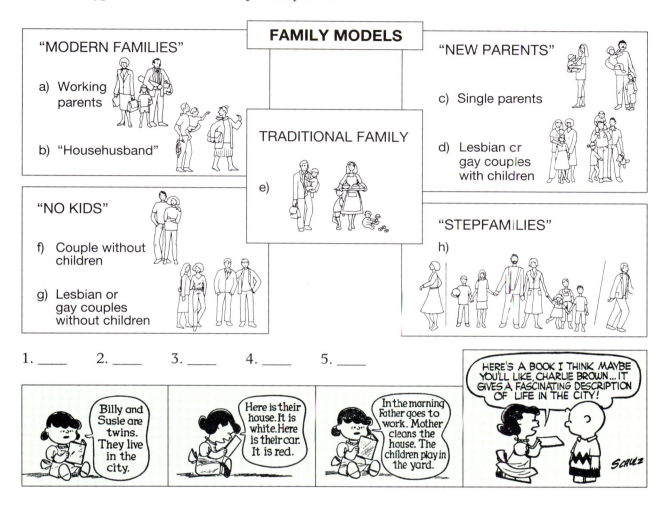

1. ___ 2. ___ 3. ___ 4. ___ 5. ___

C What sort of families do Europeans prefer? Put these three models in order of popularity.

Family Models

Model A Man goes out to work, woman does the housework and looks after the children.

Model B Man goes out to work, woman also does some work outside the home. Woman does most of the housework and takes care of the children.

Model C Both partners work, share the housework and take care of the children.

D Look at File 18 and check.

11

5 The future of the family

A Make predictions about the future of the family.

more fewer	children fathers lesbians gays mothers parents people	will	be bring up get have live stay	at home born children longer married on their own only children several times single parents

> People will live longer.
> Fewer people will get married.
> _____

B Choose your three most likely predictions and read them out.

6 Future prospects

A Look at the questions from the census poster and write three wishes for the baby on a card.

> I hope you'll ...
> I hope you won't ...
> I hope you'll be able to ...

When was I born?
Where will I go to school?
Where will I work?
How will I get there?

Will I get married?
What kind of house will I live in?
Will I have children?
Where will they be born?

B Compare.

C Make a wish for yourself.   *"I hope I'll ..."*

7 Parents and children

 A Look at these questions we asked a mother and her teenage daughter, then listen and make notes.

1. What do you think of your daughter/mother, generally?
2. Has she got any annoying habits?
3. What sort of things do you talk about with each other?
4. Do you have any tastes in common?
5. In what ways are you like each other?

Mother	Daughter

B Read the tapescript and check.

 C Compare. Do you think this mother and daughter get on well together?

8 Parental wisdom

 A What advice would a Viking give his son?

Three things a Viking needs: _____

Three things a Viking should watch out for: _____

Something a Viking should never eat: _____

cold	cash
dry	chicken
hard	cousins
left-handed	ladies
one-legged	socks
red-headed	steel
second	swordsmen

B Look at the complete cartoon in File 12 and check.

C What did your parents tell you?

"Don't forget to wash behind your ears."   *"Eat up all your vegetables."*   *"Don't talk to strangers."*

11

9 Dear Wendy

 A Choose two or three problems to reply to.

Dear Wendy
Britain's top agony aunt

I have read that it is now possible to choose the sex of your child. Is this a good idea? I would like to have a baby soon.

("Future Mother")

My son (17) wants to stay overnight at his girlfriend's place. Should I let him?

("Anxious Mother")

I think my son has started to smoke. We are a non-smoking family. What should we do?

("No Smoking!")

My father-in-law has been a widower for several years and has got bored with living on his own. He would like to move in with us. We don't think this is a good idea. How can we tell him?

("Reluctant Daughter-in-Law")

If we go to my parents-in-law at Christmas, my parents are upset; if we go to my parents, the others complain. We can't invite them all here because we haven't got enough space. What should we do? My husband says we should take a winter holiday to get away from all of them. What do you think?

("Christmas Compromiser")

Our children don't want to go on holiday with us any more. We think they are too young (16, 15) to go away or to be left in the house on their own. Have you got any ideas?

("Holiday Harmonists")

My grandchildren call their parents by their names rather than "Mum" and "Dad". Should I let them call me "Betty"?

("Granny Betty")

B Write short replies giving advice.

Dear Anxious Mother, …

MEMO PAD

If I were you, I'd …
I think I wouldn't …
I don't think you should …

C Read out your replies and discuss them.

10 Word relations

Look through the unit and find words that are related in some way. How many can you find in ten minutes?

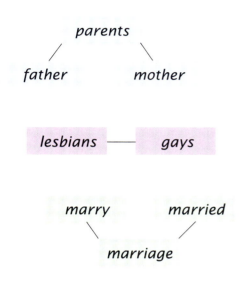

"Darling!"

11 PRONUNCIATION

 A Listen and mark the intonation (↘) or (↗) on the underlined sections.

My <u>mother's</u> from <u>Leeds</u>, but her <u>family</u> came from <u>Ireland</u>.
They arrived in <u>Leeds</u> about two or three <u>generations</u> ago.
My <u>father</u> comes from <u>Cornwall</u>. <u>Cornwall's</u> in the south-west of <u>England</u>.

 B Listen and check.

C Now practise these exchanges.

1. ❐ My father's parents were from <u>Scotland</u>.
   ○ I don't <u>know</u> where <u>my grandparents came from</u>.

2. ❐ My parents met in <u>Japan</u>.
   ○ <u>Japan</u>? What were they doing <u>there</u>?

3. ❐ My <u>mother</u> was working for a <u>company</u> in <u>Tokyo</u>.
   ○ What about your <u>father</u>?

4. ❐ My family's been in <u>this area</u> for about a hundred <u>years</u>.
   ○ <u>Oh</u>. <u>We</u> only moved here last <u>June</u>.

 D Listen and check.

ninety-seven 97

UNIT 12

On the road again

1 Means of transport

A Write down six common means of transport.

Means of transport	Characteristics
1. _____	_____
2. _____	_____
3. _____	_____
4. _____	_____
5. _____	_____
6. _____	_____

B Fill in the opposites.

+	−
_____	expensive
_____	uncomfortable
_____	inconvenient
exciting	_____
fast	_____
reliable	_____
safe	_____

✎ **C** Match these adjectives and the means of transport in A. Write them under "Characteristics".

D Complete the sentences, then compare.

1. I prefer to walk to work, even if the bus is __*quicker*__.
2. Taxis are _____, but not very _____.
3. Motorbikes are _____ than cars.
   On the other hand, they're also _____.
4. I prefer _____, even if _____ is/are _____.
5. _____ are _____, but not very _____.
6. _____ are _____ than _____. On the other hand, they're also _____.

> **York**
>
> I went round the Railway Museum in York
> there were plenty of trains
> but it was quicker to walk
>
> John Hegley

2 Things you can do in a train

A Read this first half of a British Rail advertisement.
How many ideas can you add? Make notes and report.

**The average InterCity journey takes two hours.
With no steering wheel to hold, what will you do all the time.**

A study in
time and motion.

1. See how long you can hold your breath.
2. Read a business report.
3. If you're feeling intellectual, do the Times Crossword.
4. If not, do the Times Quick Crossword.
5. Memorise your favourite poem.
6. Try and work out what your fellow travellers do for a living by studying their clothes.
7. Have a drink.
8. Persuade a total stranger to tell you their life story.
9. Have another drink.
10. Persuade a total stranger to listen to your life story.
11. Write a letter to an old friend you've lost touch with.

B Read the rest of the text in File 19 and compare.

C Write a short advert for another means of transport.

3 In ten years' time

A What do you think? Fill in.

In ten years' time:

+

will
(certainly)

will probably

might

probably won't

(certainly)
won't

−

1. there _____ be more lorries on the roads.
2. public transport in towns _____ become cheaper.
3. the railway network _____ be reduced.
4. cars and lorries _____ have to pay to enter cities.
5. car-owners _____ have to pay to park outside their houses.
6. there _____ be "intelligent" roads to help prevent traffic jams.
7. there _____ be a lot of electric cars.
8. most people _____ get rid of their cars.
9. the price of petrol _____ rise.
10. farmers _____ start to use horses again.
11. people _____ move house in order to live nearer their work.
12. speed limits _____ be lowered.

B Choose one sentence. Ask other people for their predictions and report.

12

C What are the worst transport problems in your town or area? How would you solve them? Discuss and report.

"We'd ..."   "We wouldn't ..."

4 Announcements

A You are at London Airport. Choose (✓) one of these flights and listen to the announcements. What do you have to do?

☐ AF825 to Paris
☐ BA728 to Geneva
☐ LH4029 to Frankfurt

☐ Go to Gate ___.
☐ Wait.

B You are on Platform 3 at Victoria Station in London. Choose (✓) a place and listen to the announcement. What do you have to do?

☐ Brighton
☐ Dover
☐ Gatwick Airport

☐ Get on the train.
☐ Wait on Platform 3.
☐ Go to Platform ___.

The train now arriving at Platforms 5, 6, 7 and 8 is coming in sideways.

C You are in a pub and have parked your car in the car park. Choose (✓) a car and listen to the landlord's announcement. What do you have to do?

☐ Move the car.
☐ Talk to the police.
☐ Nothing.

Black Rover ☐   Yellow Metro ☐   Blue Honda ☐

5 Giving directions

A Fill in, then listen and check.

Situation 1

come   cross   follow   go
leave   look out for   turn

_____ the motorway at junction 16 and _____ the signs for Birmingham. _____ straight on for about 3 miles till you _____ to a pub called the Coach and Horses. _____ left there, and after about a mile _____ Nelson Drive. It's on the right. It's just before a railway bridge, so if you _____ a bridge, you'll know you've gone too far.

1 mile	=	1.609 km
1 yard	=	91.44 cm
1 km	=	0.621 mile
1 km	=	1.094 yards

Situation 2

change   check   take   run   take

_____ the train from Euston to Preston and _____ there for Chorley. I think it's the Blackpool line, but you can _____ that. If you've got heavy luggage, the best thing is to _____ a taxi from the station, because it's quite a long walk. There are buses to Southport Road, but I don't know how often they _____ in the evening.

> Bradford to Bristol
> ------------------
>   from Bradford Yorkshire
>   to Bristol Temple Meads
> you don't have to change your underwear
>   but you have to change at Leeds
>
> John Hegley

B Form groups of about six. Plan a route for your teacher to visit all of you, using public transport and/or walking. Work out all the necessary details about bus numbers, bus stops, etc. Make notes and tell your teacher what to do.

"You take the ..."

12

6 Asking directions

A Write questions that a traveller in your area might want to ask.

Do you know Can you tell me	how ...? how often ...? when ...? where ...? which platform ...?

Can you tell me how to get to ...?
Do you know how often the buses to ... run?

B Ask for and give directions to something in your area (for example, the nearest phone box, the station or a post office).

"Excuse me, can you tell me the way to ...?"

"Excuse me, is there a ... near here?"

"Excuse me, do you know if there's a ... near here?"

"Excuse me, can you tell me where the ... is?"

"Yes, it's ..."

"Sorry, I'm a stranger here myself."

"Go ... and ask again."

7 The story of Thomas Cook

A Read the text and put the paragraphs in the right order.

In July 1841, Thomas Cook offered a day trip by rail from Leicester to Loughborough for one shilling (five pence in today's money). 150 years later, the company he created advertised a day trip by Concorde to Lapland for £1,595.

	Despite the problems, Thomas Cook hoped his tours would promote international peace and understanding. His son John, however, was a hard-headed businessman who did not believe in cheap tickets for Baptists, and was quite happy to arrange trips to horse races, and even to a guillotining. He gradually turned his father's company into a profitable and efficient commercial organization.		Travel in the early days of package tours was not as easy as today. When a party of 70 tourists headed for Rome in the early 1860's, it took nine stagecoaches, 432 horses, 108 men and numerous bullocks to get them over the St Gotthard Pass. Cook himself could only speak English. "Where are the ladies who know French and German?" he used to ask his tourists when he got into difficulties; "Forward please, and say what this man is jabbering about!"
	It was such a success that Cook negotiated deals with several railway companies for cheap group bookings. Soon he was advertising and selling trips in the English Midlands and in Scotland, and within a few years was also organizing trips to mainland Europe.		The man who started it all was born on November 22, 1808 in Derbyshire, England. He left school at the age of ten and worked in various jobs until 1828, when he became a Baptist missionary. He was a teetotaller and the aim of the Loughborough trip was to get working people out of the city pubs.
	What with terrible weather, illness, collapsing tents and falls from horses, Cook's first Middle East tour was not the happiest of trips. And although only one traveller actually died, it seems that many of the others thought he was the lucky one.	7	Thomas Cook died on July 18, 1892 and the business passed into John's hands. One hundred years later, Thomas Cook & Son became part of the German TUI travel group.

B Listen and check.

C Read these statements and mark them 'True' or 'False'.   True | False

1. Thomas Cook's first trip was for working people in Leicester.
2. Cook did not drink any alcohol.
3. Cook spoke several foreign languages.
4. Cook's foreign tours were famous for their standard of comfort.
5. On Cook's first Middle East tour everybody died.
6. Both Cooks were idealists.
7. John Cook was a better businessman than his father.
8. When Thomas Cook died the company was taken over by a foreign firm.

12

8 Road accidents

Complete these accident descriptions given by drivers to their insurance companies. In each case, put one verb in the Past Simple and the other one in the Past Continuous.

1. I __was coming__ (come) home when I __drove__ (drive) into the wrong house and collided with a tree I don't have.

2. I _____ (crash) into a parked car which _____ (come) the other way.

3. I _____ (drive) along the road when a pedestrian _____ (hit) me and went under my car.

4. The old lady didn't know where she _____ (go), so I _____ (run over) her.

5. I _____ (drive) into a lamp-post because I _____ (try) to kill a fly.

6. As I _____ (approach) the junction a sign suddenly _____ (appear) in a place where no stop sign had ever appeared before. I was unable to stop in time to avoid the accident.

9 Travel experiences

A Find someone who: has travelled on a train without a ticket.
has got on the wrong train.
has got off a train at the wrong stop.
has spent the night at an airport waiting for a plane.
has walked on a motorway.
has broken the speed limit for a good reason.

"What happened when …?"   "And where was …?"   "Why did you …?"

"I was on the way to …"   "We were visiting friends in England and …"

B Report something interesting.

104   one hundred and four

10 The unit rally

 A Each group writes six questions about things in this unit.

> *What is the opposite of dangerous?*
> *What is the fifth thing you can do in a train?*
> *What colour is the Metro in the pub car park?*

B Read your questions to the other groups.
The first group to answer correctly gets a point.
The winner is the group with the most points.

11 PRONUNCIATION

 A Listen and mark the intonation (↗) or (↘)
on the underlined sections.

In July eighteen forty-<u>one</u>, Thomas <u>Cook</u> offered a day trip by <u>rail</u> from Leicester to <u>Loughborough</u> for one <u>shilling</u> (five <u>pence</u> in to<u>day's money</u>). A hundred and fifty years <u>later</u>, the company he cre<u>ated</u> advertised a day trip by <u>Concorde</u> to <u>Lapland</u> for one thousand five hundred and ninety-five <u>pounds</u>.

 B Listen again and check, then practise reading the paragraph yourself.

C Read this paragraph and mark the intonation on the underlined sections.

The man who <u>started it all</u> was <u>born</u> on November the twenty-<u>second</u>, eighteen hundred and <u>eight</u> in <u>Derbyshire</u>, <u>England</u>.
He left school at the age of <u>ten</u> and worked in various <u>jobs</u> until eighteen twenty-<u>eight</u>, when he became a Baptist <u>missionary</u>.
He was a teet<u>otaller</u> and the <u>aim of the Loughborough trip</u> was to get working people out of the city <u>pubs</u>.

 D Listen and check.

PREVIEW D

1 Name five

 A Choose a topic and write down five items.

Relatives
Luxuries
Pieces of good advice
Places associated with transport
Things parents tell their children
Things people do every morning
Things people do in their living rooms
Things there will be more of in 10 years' time
Things water is used for
Things you find in a bathroom

RELATIVES   mother
            uncle
            father-in-law
            husband
            daughter

B Find a pair with a different topic and try to guess their items.

2 Sentence darts

1. Form teams of three to four players. With your team, choose a number on the dartboard. There is a sentence starter for each number.

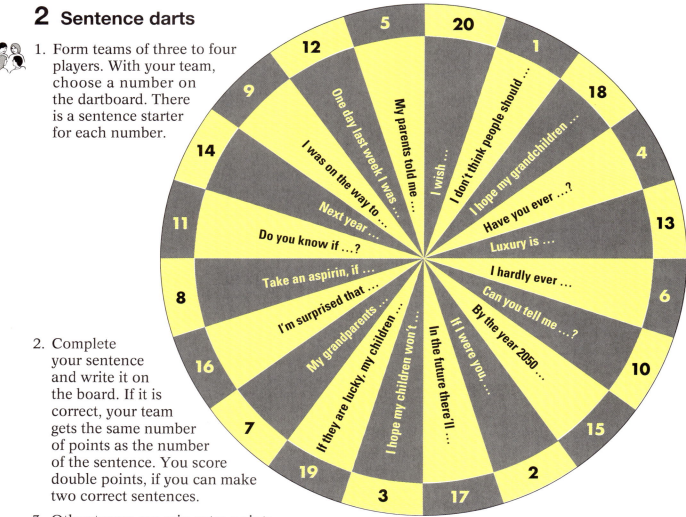

2. Complete your sentence and write it on the board. If it is correct, your team gets the same number of points as the number of the sentence. You score double points, if you can make two correct sentences.

3. Other teams can win extra points, if they make another correct sentence with your starter. The team with the most points wins.

PREVIEW D

3 Airport or station?

You are going to hear two words. Choose one of them.
If you choose the first word, go to the front of the room.
If you choose the second, go to the back.
Talk about your choice.

"Why did you choose ...?"

"Because ..."

"I just like ..."

4 Sights and sounds

A Look through the last three units and find five or six words for each of these categories.

- 👁 Things you can see: _____
- 👂 Things you can hear: _____
- 👃 Things you can smell: _____
- ✋ Things you can touch/feel: _____
- 👄 Things you can taste: _____

B Write a poem, using some of your words.

MEMO PAD _____

In the bathroom

I feel a toothbrush in my mouth
I can still taste last night
I see someone's face in the mirror
I smell toothpaste
I can still hear the alarm clock.

C Read your poem out. The other groups suggest a title.

5 Preview ⇨ ⇨ ⇨ ⇨ ⇨ ⇨ ⇨ ⇨ ⇨ ⇨ ⇨ ⇨ ⇨ ⇨ ⇨

A Match the units and topics to make predictions about the next three units.

UNIT 13 **Shopping**	will probably might	have something about	buying clothes. children and TV. the music people like. English as a world language. learning English. different TV programmes. the opening hours of shops. people's shopping habits. words that people like.
UNIT 14 **Information and entertainment**			
UNIT 15 **English and me**			

B Check your predictions.

Unit 13

Shopping

1 Good buy Beaminster

A Read the text. Underline anything in the text that you have done recently.

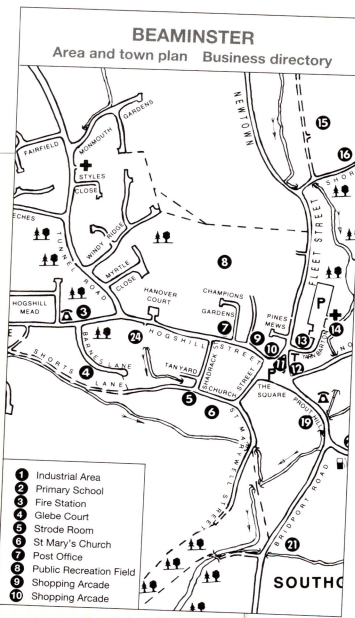

Beaminster, Dorset, population under 3,000, has a great deal to offer, apart from its beautiful surroundings and its charm.

Without leaving the town you can shop for an enormous variety of good, fresh food, locally grown, plus exotics. In addition you can drink a coffee outdoors, build a swimming pool, send a fax, make a photocopy, get married, get buried, borrow a book, advertise an event, take your cat to the vet, choose a video, post a parcel, go to evening classes, go to the doctor, do your washing in the launderette, eat out, go to the theatre, or be an actor yourself.

You can get your souvenirs, your carpets, your Sunday papers, your children's clothes, your wool, your presents, your wine, your TV, your health foods, your injections, … and you can get clothes cleaned, photos developed, furniture repaired, groceries delivered, your teeth filled and your hair done.

All this, of course, you can do in many a town besides Beaminster. But can you, in these towns, leave your shopping in the car with the window open and the keys in the ignition while you go back for more?

Okay, so I love the town. But what is the point of this article? One should appreciate things while one has them. That's what I sincerely hope everyone in Beaminster is doing. Because five years from now a lot of this will almost certainly be gone for ever.

Oh, you'll still be able to buy groceries, there will still be pubs. Some of the services may still be available. The post office may have survived. But what about the shops?

 B Compare. Find things which only one person in your group has done.

"Have you sent a fax recently?"

"Yes, I send them every day."

"Have you been to the hairdresser's recently?"

"No, I haven't." *"Neither have I."*

"Has anybody borrowed a book from the library in the last month?"

C Write down one or two things you can do in each of these places. Compare.

bank	*cash a cheque, get money,* _____
chemist's	_____
dry cleaner's	_____
florist's	_____
greengrocer's	_____
newsagent's	_____
off-licence	_____
post office	_____
stationer's	_____
video shop	_____

D Explain the last paragraph of the article. What is the author worried about?

2 Help!

A Listen and number the situations.

B Match the sentences.

1. I bought this here yesterday and I'm afraid there's something wrong with it. ____
2. I don't think this is working right. ____
3. I haven't got enough cash. ____
4. I'm looking for a pair of sandals. _f_
5. I'm interested in video cameras. ____
6. These oranges are rotten inside. ____
7. This is a bit too big for me. ____

a) Can you check it for me, please?
b) Have you got anything smaller?
c) I'd like my money back.
d) I'd like to change it.
e) Is there one you'd specially recommend?
f) What's a size 42 in English sizes?
g) Will you take a cheque?

one hundred and nine 109

13

3 Class shopping survey

A Complete these questions about shopping in you town or area.

1. Can you recommend a good _____?
2. Do you know how much a _____ costs?
3. How often do you shop for _____?
4. When did you last go to a _____?
5. Have you got a favourite _____?
6. What's your opinion of _____?
7. _____?

B Interview three people.

	Name: _____	Name: _____	Name: _____
1			
2			
3			
4			

C Report something interesting.

4 The shopping game

This is a game for two pairs. Throw a dice to move and follow the instructions in the square you land on. If the square only names a type of shop (e.g. *stationer's*), make up an appropriate dialogue with your partner.

This is your list of shopping tasks. Before you start the game, study the board and write down where you will have to go.

Pair A:

1. Buy a guide to camping in Britain. _____
2. Get something for sunburn. _____
3. Get some wine for Sunday lunch. _____
4. Post a parcel. _____
5. Take back some shoes you bought yesterday and complain. _____
6. Get some information about video cameras. _____
7. Fax a holiday booking. _____
8. Take in a coat for cleaning. _____

Pair B:

1. Buy some flowers for granny's birthday. _____
2. Buy some things for a salad. _____
3. Pick up your holiday photos. _____
4. Hire a video for the whole family. _____
5. Take back a pullover you bought yesterday and complain. _____
6. Get some information about radio alarm clocks. _____
7. Make a photocopy of a magazine article. _____
8. Buy some writing paper. _____

13

You can move in any direction along the paths. The first pair to finish all their shopping tasks and return to the START/FINISH square wins.

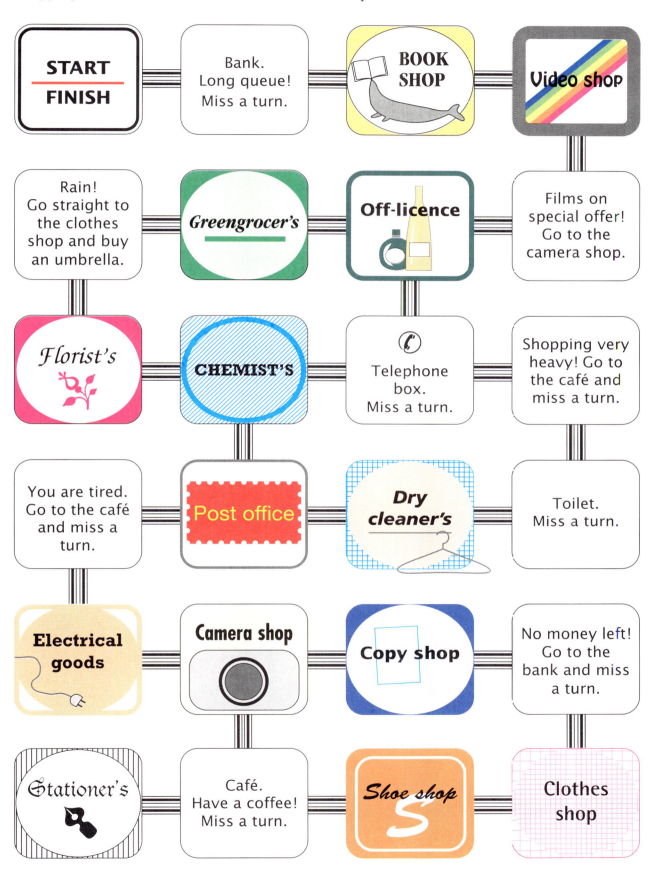

13

5 Have you got everything?

A Look at the picture for two minutes and try to remember as many objects as you can.

B Cover the picture and write down the names of all the things you can remember.

 C Compare and make a group list. Check with the picture to see how well you did.

6 Too much

A Fill in.

babies   Brie   cake   cheers   cream   drink
find   ~~jars~~   gin   pots   sweet   ten

Sweets wrapped in paper, in packets and ___jars___,
Three dozen different chocolate bars;
I can't count the types of biscuit and _____ –
It's so hard to choose I'm starting to shake.

> There's too much, just too much of all this here stuff,
> An awful lot less would be more than enough.
> (It's all sugar, isn't it? It all rots your teeth.)

Cheddar or Stilton, Chester or _____?
How shall I choose? Which cheese shall it be?
Thirty fruit yoghurts in small or large _____ –
Trying to pick one brings me out in spots.

> There's too much, just too much of all this here stuff,
> An awful lot less would be more than enough.
> (It's all animal fat, only good for a heart attack!)

Big packets, small packets, jumbos and _____;
Cornflake variety really amazes!
Ninety-five p or two pounds _____:
How many grams in each packet again?
Eight types of milk and six sorts of _____ –
Which should I take? I silently scream.

> There's too much, just too much of all this here stuff,
> An awful lot less would be more than enough.
> (Who needs breakfast? Just give me coffee, no milk!)

With so many choices I really can't think,
I feel like relaxing at home with a _____;
Just what I need for some peace of mind,
But under the DRINKS sign what do I _____?

> (The usual situation, of course!)

Sherry, martini, madeira, port – _____!
Kiwi-fruit cocktails and eighty-five beers;
Whisky and brandy and vodka and _____ –
Total confusion's the state that I'm in.
Red wine or white wine, medium dry, _____?
Please, someone, choose for me – I'm dead on my feet!

> Because, let me tell you –
> There's too much, just too much of all this here stuff,
> An awful lot less would be more than enough.
> (It's all too much for me, anyway!)

 B Listen and check.

13

7 Department stores

A Listen to some department store announcements. Which floor are these things on?

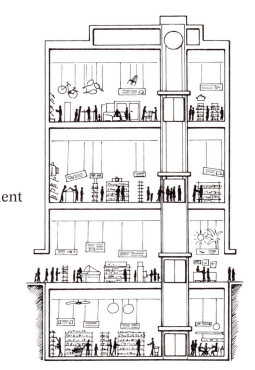

___ computer equipment
___ food
___ furniture, carpets
___ kitchen and bathroom equipment
___ music, videos
___ photoshop
___ restaurant
___ sports clothes and equipment
___ travel agency

(2) Second Floor
(1) First Floor
(G) Ground Floor
(B) Basement

 B How many more departments can you think of?

MEMO PAD

Toilettenartikel = toiletries

C Design your own department store.
Choose the departments and decide where to put them.

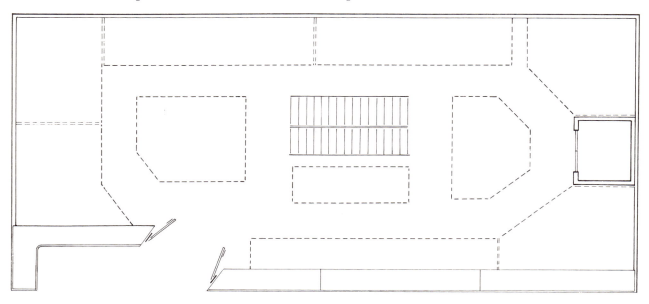

114   one hundred and fourteen

D Present your plan.   *"At the front of the store ..."*   *"Near the entrance ..."*

"In the corner ..."   *"At the back ..."*   *"On the left as you come in ..."*

8 A store manager

A Read the questions. What do you think?

In most department stores:
what kind of goods sell quickly? _____
what kind of goods sell slowly? _____
what kind of goods make a good profit? _____
what is the "best" place in a department store? _____

B Listen and compare.

C Listen again and answer the questions.

According to Peter Willems, what kind of goods do you put:
near the entrance of the store? _____
at the front of the store? _____
at the back or top of the store? _____

one hundred and fifteen   **115**

13

9 Service here and there

A Discuss. What would happen if you:

1. changed your order after they brought the food in a restaurant?
2. bought more items in the supermarket than you could afford to pay for at that moment?
3. asked for another counter to be opened to shorten the queue in the bank?
4. ordered a washing machine and asked for delivery between 12 o'clock and 2 p.m. on Monday?
5. asked someone in the petrol station to check your oil and tyres, and clean the windscreen?

"Nothing would happen."

"I think they'd do it."

"I don't think they'd do it."

"They'd probably give you a funny look."

"They'd explain why they couldn't do it."

"They'd probably tell you to …"

"I think they'd offer to …"

B A few years ago a British newspaper put the same things to the test in several cities. Read the article and find out what happened.

Service with(out) a smile

In our service economy the customer is always right. In theory at least. But just how good – or bad – is the service in this country? To find out, our reporters put five situations to the test in Birmingham ("the friendliest city in the world"), Tokyo and Los Angeles.

Situation 1
In a typical restaurant, change your entire order after five minutes (even if the food has already arrived).

Tokyo: Waiter looked a bit worried but was not annoyed. Returned a few minutes later with the new order.
Los Angeles: Waitress not at all annoyed, makes a joke and takes the fresh order.
Birmingham: "No problem at all", said our waitress.

Situation 2
Do some shopping in a busy supermarket. Queue. Discover you do not have enough money and ask to put some items back.

Tokyo: Cashier polite.
Los Angeles: No problem. Supermarkets are open 24 hours a day, seven days a week. Von's Supermarkets open a new till whenever three people queue and train staff to listen and make eye contact with customers.

Situation 3
Drive into a petrol station and ask to have your windscreen cleaned, tyres and oil checked.

Tokyo: It is normal in Japan for petrol station attendants to clean windscreens and empty ashtrays without being asked. Oil and tyres checked efficiently.
Birmingham: The assistant looks very surprised. Asks jokingly if we are disabled.

Situation 4
Ask for another counter to be opened to shorten the lunchtime queue at the bank.

Los Angeles: Wells Fargo promises to credit $5 to your account if there are more than two people in the queue.
Birmingham: All tills open except "quick service" counter. Long queues. Response to reporter's request: "Sorry, we haven't got any staff available at the moment."
Tokyo: Even a simple transaction can take half an hour or more, because everything is done with the customer present. People with questions treated poorly by Western standards because banks do not expect to be questioned. Neither friendly nor efficient.

Situation 5
Order a washing machine and ask for delivery between noon and 2 p.m. on Monday.

Tokyo: Shop will deliver at any time the customer wants during opening hours (9 a.m. to 8 p.m.).
Los Angeles: Delivery either morning, afternoon, or evening (6 to 9), Tuesday to Saturday.
Birmingham: No guaranteed delivery times, only morning or afternoon.

C What would you do?
Complete four of these sentences and compare results.

If _a salesperson was unfriendly_____, I'd complain.
If _____, I wouldn't go there again.
If _____, I'd ask for the manager.
If _____, I'd want my money back.
If _____, I'd write to the newspaper.
If _____, I'd take it back.

10 Review puzzles

A Complete this word puzzle and make up clues for it.

1. _____ pre **S** ent _____
2. _____ **H** _____
3. _____ **O** _____
4. _____ **P** _____
5. _____ **P** _____
6. _____ **I** _____
7. _____ **N** _____
8. _____ **G** _____

Clues

1. _something you give somebody for their birthday_
2. _____
3. _____
4. _____
5. _____
6. _____
7. _____
8. _____

B Now make another puzzle with a different word from this unit.

11 PRONUNCIATION

A Match the sentences and the rhythms.

1. I'm looking for a pair of sandals.
2. I'd ask for the manager.
3. This is a bit too big for me.
4. They'd probably give you a funny look.
5. Have you sent a fax recently?
6. Can you recommend a good hairdresser?

a) ooooOooOoo
b) oOoooOoOo
c) oOooOoo
d) ooOoOooo
e) oooOoOoo
f) oOooOooOoO

B Listen and check.

Unit 14

Information and entertainment

1 Television and newspapers

A Add some words.

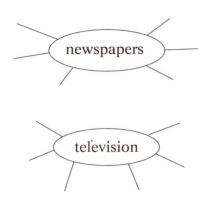

B Student A: Look at File 10.
Student B: Look at File 17.

2 Square-eyed Europe

A Look at these types of TV programme. Tick the ones that are mentioned in the text.

- [ ] series
- [ ] films
- [ ] TV films
- [ ] sports programmes
- [ ] documentaries
- [ ] game shows

Who watches what in Europe?

Despite what many people think, television is not the same everywhere.

In Italy, the programmes that attract the most viewers are football matches. In Germany it is game shows, followed by football and "soap operas" (TV series like "Neighbours" or "Lindenstrasse"). The French go for films, especially French films, whereas week for week the most popular British TV programmes are soaps, followed by comedy, TV films and movies.

National success is no guarantee of international popularity. In Germany the 13-part film "Heimat" was seen by about 20% of TV viewers, in France only 3% were interested. The French family saga "Chateauvallon" was seen by 31% of French people, but only 2.5% of British viewers.

Different countries also watch TV at different times. In Spain, the most popular times are between two o'clock and four o'clock in the afternoon, and from ten to eleven in the evening while in Germany Saturday night is the traditional TV night. More people watch breakfast TV in Britain than anywhere else in Europe.

3 Your own TV programme

A You own your own European TV station: "EUROWN TV". You have to attract a high number of viewers so that you can charge the maximum for advertising time. Work out an evening's TV programme from six p.m. to midnight. You can choose from the programmes below and also commission new programmes. All the times given (30, 45 minutes, etc.) include advertising time. You can show adverts every 15 minutes, and between programmes.

"I think it would be a good idea to …"

"Don't you think we should … ?"

"If you like, we could …"

"Wouldn't it be better to…?"

"We may get more viewers if …"

"We'll definitely get more if we show …"

On the Couch
Interview with the President of the European Commission (45 mins)

Cardboard Cities
Documentary on homelessness in Europe (45 mins)

On Top
Series on famous European families. No. 1: The Bourbons (30 mins)

Early News
National and international news programme (30 mins)

Late News
National and international news programme (30 mins)

Tomorrow's Weather
(5 mins; can be shown more than once)

News Nuggets
News highlights (10 mins; can be shown more than once)

Around and About
Regional and local news (15 mins)

In the nEUs
What's happening in Europe (45 mins)

The Street
British soap (30 mins)

A Castle in the Black Forest
German soap (30 mins)

The Road to Strasbourg
New Eurosoap featuring a group of long-distance lorry drivers (30 mins)

Golden Baldies
American situation comedy featuring three old men who share a flat (30 mins)

On the Ball
Sports programme (30 mins)

European Cup Football
(2 x 45 mins plus 15 minute break)

Concert Hall
Concert of classical music (45, 60 or 120 mins)

Eurotop Ten
Videos of the week's top hits (30 mins)

Blackbirds in September, Part 1
Television film based on best-selling romantic novel (75 mins)

Classic Re-runs
Viewers' choice of 3 Hollywood classics (90 mins)

Ecus for You, Ecus for Me
Game show (30 mins)

Eurcity
Portraits of European cities (30 mins)

EUrown Holiday
A guide to this summer's best European holiday bargains (20 mins)

B Present your schedule and explain your choices.

"We're going to start with the news at 6 o'clock because …"

"The whole of Europe will want to watch …"

14

4 Too much TV?

A This poem warns about the dangers of TV. Fill in the rhymes.

"Well, you did say they should go outside and get some fresh air."

> The most important thing we've learned,
> So far as children are ___concerned___
> Is never, never, never _____
> Them near your television set –
> Or better still, just don't _____
> The idiotic thing at all.
> In almost every house _____
> We've watched them gaping at the screen.
> They sit and stare and stare and _____
> Until they're hypnotized by it.
> Oh yes, we know it keeps them _____,
> They don't climb out the window sill,
> They never fight or kick or punch,
> They leave you free to cook the _____
> And wash the dishes in the sink –
> But did you ever stop to _____,
> To wonder just exactly _____
> This does to your beloved tot?   Roald Dahl

what
lunch
think
~~concerned~~
we've been
install
still
let
sit

B Listen and check.

C What does the author think? Which of these statements are true, which are false?

	True	False
TV has an educational value.		
It's a good idea not to have a TV.		
Children watch too much TV.		
The TV is a useful babysitter.		
Watching TV is bad for children.		

D What do you think? Discuss and report.

5 Mood music

A Listen and imagine a scene.

B Compare.

"My scene was very peaceful."

"There were two ..."   "What did he look like?"

"They were ...ing."   "What was she saying?"

C Report something interesting.

6 Music, music

A Listen to the three pieces of music. Answer the questions for each one.

Imagine that this piece of music is:

a) **film music.**
   What is the name of the film? What is it about?

b) **music for an advertisement.**
   What is the product? What is the slogan?

c) **music for a TV documentary.**
   What is the documentary about? What is the title?

MEMO PAD

Music 1   a) _____
          b) _____
          c) _____

Music 2   a) _____
          b) _____
          c) _____

Music 3   a) _____
          b) _____
          c) _____

B Report.

"We think the film would be a western, and the name could be ..."

"The documentary would be about ..."

"If this music was used to advertise something, it could be ..."

14

7 Who does what?

A Each of the four people in this house plays a different instrument, likes different music and listens to it on a different type of equipment. Read the information and complete the grid.

	Instrument	Favourite music	Equipment
Third floor	_____	_____	_____
Second floor	_____	_____	_____
First floor	_____	_____	_____
Ground floor	_____	_____	_____

- When the person who lives on the ground floor is not playing the piano, the radio is on.
- The person on the top floor has got a large collection of jazz and blues on cassette.
- The violin player lives on the floor between the guitarist and the pianist.
- The lover of classical music prefers CDs.
- The person in the flat below has got a lot of folk music LPs.
- Which floor does the clarinet player live on?
- Who likes pop music?

B Listen and check.

C Find someone who:

	Name
sings in a choir.	_____
has not got a TV.	_____
plays an instrument.	_____
has got more than one TV.	_____
dislikes the music you like.	_____
listens to a local radio station.	_____
likes the same sort of music as you.	_____
cannot play any musical instrument.	_____
tried to learn an instrument as a child.	_____
knows what song is Number One this week.	_____

14

8 The BRIDGES talent show

1. Write these words and phrases on cards. You should have a few more cards than people in the class.

2. Take a card. Do not show it to anybody!

3. Choose one of the activities below and perform it as described on the card.

4. The others have to guess what was on your card.

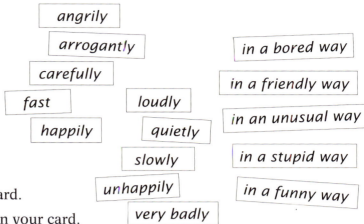

- Play Hamlet. Recite "To be or not to be, that is the question."
- Sing the Beatles song "She loves you, yeah, yeah, yeah. She loves you, yeah, yeah, yeah".
- Play a musical instrument.
- Dance with or without a partner.
- Mime something.

9 All write, all right!

A Make a list of ten words or phrases from this unit and give it to another pair.

B Write a short text including at least seven of the words or phrases you have been given. It can be anything relating to this unit, such as an ad, a story or a description of a TV programme.

C Compare.

10 PRONUNCIATION

A Listen. Underline all the [ə] sounds in these sentences.

1. We're going to start with the news at six o'clock.
2. Taxis are convenient but not very cheap.
3. Would you rather watch a programme about social problems, European history or animals?
4. What were the main stories in today's paper?
5. Can you check it for me, please?

B Listen again and practise.

UNIT 15

English and me

1 English

A Write down some things you associate with the word English.

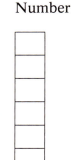

CHILDREN'S LETTERS TO GOD

Dear God,
I am English.
What are you?
Robert

B Listen. Which of the seven people talk about:

	Number
helping the children with their homework?	
a language course?	
needing a translation?	
speaking English on the phone?	
the spelling of a word?	
a trip to Britain?	
using English in their job?	

C Read this acrostic and write one yourself.

> **E** ven
> **N** ative speakers sometimes
> **G** o crazy because
> **L** earning to spell
> **I** nglish correctly is
> **S** ertainly very
> **H** ard work!

D Complete five of these sentences.

1. The nicest thing about English is _____
2. The most difficult thing about English is _____
3. Listening to English _____
4. When I'm speaking English I (don't) worry about _____
5. When I can't think of a word in English _____
6. English grammar is _____
7. The best way to learn English is _____
8. I'll stop learning English when _____

E Compare.

15

2 Sorry? What was that again?

 A Listen and fill in.

> Could you say that a bit more slowly, please?
> Can you repeat that, please?
> Did you say …?
> I'm afraid I didn't get that.
> Sorry? What was that again?

Dialogue 1

△ … and what time does it arrive?
○ Well, ten past twelve, I think.
△ _____
   ten past twelve?
○ That's right.
△ Oh, dear. That's too late, I'm afraid. Isn't there an earlier one you can take?
○ _____
△ I said, isn't there an earlier one? Ten past twelve's too late. We have to be there at 2.30 and it's a three-hour drive from the airport.
○ Oh, well, I'll have to change the booking. I'm sure there's one that gets in at about eight thirty.
△ _____
○ Half past eight; I think there's one that gets in at about half past eight.
△ Fine. You'd better take that one then.

Dialogue 2

❐ … I see, well in that case I'd like to leave a message for her.
▽ Of course, go ahead.
❐ It's about the chairs we ordered a week ago, on the twenty-fifth. The order number is TA38574.
▽ _____
❐ Of course, TA38574.
▽ TA38574. And what's the problem?
❐ Well, we'd like to change the order if that's possible. Perhaps she could ring me tomorrow and we can talk about it. It's 5674451.
▽ _____
   What was your number again?
❐ 5674451.

one hundred and twenty-five **125**

15

B Now practise dictation with your partner.

1. Student A: Look at File 20.
   Student B: Your partner is going to read this message aloud, including the missing information. Complete the text. If you need help, use the phrases from Step A.

   At motorway junction _____ you take the _____ and it's about _____ _____. As soon as you see the _____ on the left, look out for _____. That's Sydney Road. Then it's the _____ _____ and we're about _____ yards along there on the _____.
   We'll start at _____, but it's OK if you're a few minutes late.

2. Student B: Look at File 11.
   Student A: Your partner is going to read this message aloud, including the missing information. Complete the text. If you need help, use the phrases from Step A.

   It's about the _____ you're interested in. We can hold the present price till _____. After that I'm afraid it's going up. I don't know by how much exactly, but something like _____, maybe even as much as _____. So it would be a good idea to place the order _____, as today's already _____. I'll give you two numbers where you can phone me. The first's _____ and if that doesn't work, try _____.

3 Favourite words

A A few years ago a British newspaper asked its readers to name their favourite English words. Can you guess which were the top three in this list?

```
autumn      melody
castle      peace
Christmas   queen
ghost       sea
home        sunshine
love        tea
money
```

1. _____
2. _____ _____

B What are your favourite English words?

1. _____   2. _____   3. _____

C Now have a class vote on the most popular words.

D Have you got any favourite words in your own language? Compare.

4 The story of English

A Read the text and fill in.

Africa   English   French   French
Germanic   Latin   North America   Vikings
United States of America

The basis of English is the language spoken by the _____ tribes who came to Britain in the fifth century. Many everyday words like *mother* and *father*, *walk* and *run*, *eat* and *drink*, *sleep* and *speak*, *look*, *see*, *home*, *good*, *I*, *she*, *he*, *it*, and *thing*, come from Old English.

From about the year 600 on, Christianity came to Britain and brought a lot of _____ words into Old English – *monk*, *nun*, and *bishop*, for example.

From the 8th century on, the _____ (Danes and Norwegians) brought such common words as *sky*, *skin*, *want*, *they* and *their*, and two special favourites of English learners – *get* and *wrong*.

In 1066 the Normans conquered Britain and for about 150 years _____ was the language of the court, the law and the Church. In the Middle English period (1100 - 1450) thousands of _____ words entered the language, as well as many more from Italian and Latin.

When Shakespeare was writing his plays in the late 16th century, _____ was spoken by just under five million people and it is only in the last 150 years that it has become a world language.

One important reason was the growth of the British Empire, which brought English to India and many parts of _____, where it is still used as a second language. In Australia, English arrived with the first settlers in 1787, and New Zealand became British in 1841.

Probably the most important factor was the arrival of English in _____ in the 1620's. By the second half of the 18th century English was the main language of the important Atlantic coast, and in the 20th century the economic, political and cultural influence of the _____ has been enormous.

B Write one or two questions for the rest of the class.
Try to answer other people's questions with your books closed.

15

5 That's an interesting question

A Listen to the dialogues. Decide what is happening.

The person: a) does not know the answer.
b) does not understand the question.
c) does not want to answer.
d) is playing for time.

Dialogue 1 ____
Dialogue 2 ____
Dialogue 3 ____
Dialogue 4 ____

B Listen again. Tick each time you hear one of these expressions.

1. ☐ Oh, …
2. ☐ Well, …
3. ☐ Er …
4. ☐ Let me think …
5. ☐ You see …
6. ☐ I don't know really.
7. ☐ That's an interesting question.
8. ☐ What do you think?
9. ☐ I beg your pardon?
10. ☐ It's difficult to say.
11. ☐ I mean, …
12. ☐ It depends, doesn't it?
13. ☐ Oh, dear.

C On a card, write two questions you would <u>not</u> like to answer, such as:

> Who was that man I saw you with yesterday?
>
> I think butter is bad for you, don't you?
>
> Do you like me?
>
> What do you think of my new hairstyle?
>
> How old are you, actually?
>
> What do you think about the government?

D Exchange cards with a partner.
Ask and answer questions using expressions from B.

6 Riddle

A What could the apple, the house and the palace be?

> I will give my love an apple without any core
> I will give my love a house without any door
> I will give my love a palace wherein she may be
> And she may unlock it without any key.

B Listen and check.

7 Definitions

Your pair plays against another pair. One pair works out a definition, the other tries to guess the words. However, there are certain words you are not allowed to use in your definition.

Example: Define the word *key* without using the word *door*.

Here are some useful phrases:

"It's one of those things that …"

"It's something you …"   "It's that stuff that …"   "It's a way of …ing …"

"It's when you …"   "It's where you …"   "You need this to …"   "It's a sort of …"

Pair A: Look at File 9. – Pair B: Look at File 21.

8 English, English everywhere

A Tick the statements you <u>disagree</u> with.

1. There's too much English everywhere.
2. There are too many English words in German. I can hardly understand my own language any more.
3. People should sing in their own language, not in English.
4. Too many employers want staff with good English even if they never have to use it.
5. We should have more TV programmes in English. It would help me to learn the language better.
6. It's good to have one language that so many people can understand.
7. People should start learning English at primary school.
8. English should become the official European language.

B Compare and discuss.

"But wouldn't it be …?"   "But don't you think …?"

"But isn't it …?"   "But shouldn't …?"

one hundred and twenty-nine **129**

15

C What do you think about these ideas? Discuss.

1. More foreign languages should be taught in school.
2. There should be multilingual European schools.
3. Everyone should speak at least two foreign languages.

9 English is ...

Make a class poster about English.

10 PRONUNCIATION

A What do you find easy about English pronunciation and what do you find difficult?

B Discuss these statements.

1. Pronunciation isn't very important.
2. The aim of practising pronunciation is to sound like a native speaker.
3. The aim of practising pronunciation is to make yourself easily understood.
4. It is important to understand different accents.
5. The older you get, the harder it is to learn the pronunciation of a foreign language.

PREVIEW
E

1 The BRIDGES 2 game

Start on the first picture and move by throwing the dice. When you land on a square you have to invent a connection between that picture and the one you have just left. The connection could be a logical explanation or a story you make up. If you cannot make a connection, you have to go back to where you were. The first person to finish wins.

one hundred and thirty-one 131

PREVIEW E

2 Truth or lies?

Say five things about yourself. At least one of these things must be true, and at least one must be a lie.
The others guess which statements are true and which are lies.

"I have never ..."

"I often ..."   *"Last year ..."*

"Next week ..."

"I wish I ..."   *"I hope ..."*

"One day I would like to ..."   *"When I was 15 ..."*   *"When I was going home ..."*

3 Cartoon choice

A Look through the cartoons in **BRIDGES 2**.
Choose:
  a) one to advertise something.
  b) one to give to your boss or a neighbour.
  c) one to hang up in your office or in your kitchen.

B Present your choices and explain them.

4 Course project

Compile a course magazine or poster. Decide who is going to do what. There should be at least one job for everyone in the class.
Here are some suggestions. Some are better for posters, others for a magazine.

You can include:
- interviews with English-speaking people in your area;
- a short questionnaire or opinion poll with answers from members of your course;
- (unusual) information about your town or area;
- interesting information about people in your class;
- reviews of English books, TV programmes, etc;
- jokes.

You can also make your own puzzles, such as:
- crosswords and other word puzzles. There are a lot of different ideas in **BRIDGES 2**. Don't forget the **Practice Book**.
- "Hunt the picture". Choose a picture in the book, describe it and give a clue about where it is.

You can write:
- poems or rhymes (see Unit 3: haikus, Unit 15: acrostics, PREVIEW units);
- a minisaga (see Unit 4, Unit 6, Unit 11);
- a short story about something funny or unusual in connection with English.

Include pictures and drawings as well!

PREVIEW
E

5 The BRIDGES 2 Diploma

These are some of the things we hope you can now do in English.
If you can honestly answer "yes" to five of the things below, we hope
to see you in **BRIDGES 3**.

BRIDGES 2 Diploma

Yes

1. I can say hello and goodbye, and keep a conversation going for at least ten seconds.

2. I am a perfect host. I can show visitors around my area and entertain them by playing games, cooking vegetable curries, wearing clothes, pretending to play a musical instrument, talking about Shakespeare, singing Beatles songs and telling jokes.

3. I can get around by train, plane, and all other types of public or private transport. I can give, ask for and follow directions. I always arrive somewhere. I can find a hotel room and complain to the manager immediately. I can go shopping in any supermarket. With enough money I could buy anything.

4. I can describe myself and my family so well that I can identify us. I can also identify valuables, especially my own. I can name the parts of the body, the clothes I'm wearing, ten different pieces of electrical equipment, everything in my bathroom and three burglars.

5. I can talk about the past, the present and the future, especially about last year's and next year's holidays.

6. I can answer the phone or leave it to ring. I can watch TV with or without the sound.

7. I can say "Cheers!", wish people "Merry Christmas", and send greetings cards. I know how to celebrate my birthday.

8. I can write postcards, letters, thankyou notes, recipes, poems and minisagas, but I have not yet made any money out of them.

9. I can invite someone out and pay them compliments. I can give them advice. I can tell them how to plan a department store or a TV programme. I can agree or disagree with myself and can say something about any topic I can talk about.

10. I can remember everything I haven't forgotten. I am not going to worry, I am going to be happy.

F

FILES

File 1 (UNIT 0, Step 3, p. 10)

Es spielen jeweils zwei oder mehr Paare gegeneinander. Sie benötigen einen Würfel und pro Paar eine Spielfigur, z.B. eine Münze. Die Paare würfeln und ziehen der Reihe nach entsprechend der gewürfelten Punktzahl in Pfeilrichtung.

Auf den hellblauen Feldern sind Wörter zu sammeln. Die in Klammern angegebene Zahl gibt dabei die Anzahl der zu suchenden Wörter an. Auf den orangefarbenen Feldern soll ein kurzer Dialog gebildet werden, dessen Anfangs- und Schlußsatz vorgegeben sind.

Die anderen Paare entscheiden, ob die Aufgaben richtig ausgeführt wurden. Gewonnen hat, wer zuerst das Ziel *(Finish)* erreicht hat.

File 2 (PREVIEW A, Step 1, p. 33)

Für dieses Kartenspiel gibt es zwei Spielvarianten:

Spielvariante 1
Die Karten werden gemischt und verdeckt auf den Tisch gelegt. Alle Spieler/innen ziehen der Reihe nach eine Karte und vervollständigen den Satz.
Die anderen Spieler/innen entscheiden, ob der Satz richtig war.

Spielvariante 2
Gespielt wird in Gruppen von 4 – 5 Personen. Alle Karten werden an die Spieler/innen ausgeteilt. Eine Person fängt an, indem sie eine Karte hinlegt und den Satz vervollständigt. Die nächste Person soll durch Hinzufügen einer weiteren Karte den Satz zu einem zweizeiligen Dialog erweitern. Gelingt dies, darf sie die beiden Karten nehmen und behalten. Gelingt es nicht, ist die nächste Person an der Reihe.

Gewonnen hat, wer alle Karten oder nach einer vereinbarten Zeit die meisten Karten besitzt.

File 3 (UNIT 4, Step 2C, p. 36)

a) Suchen Sie neun verschiedene Küchengeräte aus und bestücken Sie damit Schaufenster 1. Nicht zeigen!

b) ‚Diktieren' Sie nun Ihr Schaufenster Ihrer Partnerin/Ihrem Partner. Wenn Sie fertig sind, vergleichen Sie, ob die beiden Schaufenster übereinstimmen.

c) Ihre Partnerin/Ihr Partner ‚diktiert' Ihnen jetzt ihr/sein Schaufenster 2.

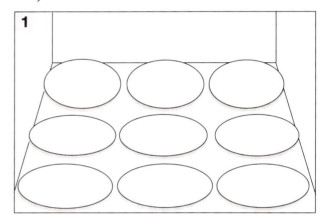

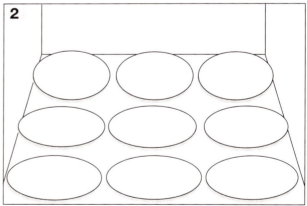

File 4 (PREVIEW B, Step 1, p. 58)

Sie sind auf einem numerierten Feld gelandet. Lesen Sie die Aufgabenstellung zu Ihrer Nummer, einigen Sie sich gegebenenfalls über die Rollenverteilung (A und B), und bilden Sie einen Dialog. Die anderen Paare entscheiden, ob der Dialog richtig ist.

1
A: Sie möchten in irgendeine europäische Stadt fliegen. Erkundigen Sie sich nach Flügen (Zeit, Preis etc.).
B: Sie arbeiten in dem Reisebüro. Geben Sie Auskunft über Flüge.

2
Unterhalten Sie sich über Ihr jeweiliges Lieblingsland oder Ihren Lieblingsort. Warum gefällt es Ihnen dort so gut?

3
A: In Ihr Hotelzimmer wurde eingebrochen. Berichten Sie der Hotelleitung Einzelheiten, z.B. was alles gestohlen wurde usw., und fragen Sie, was sie unternehmen werden.
B: Sie gehören zur Hotelleitung. Nehmen Sie sich des Problems an.

4
A: Ihr Auto wurde gestohlen. Berichten Sie darüber.
B: Drücken Sie Ihr Mitgefühl aus und fragen Sie nach, was passiert ist.

5
A: Die Waschmaschine in Ihrem Ferienapartment funktioniert nicht. Beschweren Sie sich bei der Verwaltung.
B: Nehmen Sie sich des Problems an.

6
A: Sie möchten ein Zimmer für eine Nacht reservieren. Erkundigen Sie sich im Fremdenverkehrsamt.
B: Sie arbeiten im Fremdenverkehrsamt. Geben Sie Auskunft.

7
A: Sie haben einen einwöchigen Urlaub irgendwo in Europa für zwei Personen gewonnen. Bitten Sie B, Sie zu begleiten.
B: Sagen Sie, was Sie davon halten, und machen Sie Vorschläge.

8
A: Sie sind in einem Geschäft und möchten Postkarten und die passenden Briefmarken kaufen. Erkundigen Sie sich an der Kasse.
B: Sie arbeiten in dem Geschäft. Seien Sie der Kundin/dem Kunden behilflich.

9
Unterhalten Sie sich über Ihren idealen Urlaub/Traumurlaub.

10
A: Sie möchten für eine Woche ein Auto mieten. Erkundigen Sie sich nach Preisen, Fahrzeugtypen etc.
B: Sie arbeiten in der Mietwagenagentur. Beraten Sie den Kunden/die Kundin.

11
A: Ihr Flug wurde gestrichen und Sie sind verärgert. Beschweren Sie sich und erkundigen Sie sich nach Ausweichmöglichkeiten.
B: Sie arbeiten für die Fluggesellschaft. Seien Sie dem Kunden/der Kundin behilflich.

12
A: Sie sind Hotelgast und mit Ihrem Zimmer ist etwas nicht in Ordnung. Beschweren Sie sich.
B: Sie sind Geschäftsführer/in des Hotels. Kümmern Sie sich um den Gast.

13
Erzählen Sie sich gegenseitig von Ihrem letzten Urlaub.

14
Unterhalten Sie sich über ein Land, in dem Sie noch nie waren, in welches Sie aber gerne reisen würden.

15
A: Sie haben eine Reise in ein europäisches Land Ihrer Wahl gewonnen. Berichten Sie.
B: Drücken Sie Ihre Mitfreude aus und fragen Sie nach Einzelheiten.

16
A: Sie wollen mit dem Zug durch Europa reisen. Erkundigen Sie sich am Informationsschalter nach Preisen usw.
B: Sie arbeiten bei der Bahn. Beraten Sie die Kundin/den Kunden.

17
Unterhalten Sie sich darüber, was Sie im Urlaub gerne tun.

F

File 5 (UNIT 4, Step 2C, p. 36)

a) Suchen Sie neun verschiedene Küchengeräte aus und bestücken Sie damit Schaufenster 2. Nicht zeigen!

b) Ihre Partnerin/Ihr Partner ‚diktiert' Ihnen nun ihr/sein Schaufenster 1. Richten Sie Ihr leeres Schaufenster 1 nach diesen Angaben ein und vergleichen Sie anschließend, ob die beiden Schaufenster übereinstimmen.

c) Danach ‚diktieren' Sie Ihr Schaufenster 2.

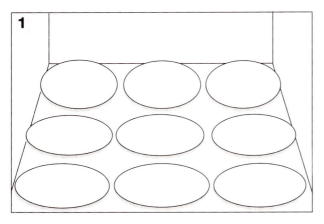

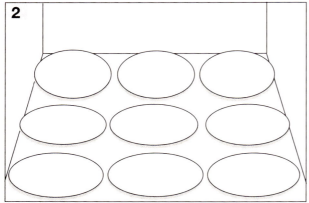

File 6 (UNIT 8, Step 4B, p. 71)

a) Sie rufen eine Freundin/einen Freund an. Begrüßen Sie sie/ihn.

b) Laden Sie sie/ihn zum Essen an einem Tag in der nächsten Woche ein.

c) Stimmen Sie dem Gegenvorschlag zu und machen Sie Vorschläge für Ort und Zeit des Treffens.

d) Verabschieden Sie sich.

File 7 (UNIT 5, Step 4B, p. 46)

1. Engländer geben sich nicht so häufig die Hand, wie es Deutsche tun. Sie sind möglicherweise überrascht und reagieren deshalb nicht.

2. Es gibt Länder und Kulturen, z. B. manche arabischen Länder, Südamerika oder auch Polen, in denen es akzeptabel ist, später als zur vereinbarten Uhrzeit zu einer Verabredung zu erscheinen.

3. Wegen der unterschiedlichen Zeitzonen (und der Telefongebühren zu verschiedenen Tageszeiten) ist es in Nordamerika nicht ungewöhnlich, Freunde oder Verwandte sehr früh morgens anzurufen.

File 8 (UNIT 7, Step 7B, p. 65)

a) Sie rufen jemanden am Arbeitsplatz an. Die Person ist jedoch nicht da. Hinterlassen Sie eine Nachricht.

b) Nun nehmen Sie ein Telefongespräch für eine Kollegin entgegen, die nicht da ist. Bieten Sie an, etwas auszurichten und schreiben Sie eine Telefonnotiz.

☎☎☎☎☎ **Telephone Message** ☎☎☎☎☎

To: _____
From: _____
About: _____
_____
_____

File 9 (UNIT 15, Step 7, p. 129)

1. Define the word *cheque* without using the word *money*.
2. Define the word *dictionary* without using the word *word*.
3. Define the word *newspaper* without using the word *read*.
4. Define the word *pet* without using the words *cat* or *dog*.
5. Define the word *time* without using the words *clock* or *watch*.

File 10   (UNIT 14, Step 1B, p. 118)

a) Beantworten Sie die Fragen Ihrer Partnerin/Ihres Partners.

b) Stellen Sie Ihrer Partnerin/Ihrem Partner die folgenden Fragen zum Thema Fernsehen:

1. What are your favourite programmes? Is there a programme you never miss?
2. What programmes can't you stand?
3. When do you watch TV?
4. What did you watch last night? What are you going to watch tomorrow?
5. At home, who decides which programmes you watch?
6. Would you rather watch a good film, a football match or something funny?
7. Would you rather watch a programme about social problems, European history or animals?

File 11   (UNIT 15, Step 2B, p. 126)

Lesen Sie Ihrer Partnerin/Ihrem Partner die folgende Mitteilung vor. Lesen Sie zügig, machen Sie keine Pausen und wiederholen Sie nichts, außer wenn Ihre Partnerin/Ihr Partner Sie darum bittet.

> It's about the XJ324 you're interested in. We can hold the present price till the end of the month. After that I'm afraid it's going up. I don't know by how much exactly, but something like five pounds, maybe even as much as six pounds fifty. So it would be a good idea to place the order next week, as today's already the twenty-third. I'll give you two numbers where you can phone me. The first's 6754312 and if that doesn't work, try 3984462.

File 12   (UNIT 11, Step 8B, p. 95)

F

File 13 (UNIT 7, Step 7B, p. 65)

a) Sie sind bei der Arbeit und nehmen ein Telefongespräch für eine Kollegin entgegen, die nicht da ist. Bieten Sie an, etwas auszurichten und schreiben Sie eine Telefonnotiz.

```
☎☎☎☎ Telephone Message ☎☎☎☎
To: _____
From: _____
About: _____
_____
_____
```

b) Nun rufen Sie jemanden am Arbeitsplatz an. Die Person ist jedoch nicht da. Hinterlassen Sie eine Nachricht.

File 14 (UNIT 8, Step 4B, p. 71)

a) Eine Freundin/Ein Freund ruft Sie an. Antworten Sie auf die Begrüßung.

b) Erklären Sie, warum Sie an diesem Tag nicht können, und schlagen Sie einen anderen Tag vor.

c) Reagieren Sie auf die Vorschläge zu Ort und Zeit des Treffens.

d) Verabschieden Sie sich.

File 15 (UNIT 10, Step 2D, p. 85)

Where the Water goes

Toilet: 47 litres
Baths and showers: 44 litres
Washing clothes: 18 litres
Washing hands, cleaning teeth, etc.: 9 litres
Washing up: 9 litres
Watering the garden: 6 litres
Cooking, drinking: 3 litres
Washing the car: 3 litres
Other: 7 litres
Total: 146 litres per day

(Source: Globus Statistics)

File 16 (UNIT 11, Step 2B, p. 91)

Twins reunited after 40 years

Identical twins Carole Wood and Sylvia Scicluna were adopted because their mother was not married when they were born in December, 1944. Each was adopted by a different family and, although the two families lived less than two miles apart, the twins never met. Later, they both trained as nurses in Portsmouth and even worked in the same hospital, although at different times. In 1967 Sylvia moved to Perth, Australia. One of the friends she left behind was Valerie White. Nearly 20 years later, Valerie White saw a woman in a street in Portsmouth who looked just like her friend Sylvia. She stopped the woman and explained the situation. As a result of this, the sisters wrote to each other and were finally reunited in Perth in August, 1985. Carole Wood says, "It's wonderful. Strangely, we have found that we like the same music, we both hate tea and drink coffee without sugar."

File 17 (UNIT 14, Step 1B, p. 118)

a) Stellen Sie Ihrer Partnerin/Ihrem Partner die folgenden Fragen zum Thema Zeitunglesen:

1. Which newspaper(s) do you read?
2. Which parts of the newspaper do you usually read first?
3. What were the main stories in today's paper?
4. What do you think of your country's press?
5. Do you read any magazines? Which ones? Why?
6. Which do you find most interesting: local news, national news or international news?
7. Which do you find most interesting: the sports pages, the financial pages or the culture pages?

b) Beantworten Sie die Fragen Ihrer Partnerin/Ihres Partners.

F

File 18 (UNIT 11, Step 4D, p. 93)

Model A	Model B	Model C
Some 25% of Europeans prefer this family model. It is particularly popular in Ireland and Luxembourg.	30% of Europeans think this is a good idea. It is particularly popular in Germany.	40% of Europeans prefer this kind of family. It is particularly popular in Denmark, England and Spain.

File 19 (UNIT 12, Step 2B, p. 99)

12. Sleep.
13. Gaze out of the window and note how England is changing.
14. Have a meal.
15. Walk up and down a bit.
16. Re-plan your life.
17. Write down your three trickiest business problems. Then work out how to solve them.
18. Read a magazine you'd never normally read.
19. Play chess.
20. Flirt outrageously with a fellow passenger of the opposite sex.
21. Invent something that will make a fortune.
22. Do whatever you please.

There's nothing quite like an InterCity journey for freeing up the mind. No phones ring. Nobody interrupts you or asks you to do things. It's a little space in your life to indulge nobody but yourself. Enjoy it.

 InterCity

File 20 (UNIT 15, Step 2B, p. 126)

Lesen Sie Ihrer Partnerin/Ihrem Partner die folgende Mitteilung vor. Lesen Sie zügig, machen Sie keine Pausen und wiederholen Sie nichts, außer wenn Ihre Partnerin/Ihr Partner Sie darum bittet.

> At motorway junction 21 you take the A25 and it's about three miles. As soon as you see the big hospital on the left, look out for a right turn. That's Sydney Road. Then it's the second on the left and we're about 500 yards along there on the right. We'll start at ten o'clock, but it's OK if you're a few minutes late.

File 21 (UNIT 15, Step 7, p. 129)

1. Define the word *English* without using the words *language* or *people*.
2. Define the word *guitar* without using the words *music* or *instrument*.
3. Define the word *shoe* without using the words *wear* or *feet*.
4. Define the word *television* without using the word *watch*.
5. Define the word *tea* without using the word *drink*.

LS

LANGUAGE SUMMARIES

Einleitung

Die *Language Summaries* sind nach Kapiteln gegliedert. Sie geben einen Überblick über die sprachlichen Lerninhalte, die in dem jeweiligen Kapitel zum ersten Mal vorkommen und aktiv geübt werden. Der in einer *Language Summary* präsentierte Stoff wird in den folgenden Kapiteln als bekannt vorausgesetzt.

Mit Hilfe der *Language Summaries* können Sie das im Unterricht Gelernte nachbereiten, aber auch möglicherweise versäumten Unterrichtsstoff nachholen.

Inhalt

Jede *Language Summary* ist untergliedert in:

- Grammatik — Dieser Abschnitt enthält die neuen grammatischen Strukturen des jeweiligen Kapitels. Durch **Fettdruck** wird hervorgehoben, worauf es ankommt. Die Numerierung richtet sich nach den Nummern der einzelnen Grammatikphänomene in der systematischen Grammatikübersicht (Anhang G) ab Seite 162.

- Sprechabsichten — In diesem Abschnitt werden die in dem Kapitel neuen Sprechabsichten bzw. die neuen Wendungen für bereits eingeführte Sprechabsichten aufgelistet. Die Numerierung richtet sich nach den Nummern der einzelnen Sprechabsichten im Anhang LF (*Language Functions*) ab Seite 157.

Die Beispiele werden in dem Kontext gegeben, in dem sie in dem jeweiligen Kapitel vorkommen.

UNIT 1

Grammar Grammatik

Id Modal Verbs Modalverben

Affirmative Form Bejahte Form	**Negative Form** Verneinte Form
You **can** (take flowers as a present).	You **can't** (wear jeans).
You **should** (phone to say you can go).	You **shouldn't** (criticize American politics).
You **have to** (take a present).	You **don't have to** (arrive at 8 o'clock).

IVc Demonstrative Pronouns Hinweisende Fürwörter

> Which of **these** statements are true?
> What are **those** strange noises?

Unit 1

IVd Relative Pronouns: "Zero" Clauses Bezügliche Fürwörter: Sätze ohne Fürwörter

people	(who)	I meet for the first time
someone	(who)	you don't know very well
a question	(which)	you would like to ask your boss
a topic	(which)	many people find boring

IVe Indefinite Pronouns Unbestimmte Fürwörter

some (Affirmative Sentences) *some* (Bejahte Sätze)
Some subjects are very boring. **someone/somebody** you don't know very well Eat **something** light.

any (Affirmative Sentences) *any* (Bejahte Sätze)	*any* (Negative Sentences) *any* (Verneinte Sätze)
Write down **any** "hellos" you know. I arrive at **any** time before 8.30.	You would not normally ask **anyone/anybody** how they voted.

any (Questions) *any* (Fragesätze)	
Are there **any** differences?	Do you need **anyone/anybody**?

■ Language Functions Sprechabsichten

1.2 **auf Vorstellung reagieren**
Pleased to meet you.

1.3 **jemanden grüßen**
Did you have a good trip?

1.5 **sich verabschieden**
Don't forget to send a postcard!
It was nice to meet you.
It was great to be here.

1.6 **gute Wünsche äußern**
Enjoy the rest of your trip!

1.8 **sich bedanken**
Thanks for everything.

1.9 **auf Entschuldigung reagieren**
Don't worry.
No problem.

2.2 **ein Gespräch einleiten**
It's a lovely day, isn't it?
Are you here on holiday/business?

2.9 **ein Beispiel geben**
(Some subjects are very boring), like (illnesses and children).

3.1 **benennen, definieren**
people (I meet for the first time)
a question (you'd like to ask your boss)

4.2 **etwas anbieten**
Can I get you a drink?

5.6 **Nichtzustimmung ausdrücken**
I disagree.

7.5 **einen Rat geben**
You should (phone to say you can go).

von etwas abraten
You shouldn't (arrive at 8 o'clock).

7.6 **sagen, daß etwas erlaubt ist**
You can (take flowers).

sagen, daß etwas nicht erlaubt ist
You can't (just go).

8.1 **sagen, daß etwas notwendig ist**
You have to (take a present).

sagen, daß etwas nicht notwendig ist
You don't have to (arrive at 8 o'clock).

LS

UNIT 2

Grammar Grammatik

IVa Personal Pronouns
Persönliche Fürwörter

> Me too. / Nor me.
> as beautiful as him
> as intelligent as her

IVd Relative Pronouns
Bezügliche Fürwörter

someone the sort of person	who that	ran away to Scotland likes hard work
something things	which that	grows on trees I want to do

Hinweis: *Who* wird bei Personen verwendet, *which* bei Gegenständen.
That kann sowohl bei Personen als auch bei Gegenständen verwendet werden.

IVe Indefinite Pronouns
Unbestimmte Fürwörter

> We **both/all** like Chinese food.
> We're **both/all** tall.
> They have **both/all** got blonde hair.

VIIa Adjectives: Comparison
Eigenschaftswörter: Steigerung

someone who is Perhaps I'm	slim**mer than** laz**ier than**	he was 10 years ago I used to be.

VIIb Other Forms of Comparison
Andere Formen des Vergleichens

I'm just **as** active **as** I used to be. I'm **not as** happy **as** I used to be.
If the children were **as** intelligent **as** him and **as** beautiful **as** her ...
He's **the same** age **as** George.

VIIIe Modifiers
Verstärkende bzw. abschwächende Umstandswörter

I find things	a bit	boring now.
I think I'm a bit	too	fat.
I'm	(not) really	short.
I'm	average	height.
I travel	quite	a lot.

VIIIf Adverbs
Umstandswörter

> I'm not very tall, but I'm **not** really short, **either**.
> Me **too**.

Language Functions
Sprechabsichten

3.1 benennen, definieren
(something) which (grows on trees)
(things) that (I want to do)

5.6 zustimmen
Me too.
Nor me.

Unit 3

Grammar Grammatik

Ic Future Tenses: *going to*
Zukunftsformen: *going to*

I'm What are you I'm not	going to	stay with a friend. wear? sit down all day.

Id Modal Verbs Modalverben

> **Shall** we take them to the …?
> I **had to** do all the shopping myself.
> Guests **should** offer to do the washing-up.
> It was so loud I **couldn't** sleep.

IVf Reflexive Pronouns
Rückbezügliche Fürwörter

> I had to do all the shopping **myself**.
> Did **he** entertain **himself**?
> **She** entertained **herself**.
> **We** had to do everything **ourselves**.
> **They** helped **themselves**.

V Quantifiers Mengenangaben

All Not many None Neither	of them	helped with the washing-up.

Language Functions Sprechabsichten

2.7 eine ausweichende Antwort geben
That depends (what time we get started).

4.2 etwas anbieten
Shall I (buy some wine)?

Hilfe anbieten
Can I help you with (the washing-up)?

5.2 Wichtigkeit ausdrücken
I think (number 3) is the most important.
I don't think (number 6) is important at all.

5.6 zustimmen
So do I!
Nor do I.

7.4 etwas vorschlagen
Why don't we (go to the theatre)?
I think it would be nice to (go to the art gallery).
We could (take them to the museum).

einen Vorschlag annehmen
Good idea!
Why not?

einen Vorschlag ablehnen/ einen Gegenvorschlag machen
Let's (go to the museum) instead.
I'd prefer to (show them the castle).

7.6 um Erlaubnis bitten
Can I (use the phone)?
Is it all right if I (use the phone)?

8.1 sagen, daß etwas notwendig ist
You should (write a thankyou letter).
(Guests) should not (come home late).

LS

UNIT 4

UNIT 4

■ Grammar Grammatik

Ic Tenses: Present Perfect Simple
Zeitformen: Present Perfect Simple

Regular Verbs	Regelmäßige Zeitwörter	
The computer	**has** chang**ed**	millions of jobs.
The television	**has** spoil**ed**	family life.

Irregular Verbs	Unregelmäßige Zeitwörter	
The microwave	**has made**	cooking a lot easier.
They	**'ve broken**	the window.
They	**'ve drunk**	the whisky.
What	**have** we **taken**?	

If Short Answers/Responses
Kurzantworten

Statement Aussage	Response Antwort
I**'ve** got a microwave.	**So have** I.
I **haven't** got a freezer.	**Nor have** I.
I **wouldn't** say that.	**Nor would** I.
I agree.	**So do** I.
I **don't** think so.	**Nor do** I.

VIIa Adjectives: Comparison (Superlative)
Eigenschaftswörter:
Steigerung (Superlativ)

Which is **the most/least** useful thing you've got?

VIIIc Adverbial Phrases of Place
Umstandsbestimmungen des Ortes

(The freezer's)	at the back/front.
(The microwave's)	on the left/right.
(The food processor's)	in the middle.

■ Language Functions
Sprechabsichten

2.7 eine ausweichende Antwort geben
It depends what you mean by …

3.1 benennen, definieren
It's (a kind of) …
You use it for …
It's something …

5.6 zustimmen
So do I.
Nor do I./Nor would I.
I think so, too.
That's true.

Nichtzustimmung ausdrücken
I wouldn't say that.
I don't think so.

6.8 Überraschung ausdrücken
Look at this!
That's surprising.

Unit 5

Grammar Grammatik

Ib Imperatives
Aufforderungssätze

| Be happy. | Don't worry. |

Ic Tenses: Present Perfect Simple Zeitformen: Present Perfect Simple

I **haven't been** to the doctor's	**for**	a long time.
Robert **hasn't had** a cold	**for**	two years.
I **haven't had** a hangover	**since**	last Christmas.
I **haven't been** in hospital	**since**	I was a child/I left school.

Hinweis: *For* und *since* entsprechen dem deutschen *seit* bzw. *seitdem*.
- *For* wird bei Zeiträumen (z. B. *for two years*) verwendet;
- *since* bei Zeitpunkten, die in der Vergangenheit liegen *(since Christmas)*.

Id Modal Verbs Modalverben

| You **must** be really pleased. |

Ig The "-ing" Form
Die "-ing"-Form

| Walk**ing** | in the woods makes me happy. |
| Get**ting** | up late on Sunday makes me happy. |

IXb Questions Fragesätze

| What **makes** you happy? |
| What **makes** you laugh? |

IXc Reported Speech
Indirekte Rede

Statement Aussage	Reported Speech Indirekte Rede
"I like to relax."	Petra **told me** she likes to relax.
"We get annoyed when ..."	A lot of people **said** they get annoyed when ...

Language Functions Sprechabsichten

1.6 Glückwünsche aussprechen
Congratulations!
Well done!

6.2 Sorgen ausdrücken
I worry about ...
What's the matter?

Hoffnung ausdrücken
Touch wood!

6.4 Freude ausdrücken
I'm happy.
I feel happy.
I'm in a good mood.
... makes me laugh.

sich mit jmd. freuen
You must be really pleased.
That's great.

6.5 Traurigkeit ausdrücken
I'm sad.
I feel (sad).

Mitleid ausdrücken
That's terrible!
How disappointing!
Oh no!
Oh, dear!
What a pity!
You must be very upset.
I'm sorry to hear that.

6.6 Ärger ausdrücken
I get annoyed when ...

LS

UNIT 6

Grammar Grammatik

Ic Tenses: Present Perfect Simple vs. Past Simple

Zeitformen:
Present Perfect Simple
vs. Past Simple

Present Perfect Simple	Past Simple
Bruce **has lived** in Mannheim.	He **lived** there from 1975 to 1979.
Have you ever **been** to France?	When **did** you **go** there?

Hinweis: Die Zeitform *Present Perfect Simple* wird benutzt, wenn es sich um die Zeit bis zum heutigen Tag handelt; die *Past Simple*-Form dagegen, wenn es um einen in der Vergangenheit abgeschlossenen Zeitraum geht.

Ig The *"ing"* Form
Die *"ing"*-Form

I **enjoy** travel**ling** around.
I **can't stand** ly**ing** in the sun.
I'm **interested in** meet**ing** people.
Go**ing** away is better than stay**ing** at home.

Hinweis: Die *"ing"*-Form wird verwendet:
1. nach bestimmten Zeitwörtern;
2. nach Verhältniswörtern;
3. als Hauptwort.

IVe Indefinite Pronouns
Unbestimmte Fürwörter

some (Questions)   *some* (Fragesätze)
Would/Could you please do **something** about it?

VIIIg Adverbs
Umstandswörter

I've **only** driven through Belgium.
Which countries have you **only** flown over?
Only one or two of us have been to Hungary.

Hinweis: Das Umstandswort *only* wird immer vor das Wort gesetzt, auf das es sich bezieht.

Language Functions Sprechabsichten

2.2 eine Äußerung einleiten
Excuse me, …

2.8 eine Aussage strukturieren
Although (your brochure says …), in fact …
In addition to this, …

4.1 versprechen, etwas zu tun
I'll (speak to them immediately).

6.1 sagen, was einem besser gefällt
I prefer (self-catering) to (hotels).

sagen, was einem nicht gefällt
I can't stand (lying in the sun).

6.6 reklamieren
Excuse me, there's (no water in the swimming pool).
We're writing to complain about (the hotel).

6.7 Gelassenheit ausdrücken
I don't mind (self-catering holidays).

7.2 eine Bitte äußern
Would/Will you please do something about it?
Can/Could you do something about it?

UNIT 7

Grammar Grammatik

Ic Present Tenses: Present Continuous
Gegenwartsformen: Present Continuous

I'm	brushing	up my English.
He's	learning	to cook.
We're	taking	a computer course.
What's	happening?	

Present Tenses: Present Simple vs. Present Continuous
Gegenwartsformen: Present Simple vs. Present Continuous

Present Simple	Present Continuous
This machine normally **works** perfectly.	It's **giving** us some trouble today.
I usually **work** in another department.	I'm **helping** out here for a few weeks.
Our company **makes** kitchen equipment.	At the moment we're **expanding** into Eastern Europe.

Future Tenses: *will*
Zukunftsformen: *will*

I'll	tell her you called.
	put you through.
	phone back tomorrow.

Ie Short forms
Kurzformen

| I'll | = | I will |

VIIIb Adverbial Phrases of Time
Umstandsbestimmungen der Zeit

At one time	he worked for an antique dealer.
For a while	he worked in a factory.
Just now	I'm preparing information material.
At the moment	we're expanding into Eastern Europe.

IXb Questions Fragesätze

| Which person | enjoys helping people? |
| Which person | likes working with children? |

IXc Reported Speech
Indirekte Rede

Statement Aussage	Reported Speech Indirekte Rede
"I trained as a nurse."	Doris **said** she trained as a nurse.

IXe *If* Clauses *If*-Sätze

Present Simple Form	Present Simple Form
It's work	if **it's** (in the office).
If **it's** in the office,	**it's** (work).

LS

UNIT 7

Language Functions
Sprechabsichten

2.7 eine ausweichende Antwort geben
It is and it isn't.
It depends how you look at it.

6.3 Wünsche äußern
I'd like to be (a nature warden).
I wouldn't mind being (a traffic warden).

Telefonkonventionen

1.1 sich am Telefon melden
Truman plc.
Mr Colby's office.

1.2 sich am Telefon vorstellen
Good morning, my name's (Roger Taylor).
Hello, this is (Liz May).

4.2 Hilfe anbieten
Can I take a message?
Would you like to leave a message?

6.3 Wünsche äußern
I'd like to speak to (Jenny Faber).
Can I speak to (Mr Colby), please?

7.2 eine Bitte äußern
Coud you tell (him) I called?

auf eine Bitte reagieren
I'll tell (her) you called.

• **Andere Telefonwendungen**
Hold on.
I'll put you through.
The line's busy.
(He's) not in (this morning).

UNIT 8

Grammar Grammatik

Ic Future Tenses: Present Continuous Zukunftsformen: Present Continuous

On Saturday	I'm meeting	Susan for lunch.
In the evening	we're going	to the disco.
Where	are they meeting?	

Hinweis: Die *Present Continuous*-Form wird nicht nur als Gegenwartsform verwendet, sondern auch für Handlungen, die für die nahe Zukunft geplant bzw. verabredet sind.

IVd Relative Pronouns
Bezügliche Fürwörter

It's a day	when	people have to ...

Vc Quantities Mengen

a pinch a tin	of	salt tomatoes

VIa Cardinal Numbers
Grundzahlen

½	**a half**
½ kg	**half a** kilo
1 ½ kg	**one and a half** kilos

UNIT 8

VId Date Datum

Written Schriftlich	Spoken Gesprochen
July 29 (th) *or* 29/7	"July **the** 29th" *or* "**the** 29th **of** July"

VIIIb Abverbial Phrases of Time
Umstandsbestimmungen der Zeit

On Saturday	I'm meeting Susan for lunch.
In the evening	we're going to the disco.
On this day	people have to ...

IXe *If* Clauses *If*-Sätze

Past Simple Form	Conditional
If I **were** a place,	**I'd** be (Paris).

Language Functions Sprechabsichten

1.6 **gute Wünsche äußern**
Merry Christmas(!)
Many happy returns(!)
Happy New Year!
Happy Anniversary!
Best wishes(!)
Happy Easter(!)
All the best!
Cheers!

1.7 **Komplimente machen**
Mm, this tastes great!
You must let us have the recipe!

1.10 **eine Einladung aussprechen**
Would you like to (go to the new Indian restaurant)?

eine Einladung annehmen
Oh, that would be nice!

eine Einladung ablehnen
I'm afraid (I'm going to the ...)

2.9 **ein Beispiel geben**
(one kg mixed vegetables) such as (carrots, leeks, etc)

3.1 **benennen, definieren**
It's a day when (people have to ...)

7.4 **etwas vorschlagen**
What we suggest is ...

7.6 **sagen, daß etwas erlaubt ist**
... people are (only) allowed to ...

sagen, daß etwas nicht erlaubt ist
... people aren't allowed to ...

UNIT 9

Grammar Grammatik

If Short Answers/Responses
Kurzantworten

When we were children we (wore jeans).	**So did we**.

Question Tags Frageanhängsel

That's a new blouse,	**isn't it?**
It could also be "shoes",	**couldn't it?**

one hundred and forty-nine

LS

UNIT 9

Ih Passive: Past Tense Passiv: Vergangenheitsform

In 1849 gold	**was** discover**ed**	in California.
Jeans	**were** introduc**ed**	to Europe by American soldiers.

IIa Nouns: Plural Forms Hauptwörter: Bildung der Mehrzahlformen

a pair of	trousers tights shoes socks	she bought in Italy
My favourite	**piece of clothing**	is an old pullover.
colourful	**clothes**	

IVb Possessive Pronouns
Besitzanzeigende Fürwörter

What's **mine** is mine.
What's **yours** is mine, too.
His and **hers**
Theirs

IVd Relative Pronouns
Bezügliche Fürwörter

Bavaria's the place	**where**	(Levi Strauss was born).

VIIa Adjectives: Comparison Eigenschaftswörter: Steigerung

The better	you look,	**the happier**	you are.
The more	you waste,	**the happier**	you are.
The quicker	fashions change,	**the more**	clothes you buy.
The more	clothes you buy,	**the more**	you throw away.

Language Functions Sprechabsichten

1.7 Komplimente machen
I like (your new glasses).
(Those jeans) look really great.
(That pullover) really suits you.
That's a beautiful (ring).
That's a new (blouse), isn't it?
It's very nice.

auf Komplimente reagieren
Oh, thank you.
Oh, do you think so?
Do you like it?
I'm glad you like it.

3.1 benennen, definieren
(Bavaria's) the place where
(Levi Strauss was born).

5.6 zustimmen
So did we.

8.9 vergleichen
That sounds familiar!
That reminds me of (my children)!
That's just like (my daughter)!

UNIT 10

Grammar Grammatik

Ic Past Tenses: Past Simple
Vergangenheitsformen: Past Simple

I wish	my flat	was	on the ground floor.
I wish	I	had	one more room.

Hinweis: Die Vergangenheitsform *Past Simple* wird auch bei Wunschvorstellungen verwendet.

Past Tenses: Past Continuous
Vergangenheitsformen: Past Continuous

I	was ironing	a shirt when …
My father-in-law	was painting	his front door when …
My sister	was boiling	some milk when …

Ie Short Forms Kurzformen

You'll = You will
It'll = It will

Ig The "-ing" Form
Die "-ing"-Form

Luxury is living on your own in a big flat. Counting sheep's good for insomnia.
… instead of putting on a pullover
Stop talking. Keep moving. Try going for a walk.

III Indefinite Article
Unbestimmter Artikel

(I've got)	a headache.
If you've got	backache/stomachache/toothache …

IVb Possessive Pronouns
Besitzanzeigende Fürwörter

A friend of **mine**

VIIa Adjectives: Comparison
Eigenschaftswörter: Steigerung

Compared to 30 years ago, we use	**more**	energy for heating.
Compared to 30 years ago, washing machines use	**less**	electricity.

IXe If Clauses If-Sätze

Past Simple Form	Conditional
If I **could** afford it,	I'**d** have my own sauna.

LS

UNIT 10

■ Language Functions Sprechabsichten

6.3 Wünsche äußern
I wish (my flat) was (on the ground floor).
I wish I had (one more room).

6.8 Überraschung ausdrücken
I didn't realise that ...
I'm surprised that ...
I find it difficult to believe that ...

7.5 einen Rat geben
Why don't you (get some fresh air)? You'll feel much better.
If you want to (feel happy, just laugh).
(Keep moving) is good advice if you've got (backache).
(Counting sheep) is good for (insomnia).

8.9 vergleichen
Compared to (30 years ago, heating systems are more efficient).

UNIT 11

■ Grammar Grammatik

Ib Imperatives
Aufforderungssätze

Affirmative Bejaht	Negative Verneint
Eat up all your vegetables.	**Don't talk** to strangers.

Ic Future Tenses: will
Zukunftsformen: will

I hope I	'll	be happy.
I hope you	won't	be unemployed.
Where	will	I go to school?

Id Modal Verbs
Modalverben

I hope you**'ll be able to** (find a good job).

Hinweis: Das Modalverb *can* hat keine Zukunftsform. Es wird auf *be able to* zurückgegriffen.

Ie Short Forms Kurzformen

wo**n't** = **will** not

IIb s' Genitive
Genitiv mit s'

since your grandparents**'** days

Hinweis: Wenn das Hauptwort in der Mehrzahl mit s endet, wird der Apostroph (') nach dem s gesetzt.

IVa Personal Pronouns
Persönliche Fürwörter

There was just **me**.
There is only **me**.

Hinweis: Nach dem Zeitwort *be* wird die Satzergänzungsform verwendet.

IVe Indefinite Pronouns
Unbestimmte Fürwörter

Each was adopted by a different family.
The sisters wrote to **each other**.
In what ways are you like **each other**?

UNIT 11

Vb Quantifiers
Mengenangaben

More	
Fewer	people will get married.

IXe *If* Clauses *If*-Sätze

Past Simple Form	Conditional
If I **were** you,	I'**d**/I **wouldn't** …

Language Functions Sprechabsichten

6.2 **Hoffnung ausdrücken**
I hope you'll …
I hope you won't …

7.5 **einen Rat geben**
If I were you, I'd …
If I were you, I wouldn't …

I think you should …
I don't think you should …
Don't forget to …!

UNIT 12

Grammar Grammatik

Ic Past Tenses: Past Continuous vs. Past Simple
Vergangenheitsformen: Past Continuous vs. Past Simple

Past Continuous	Past Simple
I **was coming** home when	I **drove** into the wrong house.
I **was driving** along the road when	a pedestrian **hit** me.

Id Modal Verbs Modalverben

Farmers **might** start to use horses again.
Cars and lorries **will have to** pay to enter cities.
I **was unable to** stop in time.

Hinweis: Das Modalverb *must* hat keine Zukunftsform. Es wird auf *have to* zurückgegriffen.

Ih Passive: *will* / Modal Verbs
Passiv: *will* / Modalverben

Speed limits **will/might be** lower**ed**.
The railway network **won't be** reduce**d**.

IIb *s'* Genitive Genitiv mit *s'*

in ten year**s'** time

IXb Questions Fragesätze

Which	means of transport do you use?
What	colour is the Metro?

LS

UNIT 12

IXd Indirect Questions Indirekte Fragen

Direct Questions Direkte Fragen	Indirect Questions Indirekte Fragen	
Is there a bank near here?	**Do you know**	if there's a bank near here?
How often do the buses run?	**Do you know**	how often the buses run?
Where's the nearest post office?	**Can you tell me**	where the nearest post office **is**?

Language Functions Sprechabsichten

2.8 eine Aussage strukturieren
(I prefer to walk), even if (the bus is cheaper).
On the other hand, (motorbikes are also more dangerous).

5.1 Gewißheit ausdrücken
(There) will certainly (be more lorries on the roads).
(The railway network) certainly won't (be reduced).

5.3 Ungewißheit ausdrücken
(There) will probably (be "intelligent" roads).
(Most people) probably won't (get rid of their cars).
(Cars and lorries) might (have to pay to enter cities).

7.1 nach dem Weg fragen
Excuse me,
– can you tell me the way to ...
– can you tell me how to get to ...
– do you know if there's a (phone box) near here?
– can you tell me where the (station) is?

... und darauf reagieren
Yes, it's ...
Go ... and ask again.
Sorry, I'm a stranger here myself.

UNIT 13

Grammar Grammatik

Ih Passive: *get* Passiv: *get*

		clothes	**cleaned**.
You can	get	furniture	**repaired**.
		your hair	**done**.

If Short Answers/Responses
Kurzantworten

Neither have I.

IIa Nouns: Plural Forms
Hauptwörter: Bildung der Mehrzahlformen

Singular Einzahl	**Plural** Mehrzahl
furniture	–
equipment	–
–	clothes
–	goods

IVb Possessive Pronouns
Besitzanzeigende Fürwörter

It's something you give **somebody** for **their** birthday.

Unit 13

IXe *If* Clauses *If*-Sätze

Past Simple Form	Conditional
If a salesperson **was** unfriendly,	**I'd** complain.
If I **couldn't** (change my order),	I **wouldn't** go there again.

Conditional	Past Simple Form
What **would** happen	if you **changed** your order?

Language Functions Sprechabsichten

1.1 eine/n Verkäufer/in ansprechen
I'm looking for (a pair of sandals).
I'm interested in (video cameras).
Have you got …?

5.1 nach einer Meinung fragen
What's your opinion of …?

5.6 zustimmen
Neither (have I).

6.1 fragen, was einem gefällt
Have you got a favourite …?

6.6 Unzufriedenheit ausdrücken, reklamieren
I don't think this is working right.
I'd like my money back.
I'd like to change it.
I'm afraid there's something wrong with it.
This is (a bit) too (big for me).

7.2 eine Bitte äußern
Can you (check) it for me, please?
Will you take (a cheque)?

7.5 einen Rat erfragen
Can you recommend (a good butcher's)?
Is there one you'd specially recommend?

Unit 14

Grammar Grammatik

Id Modal Verbs: *may*
Modalverben: *may*

> We **may** get more viewers if (we show a lot of soaps).

IIb *'s* Genitive
Genitiv mit *'s*

> this summer**'s** best holiday bargain
> an evening**'s** TV
> tomorrow**'s** weather

VIIIh Formation of Adverbs
Bildung von Umstandswörtern

bad	bad**ly**
slow	slow**ly**
loud	loud**ly**
angry	ang**rily**
happy	happ**ily**

careful	careful**ly**
bored	**in a** bored **way**
friendly	**in a** friendly **way**
fast	fast

LS

UNIT 14

IXe If Clauses If-Sätze

will Future Form	Present Simple Form
We'll get more viewers	if we **show** (more sports programmes).

Past Simple Form	Conditional
If this music **was** used to advertise something,	it **could** be (a car).

Language Functions Sprechabsichten

5.1 **Gewißheit ausdrücken**
(We)'ll definitely (get more viewers).

6.1 **fragen, was einem besser gefällt**
Would you rather (watch TV)?

sagen, was einem nicht gefällt
(Someone who) dislikes (the music you like).

7.4 **etwas vorschlagen**
Don't you think we should …?
If you like, we could …
I think it would be a good idea to …

einen Gegenvorschlag machen
Wouldn't it be better to …?

8.5 **eine Handlung nach der Art und Weise einordnen**
… in a friendly/unusual way

UNIT 15

Grammar Grammatik

IXb Negative Questions
Verneinte Fragen

Don't	you think …?
Wouldn't	it be great if …?

Language Functions Sprechabsichten

2.5 **um eine Wiederholung bitten**
Could you say that a bit more slowly, please?
Can you repeat that, please?
Did you say …?
I'm afraid I didn't get that.
Sorry?
What was that again?

2.6 **Zeit gewinnen**
Er …
Let me think.
Well, I don't know really.
That's an interesting question.
What do you think?
I beg your pardon?

It's difficult to say.
I mean, …
It depends, doesn't it?

2.10 **umschreiben**
It's one of those things that …
It's that stuff that …
It's a way of …ing
It's when/where you …
You need this to …
It's a sort of …

5.5 **widersprechen**
But wouldn't it be …?
But don't you think …?
But isn't it …?
But shouldn't …?

LF

LANGUAGE FUNCTIONS

Einleitung

Die folgende Liste bietet einen Überblick über sämtliche Sprechabsichten (*Language Functions*), die in **BRIDGES 2** vorkommen, mit Ausnahme der Ausdrücke, die in **BRIDGES 1** schon eingeführt wurden.

Die Sprechabsichten untergliedern sich in acht Hauptbereiche. Jede Sprechabsicht ist mit einer Verweisnummer versehen, wobei die Numerierung den Vorgaben des ICC/VHS-Zertifikats folgt, die dem Lehrwerk **BRIDGES** zugrundeliegt, z.B.

    2.5   um eine Wiederholung bitten.

Diese Numerierung wird auch in den LANGUAGE SUMMARIES (Abschnitt: *Language Functions*) verwendet.

Am Ende des Kapitels sind die wichtigsten Telefon- bzw. Briefkonventionen aufgelistet.

INDEX   STICHWORT-VERZEICHNIS

1 Soziale Kontakte

1.1 eine/n Verkäufer/in ansprechen
- Unit 13 I'm looking for (a pair of sandals).
- Unit 13 I'm interested in (video cameras).
- Unit 13 Have you got …?

1.2 auf Vorstellung reagieren
- Unit 1   Pleased to meet you.

1.3 jemanden grüßen
- Unit 1   Did you have a good trip?

1.5 sich verabschieden
- Unit 1   Don't forget to send a postcard!
- Unit 1   It was nice to meet you.
- Unit 1   It was great to be here.

1.6 gute Wünsche äußern
- Unit 1   Enjoy the rest of your trip!
- Unit 8   Merry Christmas(!)
- Unit 8   Many happy returns(!)
- Unit 8   Happy New Year!
- Unit 8   Happy Anniversary!
- Unit 8   Best wishes(!)
- Unit 8   Happy Easter(!)
- Unit 8   All the best!
- Unit 8   Cheers!

Glückwünsche aussprechen
- Unit 5   Congratulations!
- Unit 5   Well done!

1.7 Komplimente machen
- Unit 8   Mm, this tastes great!
- Unit 8   You must let us have the recipe!
- Unit 9   I like (your new glasses).
- Unit 9   (Those jeans) look really great.
- Unit 9   (That pullover) really suits you.
- Unit 9   That's a beautiful (ring).
- Unit 9   That's a new (blouse), isn't it?
- Unit 9   It's very nice.

auf Komplimente reagieren
- Unit 9   Oh, thank you.
- Unit 9   Oh, do you think so?
- Unit 9   Do you like it?
- Unit 9   I'm glad you like it.

1.8 sich bedanken
- Unit 1   Thanks for everything.

LF

1.9 auf eine Entschuldigung reagieren
- *Unit 1* — Don't worry.
- *Unit 1* — No problem.

1.10 eine Einladung aussprechen
- *Unit 8* — Would you like to (go to the new Indian restaurant)?

eine Einladung annehmen
- *Unit 8* — Oh, that would be nice!

eine Einladung ablehnen
- *Unit 8* — I'm afraid (I'm going to the ...).

2 Gesprächsstrategien

2.2 ein Gespräch einleiten
- *Unit 1* — It's a lovely day, isn't it?
- *Unit 1* — Are you here on holiday/business?

eine Äußerung einleiten
- *Unit 6* — Excuse me ...

2.5 um eine Wiederholung bitten
- *Unit 15* — Could you say that a bit more slowly, please?
- *Unit 15* — Can you repeat that, please?
- *Unit 15* — Did you say ...?
- *Unit 15* — I'm afraid I didn't get that.
- *Unit 15* — Sorry?
- *Unit 15* — What was that again?

2.6 Zeit gewinnen
- *Unit 15* — Er ...
- *Unit 15* — Let me think.
- *Unit 15* — Well, I don't know really.
- *Unit 15* — That's an interesting question.
- *Unit 15* — What do you think?
- *Unit 15* — I beg your pardon?
- *Unit 15* — It's difficult to say.
- *Unit 15* — I mean, ...
- *Unit 15* — It depends, doesn't it?

2.7 eine ausweichende Antwort geben
- *Unit 3* — That depends (what time we get started).
- *Unit 4* — It depends what you mean by ...
- *Unit 7* — It is and it isn't.
- *Unit 7* — It depends how you look at it.

2.8 eine Aussage strukturieren
- *Unit 6* — Although (your brochure says ...), in fact ...
- *Unit 6* — In addition to this, ...
- *Unit 12* — (I prefer to walk), even if (the bus is cheaper).
- *Unit 12* — On the other hand, (motorbikes are also more dangerous).

2.9 ein Beispiel geben
- *Unit 1* — (Some subjects are very boring), like (illnesses and children).
- *Unit 8* — (one kg mixed vegetables) such as (carrots, leeks, etc).

2.10 umschreiben
- *Unit 15* — It's one of those things that ...
- *Unit 15* — It's that stuff that ...
- *Unit 15* — It's a way of ...ing
- *Unit 15* — It's when/where you ...
- *Unit 15* — You need this to ...
- *Unit 15* — It's a sort of ...

3 Mitteilungen

3.1 benennen, definieren
- *Unit 1* — people (I meet for the first time)
- *Unit 1* — a question (you'd like to ask your boss)
- *Unit 2* — (something) which (grows on trees)
- *Unit 2* — (things) that (I want to do)
- *Unit 4* — It's (a kind of) ...
- *Unit 4* — You use it for ...
- *Unit 4* — It's something ...
- *Unit 8* — It's a day when (people have to) ...
- *Unit 9* — (Bavaria's) the place where ...

4 Versprechen, anbieten

4.1 versprechen, etwas zu tun
- *Unit 6* — I'll (speak to them immediately).

4.2 etwas anbieten
- *Unit 1* — Can I get you a drink?
- *Unit 3* — Shall I (buy some wine)?

Hilfe anbieten
Unit 3 Can I help you with (the washing-up)?

5 Stellungnahmen

5.1 **eine Meinung mitteilen; Gewißheit ausdrücken**
Unit 12 (There) will certainly (be more lorries on the roads).
Unit 12 (The railway network) certainly won't (be reduced).
Unit 14 (We)'ll definitely (get more viewers).

nach einer Meinung fragen
Unit 13 What's your opinion of …?

5.2 **Wichtigkeit ausdrücken**
Unit 3 I think (number 3) is the most important.
Unit 3 I don't think (number 6) is important at all.

5.3 **Ungewißheit ausdrücken**
Unit 12 (There) will probably (be "intelligent" roads).
Unit 12 (Most people) probably won't (get rid of their cars).
Unit 12 (Cars and lorries) might (have to pay to enter cities).

5.5 **widersprechen**
Unit 15 But wouldn't it be …?
Unit 15 But don't you think …?
Unit 15 But isn't it …?
Unit 15 But shouldn't …?

5.6 **zustimmen**
Unit 2 Me too.
Unit 2 Nor me.
Unit 3 So do I!
Unit 3 Nor do I!
Unit 4 So do I.
Unit 4 Nor do I. / Nor would I.
Unit 4 I think so, too.
Unit 4 That's true.
Unit 9 So did we.
Unit 13 Neither (have I).

Nichtzustimmung ausdrücken
Unit 1 I disagree.
Unit 4 I wouldn't say that.
Unit 4 I don't think so.

6 Gefühle

6.1 **fragen, was einem gefällt**
Unit 13 Have you got a favourite …?

sagen, was einem besser gefällt
Unit 6 I prefer (self-catering) to (hotels).

fragen, was einem besser gefällt
Unit 14 Would you rather (watch TV)?

sagen, was einem nicht gefällt
Unit 6 I can't stand (lying in the sun).
Unit 14 (Someone who) dislikes (the music you like).

6.2 **Sorgen ausdrücken**
Unit 5 I worry about …
Unit 5 What's the matter?

Hoffnung ausdrücken
Unit 5 Touch wood!
Unit 11 I hope you'll …
Unit 11 I hope you won't …

6.3 **Wünsche äußern**
Unit 7 I'd like to be (a nature warden).
Unit 7 I wouldn't mind being (a traffic warden).
Unit 10 I wish I had (one more room).
Unit 10 I wish (my flat) was (on the ground floor).

6.4 **Freude ausdrücken**
Unit 5 I'm happy.
Unit 5 I feel happy.
Unit 5 I'm in a good mood.
Unit 5 … makes me laugh.

sich mit jmd. freuen
Unit 5 You must be really pleased.
Unit 5 That's great.

6.5 **Traurigkeit ausdrücken**
Unit 5 I'm sad.
Unit 5 I feel sad.

LF

Mitleid ausdrücken
- *Unit 5* That's terrible!
- *Unit 5* How disappointing!
- *Unit 5* Oh no!
- *Unit 5* Oh, dear!
- *Unit 5* What a pity!
- *Unit 5* You must be very upset.
- *Unit 5* I'm sorry to hear that.

6.6 Unzufriedenheit ausdrücken, reklamieren
- *Unit 6* Excuse me, there's (no water in the swimming pool).
- *Unit 6* We're writing to complain about (the hotel).
- *Unit 13* I don't think this is working right.
- *Unit 13* I'd like my money back.
- *Unit 13* I'd like to change it.
- *Unit 13* I'm afraid there's something wrong with it.
- *Unit 13* This is (a bit) too (big for me).

Ärger ausdrücken
- *Unit 5* I get annoyed when …

6.7 Gelassenheit ausdrücken
- *Unit 6* I don't mind (self-catering holidays).

6.8 Überraschung ausdrücken
- *Unit 4* Look at this!
- *Unit 4* That's surprising.
- *Unit 10* I didn't realize that …
- *Unit 10* I'm surprised that …
- *Unit 10* I find it difficult to believe that …

7 Aufforderungen zum Sprechen/Handeln

7.1 nach dem Weg fragen
- *Unit 12* Excuse me,
  - can you tell me the way to …
  - can you tell me how to get to …
  - do you know if there's a (phone box) near here?
  - can you tell me where the (station) is?

… und darauf reagieren
- *Unit 12* Yes, it's …
- *Unit 12* Go … and ask again.
- *Unit 12* Sorry, I'm a stranger here myself.

7.2 eine Bitte äußern
- *Unit 6* Would/Will you please do something about it?
- *Unit 6* Can/Could you do something about it?
- *Unit 13* Can you (check it) for me, please?
- *Unit 13* Will you take (a cheque)?

7.4 etwas vorschlagen
- *Unit 3* Why don't we (go to the theatre)?
- *Unit 3* I think it would be nice to (go to the art gallery).
- *Unit 3* We could (take them to the museum).
- *Unit 8* What we suggest is …
- *Unit 14* Don't you think we should …?
- *Unit 14* If you like, we could …
- *Unit 14* I think it would be a good idea to …

einen Vorschlag annehmen
- *Unit 3* Good idea!
- *Unit 3* Why not?

einen Vorschlag ablehnen/ einen Gegenvorschlag machen
- *Unit 3* Let's (go to the museum) instead.
- *Unit 3* I'd prefer to (show them the castle).
- *Unit 14* Wouldn't it be better to …?

7.5 einen Rat geben
- *Unit 1* You should (phone to say you can go).
- *Unit 10* Why don't you (get some fresh air)? You'll feel better.
- *Unit 10* If you want to (feel happy, just laugh).
- *Unit 10* (Keep moving) is good advice if you've got (backache).
- *Unit 10* (Counting sheep) is good for (insomnia).
- *Unit 11* If I were you, I'd …
- *Unit 11* If I were you, I wouldn't …
- *Unit 11* I think you should …
- *Unit 11* I don't think you should …
- *Unit 11* Don't forget to …!

LF

einen Rat erfragen
Unit 13 Can you recommend (a good butcher's)?
Unit 13 Is there one you'd specially recommend?

von etwas abraten
Unit 1 You shouldn't (arrive at 8 o'clock).

7.6 um Erlaubnis bitten
Unit 3 Can I (use the phone)?
Unit 3 Is it all right if I (use the phone)?

sagen, daß etwas erlaubt ist
Unit 1 You can (take flowers).
Unit 8 ... people are (only) allowed to ...

sagen, daß etwas nicht erlaubt ist
Unit 1 You can't (just go).
Unit 8 ... people aren't allowed to ...

8 Andere Sprechabsichten

8.1 sagen, daß etwas notwendig ist
Unit 1 You have to (take a present).
Unit 3 You should (write a thankyou letter).
Unit 3 (Guests) should not (come home late).

sagen, daß etwas nicht notwendig ist
Unit 1 You don't have to (arrive at 8 o'clock).

8.5 eine Handlung nach der Art und Weise einordnen
Unit 14 ... in a friendly/unusual way.

8.9 vergleichen
Unit 9 That sounds familiar!
Unit 9 That reminds me of (my children)!
Unit 9 That's just like (my daughter)!
Unit 10 Compared to (30 years ago, heating systems are more efficient).

Telefonkonventionen

1.1 sich am Telefon melden
Unit 7 Truman plc.
Unit 7 Mr Colby's office.

1.2 sich am Telefon vorstellen
Unit 7 Good morning, my name's (Roger Taylor).
Unit 7 Hello, this is (Liz May).

4.2 Hilfe anbieten
Unit 7 Can I take a message?
Unit 7 Would you like to leave a message?

6.3 Wünsche äußern
Unit 7 I'd like to speak to (Jenny Faber).
Unit 7 Can I speak to (Mr Colby), please?

7.2 eine Bitte äußern
Unit 7 Could you tell (him) I called?

auf eine Bitte reagieren
Unit 7 I'll tell (her) you called.

- **Andere Telefonwendungen**
Unit 7 Hold on.
Unit 7 I'll put you through.
Unit 7 The line's busy.
Unit 7 (He's) not in (this morning).

Briefkonventionen

- *Unit 3* Dear (Bridget), Love, (Shirley)
  Unit 6 Dear Sir or Madam, Yours faithfully,

- **Nützliche Wendungen für Briefe**
  Unit 3 Well, that's all for now,

G
GRAMMAR

Einleitung

In diesem Anhang finden Sie eine Zusammenstellung der in **BRIDGES 2** enthaltenen Grammatik. Zur besseren Übersicht gibt es ein Inhaltsverzeichnis, mit dessen Hilfe die einzelnen Strukturen gefunden werden können. Die Numerierung entspricht der Systematik der *Language Summaries*.

Bei allen grammatischen Strukturen in dieser Zusammenstellung handelt es sich um aktive Lerninhalte, das heißt Strukturen, die im *Classroom Book* geübt und angewendet werden. In Klammern wird auf die jeweilige *Unit* verwiesen, in der die Struktur zum ersten Mal vorkommt.

INDEX

INHALTSVERZEICHNIS

I The Verb
- a Infinitives
- b Imperatives
- c Tenses
  - Present
  - Past
  - Future
  - Present Perfect
  - Conditional
- d Modal Verbs
  - *be allowed to*
  - *can/be able to*
  - *may*
  - *might*
  - *must/have to*
  - *shall*
  - *should*
- e Short Forms
- f Short Answers/Responses
- g "*-ing*" Form
- h Passive
  - Past Tense
  - Future Tense
  - Passive with *get*

II Nouns
- a Plural Forms
- b '*s/s*' Genitive

III Definite*/Indefinite Article

Das Zeitwort
Die Grundform des Zeitworts
Aufforderungssätze
Zeitformen
- Gegenwart
- Vergangenheit
- Zukunft
- Present Perfect
- Conditional
Modalverben
- *be allowed to*
- *can/be able to*
- *may*
- *might*
- *must/have to*
- *shall*
- *should*
Kurzformen
Kurzantworten
Die "*-ing*"-Form
Die Passivform
- Vergangenheitsform
- Zukunftsform
- Passivform mit *get*

Hauptwörter
Mehrzahlformen
Genitiv mit '*s/s*'

Bestimmter*/Unbestimmter Artikel

IV Pronouns
- a Personal Pronouns
- b Possessive Pronouns
- c Demonstrative Pronouns
- d Relative Pronouns
- e Indefinite Pronouns
  - *both/all, neither/none*
  - *some/any* + compounds
  - *everybody/nobody**
  - *each/each other*
- f Reflexive Pronouns

V Quantifiers
- a *all/most/a lot/some/several,* etc.
- b • *much/many/a lot of*
  - *more/less/fewer*
- c Quantities

VI Numerals
- a Cardinal Numbers
- b Ordinal Numbers*
- c Time of Day*
- d Date
- e Telephone Numbers*

VII Adjectives
- a Comparison
- b Other Forms
  - *as ... as*
  - *the same as*

VIII Adverbs/Adverbial Phrases
- a Frequency*
- b Time
- c Place
- d Sequence of Adverbs*
- e Modifiers
- f *too/not ... either*
- g *only*
- h Formation of Adverbs

IX Sentence Patterns
- a Statements*
- b Questions
- c Reported Speech
- d Indirect Questions
- e *If* Clauses

◆ **List of Irregular Verbs**

Fürwörter
- Persönliche Fürwörter
- Besitzanzeigende Fürwörter
- Hinweisende Fürwörter
- Bezügliche Fürwörter
- Unbestimmte Fürwörter
  - *both/all, neither/none*
  - *some/any* + Zusammensetzungen
  - *everybody/nobody**
  - *each/each other*
- Rückbezügliche Fürwörter

Mengenangaben
- *all/most/a lot/some/several,* etc.
  - *much/many/a lot of*
  - *more/less/fewer*
- Mengen

Zahlen
- Grundzahlen
- Ordnungszahlen*
- Uhrzeit*
- Datum
- Telefonnummern*

Eigenschaftswörter
- Steigerungsformen
- Andere Formen
  - *as... as*
  - *the same as*

Umstandswörter/Umstandsbestimmungen
- Häufigkeitsangaben*
- Zeitangaben
- Ortsangaben
- Reihenfolge bei zwei Umstandsbestimmungen*
- Verstärkende bzw. abschwächende Umstandswörter
- *too/not ... either*
- *only*
- Bildung von Umstandswörtern

Satzmuster
- Aussagesätze*
- Fragesätze
- Indirekte Rede
- Indirekte Fragen
- *If*-Sätze

Liste unregelmäßiger Zeitwörter

---

*see BRIDGES 1   *siehe BRIDGES 1

G

I The Verb   Das Zeitwort

Ia Infinitives   Die Grundform des Zeitworts   [Units 3, 7, 8]

I'd prefer **to show** them the castle. He decided **to train** as a librarian.	Ich würde ihnen lieber das Schloß zeigen. Er beschloß, sich zum Bibliothekar ausbilden zu lassen.
You must **let** us **have** the recipe!	Sie müssen uns unbedingt das Rezept geben!

Hinweis: Bei einigen Zeitwörtern wird der Grundform *to* vorangesetzt.

Ib Imperatives   Aufforderungssätze   [Units 5, 11]

Affirmative   Bejaht

Be happy. **Eat** up all your vegetables.	Sei glücklich. Iß dein Gemüse auf.

Negative   Verneint

Don't worry. **Don't talk** to strangers.	Machen Sie sich keine Sorgen. Rede nicht mit Fremden.

Ic Tenses   Zeitformen

Present Tenses   Gegenwartsformen

Present Continuous   [Unit 7]

I'm	brush**ing** up	my English.	Ich frische gerade mein Englisch auf.
He's	look**ing**	for a new job.	Er sucht zur Zeit eine neue Stelle.
My daughter's	learn**ing**	Italian.	Meine Tochter lernt gerade Italienisch.
What's	happen**ing**?		Was passiert gerade?
We're	tak**ing**	a computer course.	Wir machen einen Computer-Kurs.
My parents are	look**ing** forward to	retiring.	Meine Eltern freuen sich auf den Ruhestand.

Hinweis: Die *Present Continuous*-Form wird mit dem Zeitwort *be* und der "*ing*"-Form (siehe Ig) gebildet.
Der Gebrauch dieser Zeitform wird in der nächsten Tabelle erläutert.

G

Present Simple vs. Present Continuous [Unit 7]

Present Simple	Present Continuous
I usually **work** in another department. Normalerweise arbeite ich in einer anderen Abteilung.	I'm **helping** out here for a few weeks. Ich bin hier einige Wochen zur Aushilfe.
This machine normally **works** perfectly. Normalerweise funktioniert diese Maschine einwandfrei.	It's **giving** us some trouble today. Heute macht sie uns einige Schwierigkeiten.
Our company **makes** kitchen equipment. Unsere Firma produziert Küchengeräte.	At the moment we're **expanding** into Eastern Europe. Zur Zeit expandieren wir nach Osteuropa.
Hinweis: Die *Present Continuous*-Form als Gegenwartsform drückt aus, daß die Handlung gerade stattfindet, im Gegensatz zur *Present Simple*-Form, die den Normal- bzw. Dauerzustand beschreibt. Dementsprechend werden die beiden Zeitformen mit unterschiedlichen Zeitangaben (z.B. *usually*, *at the moment*) kombiniert.	

Past Tenses Vergangenheitsformen

Past Simple [Unit 10]

He **lived** in Mannheim from 1975 to 1979. It **was** so loud I **could**n't sleep.	Er lebte von 1975 bis 1979 in Mannheim. Es war so laut, daß ich nicht schlafen konnte.
I wish my flat **was** on the ground floor. **I wish** I **had** one more room.	Ich wünschte, meine Wohnung wäre im Erdgeschoß. Ich wünschte, ich hätte noch ein Zimmer.
Hinweis: Die *Past Simple*-Form wird für abgeschlossene Handlungen in der Vergangenheit verwendet. Bei Wunschvorstellungen wird das Gewünschte auch in der Vergangenheitsform ausgedrückt.	

Past Continuous [Unit 10]

I **was** iron**ing** a shirt ... My father-in-law **was** paint**ing** ... My sister **was** boil**ing** some milk ...	Ich bügelte gerade ein Hemd ... Mein Schwiegervater strich gerade ... Meine Schwester kochte gerade etwas Milch ...
Hinweis: Die *Past Continuous*-Form wird mit dem Zeitwort *be* und der "*ing*"-Form (siehe Ig) gebildet. Der Gebrauch dieser Zeitform wird in der nächsten Tabelle erläutert.	

G

Past Continuous vs. Past Simple [Unit 12]

Past Continuous	Past Simple
I **was coming** home Ich fuhr gerade nach Hause,	when I **drove** into the wrong house. als ich in das falsche Haus hineinfuhr.
I **was driving** along the road Ich fuhr gerade die Straße entlang,	when a pedestrian **hit** me. als mich ein Fußgänger traf.
Hinweis: Die *Past Continuous*-Form drückt aus, was in einem Augenblick in der Vergangenheit gerade geschah. Sie wird häufig bei Berichten und Anekdoten verwendet, um den zeitlichen Rahmen für die eigentliche Handlung festzulegen, die dann in der *Past Simple*-Form erzählt wird.	

Future Tenses Zukunftsformen

going to [Unit 3]

I'm What am I I'm not	**going to**	stay with a friend. wear? sit down all day.	Ich werde bei einem Freund wohnen. Was soll ich anziehen? Ich will nicht den ganzen Tag sitzen.
Hinweis: Die *going to*-Form drückt aus, was in absehbarer Zeit geschehen soll. Sie wird oft verwendet, wenn es um Zukunftspläne bzw. Absichten geht.			

Present Continuous as Future Present Continuous als Zukunftsform [Unit 8]

On Saturday	**I'm meeting**	Susan for lunch.	Am Samstag treffe ich mich mit Susan zum Mittagessen.
In the evening	**we're going**	to the disco.	Abends gehen wir in die Disco.
When	**are they meeting**?		Wann treffen sie sich?
Hinweis: Die *Present Continuous*-Form wird als Zukunftsform verwendet, wenn es sich um Pläne für die unmittelbare Zukunft handelt. Normalerweise ist eine Zeitangabe (*on Saturday*, *in the evening*, usw.) vorhanden oder zumindest impliziert.			

will [Units 7, 11]

It**'ll** really help. I hope I**'ll** be happy. People **will** live longer.	Das wird wirklich helfen. Ich hoffe, ich werde glücklich sein. Die Menschen werden länger leben.
I**'ll** tell her you called. Where **will** I go to school? I hope you **won't** be unemployed.	Ich sage ihr, daß Sie angerufen haben. Wo werde ich zur Schule gehen? Ich hoffe, daß du nicht arbeitslos wirst.
Hinweis: Die *will*-Form wird in erster Linie für Versprechungen, Hoffnungen und Voraussagen verwendet (siehe auch *going to* und *Present Continuous*). Die Form ist in allen Personen gleich.	

G

Present Perfect Simple

Regular Verbs Regelmäßige Zeitwörter [Unit 4]

The computer **has** chang**ed** millions of jobs.	Der Computer hat Millionen Arbeitsplätze verändert.
The television **has** spoil**ed** family life.	Das Fernsehen hat das Familienleben verdorben.

Hinweis:	Die *Present Perfect Simple*-Form wird mit dem Hilfszeitwort *have* gebildet. Bei regelmäßigen Zeitwörtern wird *-(e)d* an die Grundform angehängt. Der Gebrauch dieser Zeitform wird weiter unten erläutert.

Irregular Verbs Unregelmäßige Zeitwörter [Units 4, 5, 6]

The microwave **has made** cooking easier. What **have** we **taken**? They**'ve broken** the window. They**'ve drunk** the whisky.	Die Mikrowelle hat das Kochen einfacher gemacht. Was haben wir mitgenommen? Sie haben das Fenster zerbrochen. Sie haben den Whisky getrunken.

Hinweis:	Eine Liste aller in BRIDGES 1+2 vorkommenden unregelmäßigen Zeitwörter finden Sie auf S. 182 – 183. Der Gebrauch dieser Zeitform wird weiter unten erläutert.

Present Perfect with *for/since* [Unit 10]

I **haven't been** to the doctor's	**for** a long time.	Ich war schon lange nicht mehr beim Arzt.
Robert **hasn't had** a cold	**for** two years.	Robert hat seit zwei Jahren keine Erkältung mehr gehabt.
I **haven't had** a hangover	**since** Christmas.	Ich habe seit Weihnachten keinen Kater mehr gehabt.
I **haven't been** in hospital	**since** I was a child.	Ich bin seit meiner Kindheit nicht mehr im Krankenhaus gewesen.

Hinweis:	*For* und *since* entsprechen dem deutschen *seit* bzw. *seitdem*. *For* wird bei Zeiträumen (z.B. *two years*) verwendet; *since* bei Zeitpunkten, die in der Vergangenheit zurückliegen (z.B. *Christmas*).

Present Perfect Simple vs. Past Simple [Unit 6]

Present Perfect Simple	**Past Simple**
Bruce **has lived** in Mannheim. Bruce hat auch schon in Mannheim gelebt.	He **lived** there from 1975 to 1979. Er lebte von 1975 bis 1979 dort.
Have you ever **been** to France? Waren Sie schon einmal in Frankreich?	When **did** you **go** there? Wann sind Sie dort gewesen?

Hinweis:	Die Zeitform *Present Perfect Simple* wird benutzt, wenn es sich um die Zeit bis zum heutigen Tag handelt; die Zeitform *Past Simple* dagegen, wenn es um eine abgeschlossene Zeit in der Vergangenheit geht (z.B. *1975* oder die Frage *When?*).

G

Conditional [Units 8, 10, 11]

I'd have my own sauna. If I were a place, I'd be Paris. If I were you, I wouldn't …	Ich würde meine eigene Sauna haben. Wenn ich ein Ort wäre, würde ich Paris sein. An Ihrer Stelle würde ich nicht …
Hinweis: Die Co*nditional*-Form wird in allen Personen mit *would* und der Grundform des Zeitworts gebildet. Die *Conditional*-Form wird häufig in *If*-Sätzen (siehe IXe) verwendet.	

Id Modal Verbs Modalverben

be allowed to [Unit 8]

A day when people **are allowed to** … A day when people **aren't allowed to** …	Ein Tag, an dem es den Leuten erlaubt ist, … Ein Tag, an dem es den Leuten nicht erlaubt ist, …
Hinweis: *Be allowed to* drückt aus, was erlaubt bzw. nicht erlaubt ist.	

can/be able to [Units 1, 3, 11, 12]

Present Tense Gegenwartsform	
You **can** take flowers.	Sie können Blumen mitbringen.
Past Tense Vergangenheitsform	
We **could** not stand it any more.	Wir konnten es nicht mehr aushalten.
Future Tense Zukunftsform	
I hope **you'll be able to** find a good job.	Ich hoffe, du wirst eine gute Stelle finden können.
Conditional	
Things you **could** talk about.	Dinge, über die Sie reden könnten.

Hinweis: Das Modalverb *can* hat keine Zukunftsform. Es wird auf *be able to* zurückgegriffen. *Can/Be able to* werden verwendet, um
  1. Fähigkeiten und Möglichkeiten auszudrücken, z.B. *I can't sleep at night;*
  2. Bitten (auch um Erlaubnis) zu äußern, z.B. *Can you do something about it?;*
  3. Warnungen auszudrücken, z.B. *You can't wear jeans;*
  4. Angebote zu machen, z.B. *Can I get you a drink?*
Für weitere Hinweise zum Gebrauch siehe *Language Summaries* (LS) S. 152 – 153.	

may [Unit 14]

We **may** get more viewers.	Vielleicht bekommen wir mehr Zuschauer.
Hinweis: *May* drückt aus, was sein kann. *May* ist in allen Personen gleich.	

might [Unit 12]

Farmers **might** start to use horses again.	Es könnte sein, daß Landwirte wieder Pferde benutzen.
Hinweis:	*Might* wird verwendet, um zum Ausdruck zu bringen, was möglicherweise geschehen könnte, z.B. *There might be more lorries on the roads. Might* bleibt in allen Personen gleich.

must/have to [Units 1, 3, 4, 5, 12]

Present Tense	Gegenwartsform
You **must** be really pleased. At home you **have to** do the cooking. You **don't have to** arrive at eight o'clock.	Sie müssen sehr erfreut sein. Zu Hause muß man kochen. Sie müssen nicht um acht Uhr ankommen.
Past Tense	Vergangenheitsform
I **had to** do all the shopping myself. Which things **did** Geoff **have to** do?	Ich mußte alle Einkäufe selbst erledigen. Welche Dinge mußte Geoff tun?
Future Tense	Zukunftsform
Cars and lorries **will have to** pay to enter cities.	Um in die Städte zu gelangen, werden Autos und Lastwagen Gebühren bezahlen müssen.
Hinweis:	• *Must* wird eher bei Anweisungen und logischen Schlußfolgerungen gebraucht. • *Must* hat keine Zukunfts- bzw Vergangenheitsform. Es wird auf *have to* zurückgegriffen. • *Have to* wird verwendet, um Notwendigkeiten zum Ausdruck zu bringen.

shall [Unit 3]

Shall I buy some wine? **Shall we** take them to the museum?	Soll ich Wein kaufen? Sollen wir ihnen das Museum zeigen?
Hinweis:	*Shall* wird bei Vorschlägen und Hilfsangeboten verwendet. *Shall* wird nur bei den Personen *I* und *we* verwendet.

should [Units 1, 3]

You **should** phone to say you can go. Guests **shouldn't** smoke in the house.	Du solltest anrufen, um zu sagen, daß du kommen kannst. Gäste sollten im Haus nicht rauchen.
Hinweis:	*Should* wird verwendet, um Ratschläge zu geben, z.B. *You should write a thankyou letter.* bzw. um zum Ausdruck zu bringen, daß etwas wichtig ist, z.B. *Guests should help with the cooking.* Die Form *should* ist in allen Personen gleich.

G

Ie Short Forms — Kurzformen [Units 6, 10, 11]

I'll	(= I will)	do it.	Ich mache es./Ich werde es machen.
You'll	(= You will)	feel much better.	Sie werden sich viel besser fühlen.
It'll	(= It will)	really help.	Das hilft bestimmt.
You **won't**	(= You will not)	be unemployed.	Du wirst nicht arbeitslos sein.

If Short Answers/Responses — Kurzantworten [Units 2, 4]

I'm just as fit as I used to be. Ich bin genauso fit wie früher.	**So am I.** Ich auch.	**I'm not.** Ich nicht.
I'm not as slim as I used to be. Ich bin nicht mehr so schlank wie früher.	**Nor/Neither am I.** Ich auch nicht.	**I am.** Ich schon.
I've got a microwave. Ich habe eine Mikrowelle.	**So have I.** Ich auch.	**I haven't.** Ich nicht.
I haven't got a freezer. Ich habe keinen Gefrierschrank.	**Nor/Neither have I.** Ich auch nicht.	**I have.** Ich schon.

I **agree**. Ich stimme zu.	**So do I.** Ich auch.
I **don't** think so. Ich bin nicht der Meinung.	**Nor/Neither do I.** Ich auch nicht.
I **wouldn't** say that. Das würde ich nicht sagen.	**Nor/Neither would I.** Ich auch nicht.

> Hinweis: Das Zeitwort in der Kurzantwort richtet sich nach dem Ausgangssatz. Hilfszeitwörter wie *be, do, have* sowie Modalverben werden wiederholt. Bei anderen Zeitwörtern wird das Zeitwort *do* in der entsprechenden Form (*do, does, did*) gebraucht. Bei positiver Zustimmung wird *so* verwendet, bei negativer Zustimmung *nor* oder *neither*.

Question Tags — Frageanhängsel [Units 1, 9]

It's a lovely day, **isn't it**? **It could** also be "shoes", **couldn't it**?	(Es ist) Ein schöner Tag, nicht wahr? Es könnte auch "*shoes*" sein, nicht wahr?

> Hinweis: Die Form der *question tags* richtet sich nach dem Ausgangssatz. Bejahte Ausgangssätze bilden verneinte *question tags*. *Question tags* werden verwendet, um indirekte Fragen zu bilden. Allerdings geht die fragende Person dabei von einer *Ja*-Antwort aus, z.B. *That's a nice blouse, isn't it?* Sie werden oft als Gesprächseröffnung gebraucht, z.B. *Nice day, isn't it?*

Ig The "-ing" Form   Die "-ing"-Form   [Units 5, 6, 10]

I **enjoy** travel**ling** around.	Ich genieße es herumzureisen.
I **can't stand** ly**ing** in the sun.	Ich hasse es, in der Sonne zu liegen.
Stop talk**ing**.	Hör auf zu reden.
Try go**ing** for a walk.	Versuch's doch mal mit einem Spaziergang.
Keep mov**ing**.	Bleiben Sie in Bewegung.
I'm interested **in** meet**ing** people.	Ich interessiere mich dafür, Menschen kennenzulernen.
My parents are looking forward **to** retir**ing**.	Meine Eltern freuen sich auf den Ruhestand.
Luxury is liv**ing** on your own.	Luxus ist, allein zu leben.

Hinweis: Die "-ing"-Form wird verwendet
1. nach bestimmten Zeitwörtern; 2. nach Verhältniswörtern; 3. als Hauptwort.

Ih Passive   Passivform   [Units 9, 11, 12]

Past Tense   Vergangenheitsform

In 1849 gold **was** discover**ed** in California.	1849 wurde in Kalifornien Gold entdeckt.
My father **was** **born** in Hamburg.	Mein Vater ist in Hamburg geboren.
Jeans **were** introduc**ed** to Europe **by** American soldiers.	Jeans wurden von amerikanischen Soldaten nach Europa gebracht.

Future Tense   Zukunftsform

Speed limits **will be** lower**ed**.	Das Tempolimit wird gesenkt werden.
Where **will** they **be born**?	Wo werden sie geboren werden?
The railway network **won't be** reduc**ed**.	Das Bahnnetz wird nicht reduziert werden.

Hinweis: Die Passivform wird mit dem Zeitwort *be* in der entsprechenden Zeitform gebildet. Die Person, die die Handlung vollzog, wird mit *by* eingeleitet.

Passive with *get*   [Unit 13]

You can	get	clothes **cleaned**.	Man kann Kleider reinigen lassen.
You can	get	your hair **done**.	Man kann sich die Haare machen lassen.
You can	get	furniture **repaired**.	Man kann Möbel reparieren lassen.

G

II Nouns Hauptwörter

IIa Irregular Plural Forms Unregelmäßige Mehrzahlformen [Units 2, 9, 10, 13]

Nouns without a Singular Form Hauptwörter ohne Einzahlform	**Nouns with the Same Form for Singular and Plural** Hauptwörter mit der gleichen Form in der Ein- und Mehrzahl
clothes goods	means (of transport)
Nouns without a Plural Form Hauptwörter ohne Mehrzahlform	Hinweis: Einige Hauptwörter haben im Gegensatz zu den entsprechenden deutschen Vokabeln keine Mehrzahl- bzw. Einzahlform.
backache/stomachache/toothache information/advice furniture/clothing/equipment	

IIb 's/s' Genitive Genitiv mit 's/s' [Units 11, 12, 13, 14]

's		Hinweis: Der Apostroph kommt vor das s, 1. wenn das Hauptwort in der Einzahl ist; 2. wenn die Mehrzahlform des Hauptwortes nicht mit s gebildet wird. Der Apostroph wird hinter das s gesetzt, wenn die Mehrzahlform mit s gebildet wird.
my mother's parents today's paper children's stories	die Eltern meiner Mutter die heutige Zeitung Kindergeschichten	
s'		
since your grandparents' days in ten years' time	seit der Zeit Deiner Großeltern in zehn Jahren	

III Indefinite Article Unbestimmter Artikel

a [Unit 10]

I've got **a** headache.	Ich habe Kopfschmerzen.
I've got **backache/stomachache/toothache**. Keep moving is good **advice**.	Ich habe Rücken-/Magen-/Zahnschmerzen. Es ist ein guter Ratschlag, in Bewegung zu bleiben.
Hinweis: Einige englische Hauptwörter können nicht mit dem unbestimmten Artikel verwendet werden. Man verwendet *some* oder läßt den Artikel weg.	

a pair of/a piece of [Units 4, 9]

(a pair of) **trousers/glasses** (a pair of) **shoes**	eine Hose/Brille ein Paar Schuhe	Hinweis: Wenn man zum Ausdruck bringen will, daß es sich um nur eine Sache handelt, wird mit *a pair of* oder *a piece of* umschrieben.
my favourite **piece of clothing**	mein Lieblingskleidungsstück	
a useful **piece of equipment**	ein nützliches Gerät	

IV Pronouns — Fürwörter

IVa Personal Pronouns — Persönliche Fürwörter [Units 2, 11]

Me too./Nor **me**.	Ich auch./Ich auch nicht.
There is only **me**.	Es gibt nur mich.
as beautiful as **her**	so attraktiv wie sie
as intelligent as **him**	so intelligent wie er

IVb Possessive Pronouns — Besitzanzeigende Fürwörter [Units 9, 10, 13]

What's **mine** is mine.	Was meins ist, ist meins.
What's **yours** is mine, too.	Was deins ist, ist auch meins.
His and **hers**	seins und ihrs
ours	unsers
yours	euers/Ihrs
theirs	ihrs
It's something you give **somebody** for **their** birthday.	Es ist etwas, das man jemandem zum Geburtstag schenkt.
Hinweis: Wenn es bei somebody nicht bekannt ist, ob es sich um eine männliche oder eine weibliche Person handelt, wird im heutigen Englisch das neutrale Wort *their* verwendet.	

IVc Demonstrative Pronouns — Hinweisende Fürwörter [Unit 1]

Which of **these** statements are true?	Welche dieser Aussagen sind richtig?
What are **those** strange noises?	Was sind das für komische Geräusche?

IVd Relative Pronouns — Bezügliche Fürwörter

who/which/that [Unit 2]

someone	**who**	ran away to Scotland	jemand, der sich nach Schottland absetzte
the sort of person	**that**	likes hard work	die Sorte Mensch, die gern hart arbeitet
something	**which**	grows on trees	etwas, was an Bäumen wächst
things	**that**	I want to do	die Dinge, die ich machen will
Hinweis: Who wird bei Personen verwendet, which bei Gegenständen. *That* kann bei Personen oder Gegenständen gebraucht werden.			

when/where [Units 8, 9]

It's a day	**when**	people have to …	Es ist ein Tag, an dem die Menschen …
Bavaria's the place	**where**	Levi Strauss …	Bayern ist die Gegend, wo Levi Strauss …

G

"Zero" Clauses   Sätze ohne Fürwörter [Units 1, 9]

people	(who/that)	I meet for the first time	Menschen, die ich zum ersten Mal treffe
someone	(who/that)	you don't know very well	jemand, den Sie nicht gut kennen
a question	(which/that)	you would like to ask your boss	eine Frage, die Sie Ihrem Chef stellen möchten
a topic	(which/that)	many people find boring	ein Thema, das viele Leute langweilig finden
the year	(when)	gold was discovered	das Jahr, in dem Gold entdeckt wurde
Hinweis:	Wenn das bezügliche Fürwort Satzgegenstand ist, kann es weggelassen werden.		

IVe Indefinite Pronouns   Unbestimmte Fürwörter

both/all [Units 0, 2]

We We are They have	**both/all**	like Chinese food. very tall. got blonde hair.	Wir mögen beide/alle chinesische Gerichte. Wir sind beide/alle sehr groß. Sie haben beide/alle blondes Haar.
Hinweis:	*Both/All* werden normalerweise vor das Zeitwort gesetzt, beim Zeitwort *be* allerdings hinter das Zeitwort und bei zusammengesetzten Zeitformen (z.B. beim *Present Perfect Simple* oder *Present Continuous*) zwischen die Zeitwörter.		

neither/none [Unit 3]

Neither of them helped with the cooking. **None** of them visit the school.	Keiner von den beiden half beim Kochen. Keiner von ihnen besichtigt die Schule.
Hinweis: *Neither* bezieht sich auf zwei Personen, *none* auf mehr als zwei Personen.	

some/any + compounds   *some/any* und deren Zusammensetzungen

some (Affirmative Sentences)   *some* (Bejahte Sätze) [Unit 1]

Some subjects are very boring.	Einige Themen sind sehr langweilig.
someone/somebody you don't know very well Eat **something** light.	jemand, den Sie nicht sehr gut kennen Essen Sie etwas Leichtes.
Hinweis: Grundsätzlich wird in bejahten Aussagen *some* verwendet.	

some (Questions)   *some* (Fragesätze) [Unit 6]

Can/Could you do **something** about it? Will/Would you please do **something** about it?	Könn(t)en Sie etwas dagegen unternehmen? Würden Sie etwas dagegen unternehmen?
Hinweis: In Bitten kann *some* verwendet werden.	

G

any (Affirmative Sentences)   *any* (Bejahte Sätze)   [Units 1, 3, 10]

Write down **any** "hellos" you know. I arrive at **any** time before 8.30. She helps herself **any** time she feels like it.	Schreiben Sie alle *"hellos"* auf, die Sie kennen. Ich komme irgendwann vor 8 Uhr 30 an. Sie bedient sich jedes Mal, wenn ihr danach ist.
The next time I stay with **anybody** … Neither of them helped with the cooking or **anything**. Luxury is **anything** more than food and drink.	Das nächste Mal, wenn ich bei irgendjemandem zu Besuch bin, … Keiner von den beiden hat beim Kochen oder bei sonst irgendetwas geholfen. Luxus ist alles, was über Essen und Trinken hinausgeht.
Hinweis: *Any* kann auch in bejahten Sätzen mit der Bedeutung *irgendetwas*, *irgendjemand* usw. oder *alle* benutzt werden.	

any (Questions)   *any* (Fragesätze)   [Unit 1]

Are there **any** differences? Do you need **anybody/anyone**?	Gibt es Unterschiede? Brauchen Sie jemanden?

any (Negative Sentences)   *any* (Verneinte Sätze)   [Units 1, 6]

We could not stand it **any** more.	Wir konnten es nicht länger aushalten.
You would not normally ask **anyone** how they voted. I don't tell **anybody**.	Normalerweise würde man nicht fragen, wie jemand gewählt hat. Ich erzähle es niemandem.
Hinweis: Grundsätzlich wird *any* in verneinten Aussagen sowie in Fragesätzen gebraucht.	

each/each other   [Unit 11]

Each was adopted by a different family. The sisters wrote to **each other**. In what ways are you like **each other**?	Jede wurde von einer anderen Familie adoptiert. Die Schwestern haben einander geschrieben. Worin sind Sie sich ähnlich?

IVf Reflexive Pronouns   Rückbezügliche Fürwörter   [Units 1, 3]

I had to do all the shopping **myself**. Give **yourself** a different identity. Did he entertain **himself**? She entertained **herself**. We had to do everything **ourselves**. They enjoyed **themselves**.	Ich mußte alle Einkäufe selbst erledigen. Geben Sie sich eine andere Identität. Hat er sich selbst unterhalten? Sie unterhielt sich selbst. Wir mußten alles selbst machen. Sie haben sich gut amüsiert.
Hinweis: Rückbezügliche Fürwörter werden in der Bedeutung *ich – mich, Sie – sich,* usw. verwendet oder als Betonung in der Bedeutung *(ich) selbst*.	

G

V Quantifiers   Mengenangaben

Va *all/most/a lot/some/several/not many/none/neither* [Unit 3]

All		Alle	von ihnen ...
Most		Die meisten	von ihnen ...
A lot		Viele	von ihnen ...
Some	of them ...	Einige	von ihnen ...
Several		Mehrere	von ihnen ...
Not many		Nicht viele	von ihnen ...
None		Keiner	von ihnen ...
Neither		Keiner	von den beiden ...

Vb *much/many/a lot of; more/less/fewer*

much/a lot of [Units 3, 7, 14]

Children watch **too much** TV.	Kinder sehen zu viel fern.
How much time is she going to spend in Scotland?	Wie lange wird sie in Schottland bleiben?
a lot of work	viel Arbeit

many/a lot of [Units 1, 3, 6]

topics **many** people find boring	Themen, die viele Leute langweilig finden
not many of them	nicht viele von ihnen
how many people?	wie viele Menschen?
a lot of women	viele Frauen

| Hinweis: *Much* wird mit Hauptwörtern in der Einzahl verwendet, *many* mit Hauptwörtern in der Mehrzahl. *A lot of* kann sowohl mit der Einzahl als auch mit der Mehrzahl benutzt werden. |

more/less/fewer [Units 10, 11]

Showers use **less** water.	Duschen verbrauchen weniger Wasser.
Fewer people will get married.	Weniger Menschen werden heiraten.
We use **more** energy for heating.	Wir brauchen mehr Energie zum Heizen.
More and more people prefer showers.	Immer mehr Leute bevorzugen Duschen.

| Hinweis: *Less* wird bei Hauptwörtern in der Einzahl verwendet, *fewer* in der Mehrzahl. *More* kann bei Hauptwörtern in der Einzahl sowie Mehrzahl gebraucht werden. |

Vc Quantities   Mengen [Units 4, 8]

millions		jobs	Millionen Arbeitsplätze
a pinch		salt	eine Prise Salz
a piece	of	fresh ginger	ein Stück frischer Ingwer
a tablespoon		lemon juice	ein Eßlöffel Zitronensaft
a tin		tomatoes	eine Dose Tomaten

G

VI Numerals — Zahlen

VIa Cardinal Numbers — Grundzahlen [Unit 8]

$1/2$	= **a half**	eine Hälfte
$1/2$ kg	= **half a** kilo	ein halbes Kilogramm
$1\,1/2$ kg	= **one and a half** kilos	eineinhalb Kilogramm

VId Date — Datum [Units 8, 12]

Written Schriftlich	**Spoken** Gesprochen
July 29(th) *or* 29/7	July **the** 29th *or* **the** 29th **of** July
1808 1841	eighteen hundred **and** eight *or* eighteen-**oh**-eight eighteen forty-one

VII Adjectives — Eigenschaftswörter

VIIa Comparison — Steigerung [Units 2, 4, 9, 10]

Are you Perhaps I'm	**taller than** **lazier than**	your mother? I used to be.	Sind Sie größer als Ihre Mutter? Vielleicht bin ich fauler, als ich früher war.

Hinweis: Steigerungsformen mit *than* können mit einzelnen Hauptwörtern *(mother)* oder mit Sätzen (z.B. *I used to be*) kombiniert werden.

[handwritten: 2 silbige Adjektive - Steigerung]

more efficient **the most** efficient	leistungsfähiger am leistungsfähigsten
less efficient **the least** efficient	weniger leistungsfähig am wenigsten leistungsfähig

[handwritten: short, shorter, shortest / small, smaller, smallest / Steigerung für einsilbige Adjektive]

The better you look,
    the happier you are.
	Je besser man aussieht,
	    desto glücklicher ist man.

The more you waste,
    the happier you are.
	Je mehr man verschwendet,
	    desto glücklicher ist man.

The quicker fashions change,
    the more clothes you buy.
	Je schneller die Mode wechselt,
	    desto mehr Kleidung kauft man.

The more clothes you buy,
    the more you throw away.
	Je mehr Kleidung man kauft,
	    desto mehr wirft man weg.

[handwritten: good - better - best / bad - worse - worst]

G

VIIb Other Forms of Comparison   Andere Formen des Vergleichs

as ... as /the same as   [Units 2, 9]

I'm just **as** active **as** I used to be. I'm **not as** happy **as** I used to be	Ich bin genau so aktiv wie früher. Ich bin nicht so glücklich wie früher.
If the children were **as** intelligent **as** him ... ... and **as** beautiful **as** her, ...	Wenn die Kinder so intelligent wären wie er ... ... und so schön wie sie, ...
as many **as** possible	so viele wie möglich
She's **the same** size **as** I am.	Sie hat die gleiche Größe wie ich.

VIII Adverbs/Adverbial Phrases   Umstandswörter/Umstandsbestimmungen

VIIIb Time   Zeit   [Units 7, 8]

At one time	he worked for an antique dealer.	Einmal arbeitete er für einen Antiquitätenhändler.
For a while	he worked in a factory.	Eine Zeitlang arbeitete er in einer Fabrik.
Just now	I'm preparing information material.	Jetzt bereite ich gerade Informationsmaterial vor.
At the moment	we're expanding into Eastern Europe.	Zur Zeit expandieren wir nach Osteuropa.
On Saturday	I'm meeting Susan for lunch.	Am Samstag treffe ich mich mit Susan zum Mittagessen.
In the evening	we're going to the disco.	Am Abend gehen wir in die Disco.
On this day	people have to ...	An diesem Tag müssen die Leute ...
Hinweis: Zeitangaben werden meistens an das Ende des Satzes gesetzt. Zu Kontrast- bzw. zu Betonungszwecken können sie auch an den Anfang gesetzt werden.		

VIIIc Place   Ort   [Unit 4]

The freezer is The microwave is The food processor is	**at the back/front**. **on the left/right**. **in the middle**.	Der Gefrierschrank ist hinten/vorne. Das Mikrowellengerät ist links/rechts. Die Küchenmaschine ist in der Mitte.

VIIIe Modifiers Verstärkende bzw. abschwächende Umstandswörter [Unit 2, 4, 10]

I find things	**a bit**	boring now.	Ich finde jetzt alles ein bißchen langweilig.
I think I'm a bit	**too**	fat.	Ich meine, daß ich ein bißchen zu dick bin.
I'm	**(not) really**	short.	Ich bin (nicht) wirklich klein.
I'm	**average**	height.	Ich bin durchschnittlich groß.
I travel	**quite**	a lot.	Ich reise recht viel.
We have	**a lot**	more equipment.	Wir haben viel mehr Geräte.
Which is	**particularly**	annoying?	Welches ist besonders ärgerlich?

VIIIf *too/not ... either* [Unit 2, 4]

| Me **too**.
I think so, **too**. | Ich auch.
Das finde ich auch. |
| I'm **not** very tall, but I'm not really short, **either**. | Ich bin nicht sehr groß, aber klein bin ich auch nicht. |

Hinweis: *Too* wird in positiven Äußerungen verwendet, *either* in verneinten Sätzen. Beide werden ans Ende des Satzes gesetzt.

VIIIg *only* [Unit 6]

| I've **only** driven through Belgium.
Which countries have you **only** flown over?
Only one or two of us have been to Hungary. | Ich bin durch Belgien nur durchgefahren.
Über welche Länder sind Sie nur geflogen?
Nur einige von uns waren schon in Ungarn. |

Hinweis: Das Umstandswort *only* wird immer vor das Wort gesetzt, auf das es sich bezieht.

VIIIh Formation of Adverbs Bildung von Umstandswörtern [Unit 14]

bad slow loud	bad**ly** slow**ly** loud**ly**	Hinweis: Umstandswörter werden in der Regel durch Anhängen von *-ly* an das Eigenschaftswort gebildet. Einige Eigenschaftswörter ändern sich nicht. Andere lassen sich nicht zu Umstandswörtern umformen. Stattdessen wird *in a ... way* verwendet.
angry happy	angr**ily** happ**ily**	
careful	careful**ly**	
bored friendly	**in a** bored **way** **in a** friendly **way**	
fast	fast	

G

IX Sentence Patterns   Satzmuster

IXb Questions   Fragesätze

what/which [Units 1, 5, 11, 12]

Which topics do you find boring? **What** did your parents tell you? **What colour** is the Metro?	Welche Themen finden Sie langweilig? Was haben Ihre Eltern Ihnen erzählt? Welche Farbe hat der Metro?
What makes you happy? **What makes** you laugh? **Which person** likes working with children?	Was macht Sie glücklich? Was bringt Sie zum Lachen? Welche Person arbeitet gerne mit Kindern?

Hinweis: Wenn das Fragewort Satzgegenstand ist, entfällt die Umschreibung mit *do*.

Negative Questions   Verneinte Fragen   [Unit 15]

Don't you think …? **Wouldn't** it be better if …?	Glauben Sie nicht …? Wäre es nicht besser, wenn …?

Hinweis: Verneinte Fragen sind keine Informationsfragen. Sie zeigen, daß die fragende Person die Antwort bereits kennt bzw. den Gefragten in dessen Meinung beeinflußen will.

IXc Reported Speech   Indirekte Rede   [Units 5, 7]

Statement Aussage	**Reported Speech** Indirekte Rede
"I like to relax." "Ich entspanne mich gern."	Petra **told me** she likes to relax. Petra sagte mir, daß sie sich gern entspannt.
"We get annoyed when …" "Wir ärgern uns, wenn …"	A lot of people **said** they get annoyed when … Viele Leute sagten, daß sie sich ärgern, wenn …
"I trained as a nurse." "Ich habe eine Ausbildung als Krankenschwester gemacht."	Doris **said** she trained as a nurse. Doris sagte, daß sie eine Ausbildung als Krankenschwester gemacht hat.

Hinweis: In der indirekten Rede behält das Zeitwort in der Regel die Ausgangszeitform, auch wenn die inderekte Rede mit einem Zeitwort der Vergangenheit eingeleitet wird.

IXd Indirect Questions Indirekte Fragen [Unit 12]

Direct Questions Direkte Fragen	Indirect Questions Indirekte Fragen
How often do the buses run? Wie oft fahren die Busse?	**Do you know** how often the buses run? Wissen Sie, wie oft die Busse fahren?
Is there a bank near here? Gibt es hier in der Nähe eine Bank?	**Do you know if** there's a bank near here? Wissen Sie, ob es hier in der Nähe eine Bank gibt?
Where's the nearest post office? Wo ist das nächste Postamt?	**Can you tell me** where the nearest post office **is**? Können Sie mir sagen, wo das nächste Postamt ist?

IXe *If* Clauses *If*-Sätze [Units 7, 8, 10, 11, 13, 14]

Present Simple Form	Present Simple Form
It**'s** work Es handelt sich um Arbeit,	if it**'s** in the office. wenn es im Büro ist.
If it**'s** in the office, Wenn es im Büro ist,	it**'s** work. handelt es sich um Arbeit.

Past Simple Form	Conditional Form
If this music **was** used to advertise something, Wenn diese Musik für Werbezwecke gebraucht würde,	it **could** be a car. könnte es für ein Auto sein.
If I **were** a place, Wenn ich ein Ort wäre,	I'd be Paris. würde ich Paris sein.
If I **were** you, Wenn ich Sie wäre,	I **wouldn't** ... würde ich nicht ...
If I **could** afford it, Wenn ich es mir leisten könnte,	**I'd** have my own sauna. würde ich meine eigene Sauna haben.

Conditional Form	Past Simple Form
What **would** happen Was würde passieren,	if you **changed** your order? wenn Sie die Bestellung ändern würden?

Will Future Form	Present Simple Form
We**'ll** get more viewers Wir bekommen mehr Zuschauer,	if we **have** a lot of sports programmes. wenn wir viele Sportsendungen anbieten.

G

IRREGULAR VERBS   Unregelmäßige Zeitwörter
(BRIDGES 1+2)

Infinitive Grundform	Past Simple *Past Simple*-Form	Past Participle Partizip Perfekt	
be	was/were	been	sein
bear	bore	born	tragen, ertragen
become	became	become	werden
begin	began	begun	beginnen, anfangen
bend	bent	bent	beugen, sich beugen
bite	bit	bitten	beißen
break	broke	broken	brechen, zerbrechen
bring	brought	brought	bringen, mitbringen
build	built	built	bauen
buy	bought	bought	kaufen
can	could	–	können
catch	caught	caught	fangen, ergreifen
choose	chose	chosen	wählen
come	came	come	kommen
cost	cost	cost	kosten
cut	cut	cut	schneiden
deal (with)	dealt	dealt	sich kümmern um, sich beschäftigen mit
dig	dug	dug	graben
do	did	done	tun, machen
draw	drew	drawn	zeichnen, malen
drink	drank	drunk	trinken
drive	drove	driven	(Auto) fahren
eat	ate	eaten	essen
fall	fell	fallen	fallen
feel	felt	felt	fühlen
fight	fought	fought	kämpfen, bekämpfen
find	found	found	finden, suchen
fly	flew	flown	fliegen
forget	forgot	forgotten	vergessen
get	got	got	bekommen, kommen
give	gave	given	geben
go	went	gone	gehen, fahren
grind	ground	ground	reiben, zerreiben
grow	grew	grown	wachsen
hang (up)	hung	hung	aufhängen
have	had	had	haben
hear	heard	heard	hören
hide	hid	hidden	(sich) verstecken

Infinitive Grundform	Past Simple *Past Simple*-Form	Past Participle Partizip Perfekt	
hit	hit	hit	stoßen, schlagen
hold	held	held	halten, abhalten
keep	kept	kept	halten, behalten
know	knew	known	wissen, kennen
leave	left	left	verlassen, abfahren
let	let	let	lassen
lie	lay	lain	liegen
lose	lost	lost	verlieren
make	made	made	machen, anfertigen
mean	meant	meant	bedeuten
meet	met	met	treffen, begegnen
pay	paid	paid	bezahlen
put	put	put	setzen, stellen, legen
read	read	read	lesen
ride	rode	ridden	reiten, (rad)fahren
ring	rang	rung	läuten, klingeln
run	ran	run	laufen
say	said	said	sagen
see	saw	seen	sehen
seek	sought	sought	suchen
sell	sold	sold	verkaufen
send	sent	sent	senden, schicken
shake	shook	shaken	schütteln
shine	shone	shone	leuchten, scheinen
show	showed	shown/showed	zeigen
sing	sang	sung	singen
sit	sat	sat	sitzen
sleep	slept	slept	schlafen
speak	spoke	spoken	sprechen, reden
spend	spent	spent	verbringen, ausgeben
spread	spread	spread	ausbreiten
stand	stood	stood	stehen
steal	stole	stolen	stehlen
swim	swam	swum	schwimmen
take	took	taken	nehmen, mitnehmen
teach	taught	taught	lehren, unterrichten
tell	told	told	erzählen
think	thought	thought	denken
throw	threw	thrown	werfen
understand	understood	understood	verstehen
wake (up)	woke	woken	aufwachen
wear	wore	worn	tragen (Kleidung)
win	won	won	gewinnen
write	wrote	written	schreiben

V

VOCABULARY

Phonetic alphabet   Lautschrift

[ː] bedeutet, daß der vorangehende Laut lang ist
[ˈ] bedeutet, daß die folgende Silbe eine Hauptbetonung erhält
[ˌ] bedeutet, daß die folgende Silbe eine Nebenbetonung erhält
[‿] bedeutet, daß die beiden Laute miteinander verbunden werden

[iː]	meet [miːt]	[eɪ]	name [neɪm]	[f]	fine [faɪn]
[ɑː]	father [ˈfɑːðə]	[aɪ]	my [maɪ]	[v]	evening [ˈiːvnɪŋ]
[ɔː]	morning [ˈmɔːnɪŋ]	[ɔɪ]	boiled [bɔɪld]	[θ]	thanks [θæŋks]
[uː]	blue [bluː]	[əʊ]	phone [fəʊn]	[ð]	this [ðɪs]
[ɜː]	Germany [ˈdʒɜːmənɪ]	[aʊ]	now [naʊ]	[s]	son [sʌn]
		[ɪə]	beer [bɪə]	[z]	is [ɪz]
[ɔ̃ː]	restaurant [ˈrestərɔ̃ːŋ]	[eə]	where [weə]	[ʃ]	she [ʃiː]
		[ʊə]	tourist [ˈtʊərɪst]	[ʒ]	television [ˈtelɪˌvɪʒn]
[ɪ]	in [ɪn]			[h]	he [hiː]
[e]	yes [jes]	[p]	pub [pʌb]	[m]	my [maɪ]
[æ]	thanks [θæŋks]	[b]	bye [baɪ]	[n]	now [naʊ]
[ʌ]	much [mʌtʃ]	[t]	town [taʊn]	[ŋ]	evening [ˈiːvnɪŋ]
[ɒ]	what [wɒt]	[d]	drink [drɪŋk]	[l]	like [laɪk]
[ʊ]	good [gʊd]	[k]	coffee [ˈkɒfɪ]	[r]	room [rʊm]
[ə]	number [ˈnʌmbə]	[g]	good [gʊd]	[w]	we [wiː]
		[tʃ]	church [tʃɜːtʃ]	[j]	yes [jes]
		[dʒ]	job [dʒɒb]		

Unit vocabulary   Kapitel-Wörterverzeichnis

In diesem Wörterverzeichnis finden Sie Wörter und Wendungen, die zum Verständnis und zur Durchführung der Aufgaben in BRIDGES 2 benötigt werden, in der Reihenfolge ihres Auftretens unter der Kapitel- und Schrittnummer. Wörter, die in BRIDGES 1 schon vorkommen, werden in der Regel hier nicht eingetragen.

Wenn nötig, werden die Arbeitsanweisungen (kursiv gedruckt) auch übersetzt. Alle Einträge mit Ausnahme der Arbeitsanweisungen werden zusätzlich in Lautschrift angegeben.

Die wichtigsten Einzelwörter aus den Arbeitsanweisungen und Wendungen werden anschließend auch einzeln aufgeführt.

Relevante Unterschiede zwischen britischem und amerikanischem Englisch (z. B. in Bedeutung oder Rechtschreibung) werden durch 'BE' oder 'AE' gekennzeichnet.

Unit 0

1

| getting to know each other ['getɪŋ tʊ nəʊ iːtʃ ˈʌðə] | sich gegenseitig kennenlernen |

2A

specially [ˈspeʃəli]	besonders
TV programme [ˌtiːˈviː ˈprəʊɡræm]	Fernsehsendung
magazine [ˌmæɡəˈziːn]	Zeitschrift

3

| go back [ɡəʊ bæk] | zurückgehen |

Unit 1

| meeting people [ˈmiːtɪŋ ˈpiːpl] | Menschen treffen, kennenlernen |

1B

at the beginning [ət ðə bɪˈɡɪnɪŋ]	zu Beginn, am Anfang
at the end [ət ði end]	zum Schluß, am Ende
can't say [kɑːnt seɪ]	ich weiß es nicht, kann es nicht sagen
Don't forget to send a postcard! [dəʊnt fəˈɡet tʊ send ə ˈpəʊstkɑːd]	Vergiß nicht, eine Postkarte zu schikken!
forget [fəˈɡet]	vergessen
send [send]	senden, schicken
problem [ˈprɒbləm]	Problem
It's a lovely day, isn't it? [ɪts ə ˈlʌvli deɪ ˈɪznt ɪt]	Ein schöner Tag, nicht wahr?
lovely [ˈlʌvli]	schön
great [ɡreɪt]	großartig, toll
fine [faɪn]	*hier:* gut, in Ordnung
Pleased to meet you. [pliːzd tʊ miːt jʊ]	Sehr erfreut. (*bei Vorstellungen*)
Sorry I'm late. [ˈsɒri aɪm leɪt]	Verzeihung, ich habe mich verspätet.

2

boyfriend [ˈbɔɪfrend]	Freund
girlfriend [ˈɡɜːlfrend]	Freundin
business people [ˈbɪznɪs ˈpiːpl]	Geschäftsleute

| for the first time [fə ðə fɜːst taɪm] | zum ersten Mal |
| people who first met a short time ago [ˈpiːpl huː fɜːst met ə ʃɔːt taɪm əˈɡəʊ] | Personen, die sich vor kurzem zum ersten Mal begegnet sind |

3

| shaking hands [ˈʃeɪkɪŋ hændz] | sich die Hände geben |

3A

Who do you use first names with?	Wen sprechen Sie mit dem Vornamen an?
close friends [kləʊs frendz]	enge Freunde
close [kləʊs]	*hier:* nahestehend
handshake [ˈhændʃeɪk]	Handschlag

3D

According to the speaker, which of these statements are true?	Welche dieser Aussagen sind der Sprecherin gemäß zutreffend?
speaker [ˈspiːkə]	Sprecher/in
statement [ˈsteɪtmənt]	Aussage, Darstellung
people they know [ˈpiːpl ðeɪ nəʊ]	Leute, die sie kennen
kiss [kɪs]	küssen
call each other [kɔːl iːtʃ ˈʌðə]	sich gegenseitig anreden
unusual [ʌnˈjuːʒʊəl]	ungewöhnlich

3E

| *Are there any differences in the way you and the Englishwoman do things?* | Gibt es Unterschiede zwischen Ihrem Verhalten und dem der Engländerin? |

4

| small talk [smɔːl tɔːk] | oberflächliches Gespräch, Small talk |

4A

disagree [dɪsəˈɡriː]	nicht übereinstimmen
horrible [ˈhɒrəbl]	schrecklich, furchtbar
subject [ˈsʌbdʒekt]	*hier:* Thema, Gesprächsthema
illness [ˈɪlnəs]	Krankheit
just to say something [dʒʌst tʊ seɪ ˈsʌmθɪŋ]	nur, um etwas zu sagen
rent [rent]	Miete
pay [peɪ]	bezahlen
salary [ˈsæləri]	Gehalt

V

UNIT 1

taboo [təˈbuː]	tabu	name [neɪm]	*hier:* bezeichnen
politics [ˈpɒlətɪks]	Politik	surprise, surprise [səˈpraɪz səˈpraɪz]	*etwa:* welch eine Überraschung!

4 B

topic [ˈtɒpɪk]	Thema	surprise [səˈpraɪz]	Überraschung
dangerous [ˈdeɪndʒərəs]	gefährlich	informant [ɪnˈfɔːmənt]	Informant
Which questions would you like to ask ... but feel you can't? [wɪtʃ ˈkwestʃənz wʊd ju laɪk tu ɑːsk bət fiːl ju kɑːnt]	Welche Fragen würden Sie gerne ... stellen, aber trauen sich nicht?	however [haʊˈevə]	jedoch
		religion [rɪˈlɪdʒən]	Religion
		Americans do not like foreigners to criticize American politics. [əˈmerɪkənz du nɒt laɪk ˈfɒrənəz tu ˈkrɪtɪsaɪz əˈmerɪkən ˈpɒlətɪks]	Den Amerikanern gefällt es nicht, wenn Ausländer die amerikanische Politik kritisieren.
pet [pet]	Haustier		
That's a new collar, isn't it, Rusty?	Du hast ein neues Halsband, nicht wahr, Rusty?		
Why, yes ... Do you like it?	Ja, stimmt ... Gefällt es dir?	criticize [ˈkrɪtɪsaɪz]	kritisieren
I must have chased that squirrel forever.	Ich muß diesem Eichhörnchen eine Ewigkeit hinterhergejagt sein.	vote [vəʊt]	wählen (*bei Wahlen*)
		election [ɪˈlekʃn]	Wahl
		unaskable question [ˌʌnˈɑːskəbl ˈkwestʃən]	Frage, die man nicht stellen sollte
I hear the Caldwells got a new cat.	Ich habe gehört, daß die Caldwells eine neue Katze haben.	lover [ˈlʌvə]	Geliebte/r
		strange [streɪndʒ]	seltsam, merkwürdig
Say, I just found out yesterday I've got worms.	Weißt du, ich habe gestern festgestellt, daß ich Würmer habe.	noise [nɔɪz]	Geräusch, Lärm
		through [θruː]	durch, hindurch
		wall [wɔːl]	Wand

4 C

5 A

America talking [əˈmerɪkə ˈtɔːkɪŋ]	*etwa:* worüber Amerika spricht	everything's relative [ˈevrɪθɪŋz ˈrelətɪv]	alles ist relativ
include [ɪŋˈkluːd]	einschließen, umfassen	weight [weɪt]	Gewicht
hobby [ˈhɒbɪ]	Hobby		
especially [ɪˈspeʃəlɪ]	besonders, insbesondere	**6**	
		keep talking [kiːp ˈtɔːkɪŋ]	sprich/sprechen Sie weiter
current plans and projects [ˈkʌrənt plænz ənd ˈprɒdʒekts]	gegenwärtige Pläne und Projekte	How long can you keep a conversation going?	Wie lange können Sie ein Gespräch fortführen?
indeed [ɪnˈdiːd]	in der Tat, tatsächlich	Here are some starters.	Hier sind einige Aufhänger.
stranger [ˈstreɪndʒə]	Fremde/r	on business [ɒn ˈbɪznɪs]	geschäftlich
complete family history [kəmpliːt ˈfæməlɪ ˈhɪstərɪ]	gesamte Familiengeschichte		
		on holiday [ɒn ˈhɒlɪdeɪ]	in den Ferien
complete [kəmˈpliːt]	vollständig, ganz	Can I get you a drink? [kən aɪ get ju ə drɪŋk]	Kann ich dir/Ihnen etwas zu trinken holen?
within [wɪˈðɪn]	innerhalb		
the state of the economy [ðə steɪt əv ðɪ ɪˈkɒnəmɪ]	der Zustand der (Volks-)Wirtschaft	**7**	
		disco [ˈdɪskəʊ]	Disco
the worse it is, the more they talk about it [ðə wɜːs ɪt ɪz ðə mɔː ðeɪ tɔːk əˈbaʊt ɪt]	je schlechter es ihr geht, umso mehr sprechen sie darüber.	fellow student [ˈfeləʊ ˈstjuːdənt]	Mitschüler/in, Kommilitone
		lounge [laʊndʒ]	*hier:* Aufenthaltsraum
		bar [bɑː]	Bar
		midnight [ˈmɪdnaɪt]	Mitternacht

Unit 1

7A

intensive course [ɪn'tensɪv kɔːs]	Intensivkurs
language school ['læŋgwɪdʒ skuːl]	Sprachschule
Give yourself a different identity.	Nehmen Sie eine andere Identität an.
yourself [jɔː'self]	dich/dir (selbst)
detail ['diːteɪl]	Einzelheit, Detail
profession [prə'feʃn]	Beruf
interest ['ɪntrest]	hier: Interessengebiet
take a course [teɪk ə kɔːs]	einen Kurs besuchen

8

party etiquette ['pɑːtɪ ˌetɪket]	Party Etikette (Verhaltensregeln für Partys)

8A

housewarming party ['haʊswɔːmɪŋ 'pɑːtɪ]	Einzugsparty
questionnaire [ˌkwestʃə'neə]	Fragebogen
in reply to ... [ɪn rɪ'plaɪ tuː]	als Antwort auf ...
phone [fəʊn]	anrufen, telefonieren
you just go [juː dʒʌst gəʊ]	du gehst/Sie gehen einfach hin
a few minutes to eight [ə fjuː 'mɪnɪts tʊ eɪt]	einige Minuten vor acht, kurz vor acht
any time ['enɪ taɪm]	irgendwann
wear [weə]	tragen (v. Kleidungsstücken)
ordinary ['ɔːdnrɪ]	gewöhnlich, normal
particularly [pə'tɪkjələlɪ]	besonders
formal ['fɔːml]	formell, förmlich
like a suit or dress [laɪk ə sjuːt ɔː dres]	wie zum Beispiel einen Anzug oder ein Kleid
like [laɪk]	hier: wie zum Beispiel
suit [sjuːt]	Anzug
dress [dres]	Kleid
present ['preznt]	Geschenk
take [teɪk]	hier: mitnehmen, mitbringen
bottle ['bɒtl]	Flasche
something light ['sʌmθɪŋ laɪt]	etwas Leichtes
evening meal ['iːvnɪŋ miːl]	Abendessen

8B

Give them some advice.	Geben Sie ihnen ein paar Ratschläge.
have to ['hæv tuː]	müssen
don't have to [dəʊnt 'hæv tuː]	nicht müssen
should [ʃʊd]	sollte, solltest, sollten (Ratschlag)
shouldn't ['ʃʊdnt]	sollte, solltest, sollten nicht (Ratschlag)

9

somebody ['sʌmbədɪ]	jemand
anybody ['enɪˌbɒdɪ]	irgendjemand

9B

Can you give a rule for some and any?	Können Sie eine Regel für some und any formulieren?
the Grammar Section at the back of the book	die Grammatik im Anhang des Buches

10A

Match the words and the rhythms.	Ordnen Sie die Wörter den Betonungsmustern zu.
rhythm ['rɪðm]	Rhythmus

11A

Which of these sentences go up at the end and which go down?	Bei welchen dieser Sätze wird am Ende die Stimme gehoben bzw. gesenkt?
go up [gəʊ ʌp]	ansteigen, heraufgehen
go down [gəʊ daʊn]	sinken, fallen

Unit 2

1

appearances [ə'pɪərənsɪz]	Aussehen, äußere Erscheinungsbilder
class reunion [klɑːs riː'juːnjən]	Klassentreffen
short [ʃɔːt]	klein, kurz
tall [tɔːl]	groß, lang
slim [slɪm]	schlank
fat [fæt]	dick, fett
fair hair [feə heə]	blondes Haar

V

UNIT 2

dark hair [dɑːk heə]	dunkles Haar	I'm average height, although the others always say I'm short. [aɪm ˈævərɪdʒ haɪt ɔːlˈðəʊ ðɪ ˈʌðəz ˈɔːlweɪz seɪ aɪm ʃɔːt]	Ich bin durchschnittlich groß, obwohl die anderen immer sagen, ich sei klein.
bald [bɔːld]	kahl, glatzköpfig		
moustache [məˈstɑːʃ]	Schnurrbart		
beard [bɪəd]	Bart		
glasses [ˈglɑːsɪz]	Brille		
What do they look like? [wɒt dʊ ðeɪ lʊk laɪk]	Wie sehen sie aus?	average [ˈævərɪdʒ]	Durchschnitt, durchschnittlich
look like [lʊk laɪk]	aussehen wie	height [haɪt]	Größe, Höhe
		although [ɔːlˈðəʊ]	obwohl
2		shortish, straight hair [ˈʃɔːtɪʃ streɪt heə]	recht kurzes, glattes Haar
family likeness [ˈfæməli ˈlaɪknɪs]	Ähnlichkeiten innerhalb der Familie	shortish [ˈʃɔːtɪʃ]	recht/ziemlich kurz
2A		**2B**	
Read the way the Pyes describe themselves.	Lesen Sie, wie die Pyes sich selbst beschreiben.	the members of the Pye family [ðə ˈmembəz əv ðə paɪ ˈfæməli]	die Mitglieder der Familie Pye
a bit too [ə bɪt tuː]	ein wenig/etwas zu sehr ...	member [ˈmembə]	Mitglied
really [ˈrɪəli]	eigentlich, wirklich	**2C**	
curly [ˈkɜːli]	lockig, gelockt	play [pleɪ]	spielen
reddish [ˈredɪʃ]	rötlich	twins [twɪnz]	Zwillinge
blueish [ˈbluːɪʃ]	bläulich	boy [bɔɪ]	Junge
grey [greɪ]	grau	girl [gɜːl]	Mädchen
When I was young I was very thin and my legs still are. [wen aɪ wəz jʌŋ aɪ wəz ˈveri θɪn ənd maɪ legz stɪl ɑː]	Als ich jung war, war ich sehr dünn und meine Beine sind es immer noch.	related [rɪˈleɪtɪd]	verwandt
		full name [fʊl neɪm]	vollständiger Name
		3	
		portrait [ˈpɔːtreɪt]	Porträt, Bild
young [jʌŋ]	jung	**3A**	
thin [θɪn]	schlank, dünn	close [kləʊz]	schließen
leg [leg]	Bein	**3B**	
Now, I'd like to lose a few kilos ... [naʊ aɪd laɪk tə luːz ə fjuː ˈkiːləʊz]	Jetzt möchte ich gerne ein paar Kilo abnehmen ...	description [dɪˈskrɪpʃn]	Beschreibung
		take out [teɪk aʊt]	*hier:* herausnehmen
		4A	
lose [luːz]	verlieren; *hier:* abnehmen	fit [fɪt]	fit, in Form
		5A	
I'm not very tall but I'm not really short, either. [aɪm nɒt ˈveri tɔːl bət aɪm nɒt ˈrɪəli ʃɔːt ˈaɪðə]	Ich bin nicht sehr groß, aber auch nicht gerade klein.	nasty [ˈnɑːsti]	garstig, widerlich
		weak [wiːk]	schwach
		stupid [ˈstjuːpɪd]	dumm, töricht
		lazy [ˈleɪzi]	faul, träge
not ... either [nɒt ... ˈaɪðə]	auch nicht	ugly [ˈʌgli]	häßlich
straight, fair hair [streɪt feə heə]	glattes, blondes Haar	**5B**	
straight [streɪt]	gerade; *hier:* glatt	these [ðiːz]	diese (Mz. v. *this*)
the others [ðɪ ˈʌðəz]	die anderen	Put them in the columns.	Tragen Sie sie in die Spalten ein.
figure [ˈfɪgə]	Figur		
I'm a bit too fat. [aɪm ə bɪt tuː fæt]	Ich bin etwas zu dick.	column [ˈkɒləm]	Spalte

UNIT 2

clever ['klevə]	klug, gescheit
generous ['dʒenərəs]	großzügig
good-looking [gʊd 'lʊkɪŋ]	gutaussehend
hard-working [hɑːd 'wɜːkɪŋ]	hart arbeitend
honest ['ɒnɪst]	ehrlich, aufrichtig
intelligent [ɪn'telɪdʒənt]	intelligent, klug
shy [ʃaɪ]	schüchtern
unhappy [ʌn'hæpɪ]	unglücklich
positive ['pɒzətɪv]	positiv
negative ['negətɪv]	negativ
it depends [ɪt dɪ'pendz]	es kaumt darauf an, je nachdem
To the unknown politician. [tʊ ðɪ 'ʌnnəʊn pɒlə'tɪʃn]	Dem unbekannten Politiker gewidmet.

6

lonely hearts ['ləʊnlɪ hɑːts]	einsame Herzen (Überschrift bei Kontaktanzeigen in Zeitungen)
personal ad ['pɜːsənl æd]	private Anzeige
widow ['wɪdəʊ]	Witwe
educated ['edʒʊkeɪtɪd]	gebildet
movie ['muːvɪ]	Film
eat out [iːt aʊt]	Essen gehen
the arts [ðɪ 'ɑːts]	die schönen Künste
gentleman ['dʒentlmən]	Herr, Gentleman
friendship ['frendʃɪp]	Freundschaft
box [bɒks]	hier: Postfach, Chiffre
active ['æktɪv]	aktiv, rege
non-smoker [ˌnɒn 'sməʊkə]	Nichtraucher
non-drinker [ˌnɒn 'drɪŋkə]	Nichttrinker
running ['rʌnɪŋ]	Laufen, Jogging
aerobics [eə'rəʊbɪks]	Aerobic
seek [siːk]	suchen, begehren
similar ['sɪmɪlə]	ähnlich, gleich
athletic [æθ'letɪk]	athletisch
self-employed [ˌself ɪm'plɔɪd]	selbstständig (Beruf)
sense of humor (AE) (BE: humour) [sens əv 'hjuːmə]	(Sinn für) Humor
cook [kʊk]	Köchin, Koch
picnic ['pɪknɪk]	Picknick
boxing ['bɒksɪŋ]	Boxen
a new romance [ə ˌnjuː rəʊ'mæns]	eine neue Liebe/Romanze
romance [rəʊ'mæns]	Romanze
The Fresno Bee [ðə 'freznəʊ biː]	Name einer amerikanischen Zeitung
social event ['səʊʃl ɪ'vent]	Veranstaltung (Konzert, Theater, Partys usw.), gesellschaftliches Ereignis
professional man [prə'feʃənl mæn]	Person in guter beruflicher Stellung (z.B. Arzt, Anwalt, Lehrer usw.)
the good things in life [ðə gʊd θɪŋz ɪn laɪf]	die guten Seiten des Lebens, das Schöne am Leben
golf [gɒlf]	Golf
musician [mjuː'zɪʃn]	Musiker/in
serious ['sɪərɪəs]	ernst, ernsthaft
relationship [rɪ'leɪʃnʃɪp]	Beziehung
blonde [blɒnd]	blond
inch [ɪntʃ]	Zoll (Längenmaß = 2,54 cm)
foot [fʊt]	Fuß (Längenmaß = 30,48 cm)

7

consequence ['kɒnsɪkwens]	Konsequenz, Folge
Snow White [ˌsnəʊ 'waɪt]	Schneewittchen
get married [get 'mærɪd]	heiraten

8

Those were the days(!) [ðəʊz wə ðə deɪz]	Das waren noch Zeiten!

8 A

Read the three quotes on the right.	Lesen Sie die drei Zitate auf der rechten Seite.
quote [kwəʊt]	Zitat
Which of these topics are they about?	Von welchen dieser Themen handeln sie?
leaving school ['liːvɪŋ skuːl]	die Schule verlassen, abgehen
retirement [rɪ'taɪəmənt]	Ruhestand
I'm the sort of person that likes hard work. [aɪm ðə sɔːt əv 'pɜːsn ðət laɪks hɑːd wɜːk]	Ich gehöre zu denjenigen, die gerne hart arbeiten.
hard work [hɑːd wɜːk]	harte, anstrengende Arbeit

V

UNIT 2

quite a lot [kwaɪt ə lɒt]	recht viel, häufig, oft	perfect ['pɜːfɪkt]	perfekt, vollkommen
all sorts of other things [ɔːl sɔːts əv ˈʌðə θɪŋz]	alle möglichen anderen Dinge	reply [rɪˈplaɪ]	erwidern

8 E

Compare and comment. — Vergleichen und reagieren Sie.
me too [miː tuː] — ich auch
nor me [nɔː miː] — ich auch nicht

9

wit and wisdom [wɪt ənd ˈwɪzdm] — Verstand und Weisheit

9 A

saying [ˈseɪɪŋ] — Redensart, Sprichwort
side [saɪd] — Seite
hill [hɪl] — Hügel, Berg

9 B

wooden [ˈwʊdn] — hölzern
merry [ˈmerɪ] — lustig, fröhlich
naughty [ˈnɔːtɪ] — unartig, ungezogen
run away [rʌn əˈweɪ] — fortlaufen
ground [graʊnd] — Boden, Grund
yard [jɑːd] — Yard (Längenmaß = 0,914 m)
cherry [ˈtʃerɪ] — Kirsche
wonder [ˈwʌndə] — sich fragen, sich wundern

9 C

a beautiful actress once wrote to him [ə ˈbjuːtəfʊl ˈæktrɪs wʌns rəʊt tʊ hɪm] — eine hübsche Schauspielerin hat ihm einmal geschrieben
actress [ˈæktrɪs] — Schauspielerin
once [wʌns] — einmal
suggest [səˈdʒest] — vorschlagen
they should have children together [ðeɪ ʃʊd hæv ˈtʃɪldrən təˈgeðə] — sie sollten gemeinsam Kinder bekommen
have children [hæv ˈtʃɪldrən] — Kinder bekommen
beauty [ˈbjuːtɪ] — Schönheit
intelligence [ɪnˈtelɪdʒəns] — Intelligenz, Verstand
She said their children would be perfect. [ʃiː sed ðeə ˈtʃɪldrən wʊd bɪ ˈpɜːfɪkt] — Sie sagte, daß ihre Kinder vollkommen sein würden.

9 E

feet [fiːt] — Füße (Mz. v. *foot*)
entrance [ˈentrəns] — Eingang
something which grows on trees [ˈsʌmθɪŋ wɪtʃ grəʊz ɒn triːz] — etwas, das auf Bäumen wächst
grow [grəʊ] — wachsen
poetry [ˈpəʊɪtrɪ] — Dichtung, Gedichte
equal [ˈiːkwl] — gleichen, entsprechen
metre [ˈmiːtə] — Meter

10

some you like, some you don't [sʌm juː laɪk sʌm juː dəʊnt] — *hier:* Menschen, die man mag und solche, die man nicht mag
at least [ət liːst] — wenigstens

11 A

Match the underlined sounds with the sounds in the column on the right. — Ordnen Sie die unterstrichenen Laute den Lauten in der rechten Spalte zu.
sound [saʊnd] — Laut, Ton, Klang

12 A

stressed [strest] — *hier:* betont

UNIT 3

Be my guest [biː maɪ gest] — Bitte Sehr! Bedienen Sie sich! (*Antwort, wenn man jdn. um etwas gebeten hat.*)

1 A

What do you think of when you hear the word guests? — Woran denken Sie, wenn Sie das Wort *Gäste* hören?

1 B

Write the sentence numbers in the appropriate circles. — Tragen Sie die Nummern der Sätze in die entsprechenden Kreise ein.
appropriate [əˈprəʊprɪət] — angemessen, passend

190 one hundred and ninety

UNIT 3

circle ['sɜːkl] — Kreis
washing-up ['wɒʃɪŋ ʌp] — Abwasch
cooking ['kʊkɪŋ] — Kochen
go to bed [gəʊ tʊ bed] — zu Bett gehen
at the same time [ət ðə seɪm taɪm] — zur gleichen Zeit, gleichzeitig
bring [brɪŋ] — *hier:* mitbringen
Guests should take you out for a meal. [gests ʃʊd teɪk jʊ aʊt fər ə miːl] — Die Gäste sollten Sie zum Essen einladen.
take someone out [teɪk 'sʌmwʌn aʊt] — *hier:* in ein Restaurant einladen
Guests should buy wine to go with the food. [gests ʃʊd baɪ waɪn tʊ gəʊ wɪð ðə fuːd] — Die Gäste sollten den Wein zum Essen kaufen.
entertain [ˌentə'teɪn] themselves [ðəm'selvz] — sich selbst (3. Pers. Mz.) unterhalten
thankyou letter ['θæŋkjuː 'letə] — Dankschreiben

1C

So do I! [ˌsəʊ dʊ 'aɪ] — Ich auch!
Well, ... [wel] — *hier:* Nun, ... (am Anfang eines Satzes)
I don't think 6 is important at all. [aɪ dəʊnt θɪŋk sɪks ɪz ɪm'pɔːtənt ət ɔːl] — Ich glaube überhaupt nicht, daß Nummer 6 wichtig ist.
not ... at all [nɒt ... ət ɔːl] — überhaupt nicht
Nor do I. [ˌnɔː dʊ 'aɪ] — Ich auch nicht.
nor [nɔː] — auch nicht

2

when you last had guests [wen jʊ lɑːst hæd gests] — als Sie zum letzten Mal Gäste hatten

2A

herself [hə'self] — sich (selbst) *(weiblich)*
himself [hɪm'self] — sich (selbst) *(männlich)*

2B

do the shopping [dʊ ðə 'ʃɒpɪŋ] — einkaufen gehen, Einkäufe machen
ourselves [ˌaʊə'selvz] — wir, uns (selbst)

3A

trials of a troubled host and hostess ['traɪəlz əv ə 'trʌbld həʊst ənd 'həʊstɪs] — die Geduldsproben geplagter Gastgeber
to say the least [tʊ seɪ ðə liːst] — gelinde gesagt
pipe [paɪp] — Pfeife
drop [drɒp] — fallen lassen
half of it [hɑːf əv ɪt] — die Hälfte davon
without [wɪ'ðaʊt] — ohne
ask permission [ɑːsk pə'mɪʃn] — um Erlaubnis bitten
loud [laʊd] — laut
outside [ˌaʊt'saɪd] — draußen, nach draußen
peace and quiet [piːs ənd 'kwaɪət] — Ruhe und Frieden
peace [piːs] — Frieden
quiet ['kwaɪət] — Ruhe
all that [ɔːl ðæt] — all das
enormous [ɪ'nɔːməs] — ungeheuer, riesig
smelly ['smeli] — übelriechend, stinkend
even ['iːvn] — sogar
that's all for now [ðæts ɔːl fə naʊ] — soviel für heute *(am Ende eines Briefes)*
do aerobics [dʊ eə'rəʊbɪks] — Aerobik machen
they helped themselves to food [ðeɪ helpt ðəm'selvz tʊ fuːd] — sie haben sich das Essen genommen, ohne zu fragen
help oneself to something [help wʌn'self tʊ 'sʌmθɪŋ] — sich mit etwas bedienen

3C

all right [ɔːl raɪt] — in Ordnung

3E

Do you have any memories of particularly good or bad guests? — Können Sie sich an besonders gute oder schlechte Gäste erinnern?
memory ['meməri] — Gedächtnis, Erinnerung

One of the nicest evenings I've ever spent at the Wilson's ... and then you had to go and do that on the rug! — Das war einer der schönsten Abende, den ich je bei den Wilsons verbracht habe ... und ausgerechnet heute mußtest Du auf den Teppich machen!

V

Unit 3

4A
English course ['ɪŋglɪʃ kɔːs]	Englischkurs
stay [steɪ]	Aufenthalt
day-trip [deɪ trɪp]	Tagesausflug

4C
Where is the person going to stay during the course? [weər ɪz ðə 'pɜːsn 'gəʊɪŋ tu steɪ 'dʒʊərɪŋ ðə kɔːs]	Wo wird die Person während des Kurses wohnen?
going to do something ['gəʊɪŋ tu duː 'sʌmθɪŋ]	etwas beabsichtigen, etwas tun werden
stay [steɪ]	*hier:* sich aufhalten, wohnen
during ['dʒʊərɪŋ]	während

4D
actually ['æktʃəli]	tatsächlich, eigentlich
What do you mean, …? [wɒt dʊ jʊ miːn]	Was meinst du damit, …?; Was soll das heißen, …?
get started [get 'stɑːtɪd]	*hier:* losfahren, abfahren

4E
sit down [sɪt daʊn]	sich setzen
all day [ɔːl deɪ]	den ganzen Tag lang
walk around [wɔːk ə'raʊnd]	umherspazieren, herumlaufen
wall [wɔːl]	*hier:* Stadtmauer

5A
move house [muːv haʊs]	umziehen
retire [rɪ'taɪə]	sich zur Ruhe setzen, in Rente gehen

6
return [rɪ'tɜːn]	wiederkehren, zurückkommen
share [ʃeə]	teilen, teilhaben
silent ['saɪlnt]	schweigsam, stumm
silence ['saɪləns]	Schweigen, Stille
kindness ['kaɪndnɪs]	Freundlichkeit, Liebenswürdigkeit
accept [ək'sept]	annehmen, akzeptieren

7
unusual visits [ʌn'juːʒʊəl 'vɪzɪts]	ungewöhnliche Besuche

7A
sort [sɔːt]	sortieren, einordnen
power station ['paʊə ˌsteɪʃn]	Kraftwerk
castle ['kɑːsl]	Burg, Schloß
hospital ['hɒspɪtl]	Krankenhaus, Klinik
centre for alternative technology ['sentə fə ɔːl'tɜːnətɪv tek'nɒlədʒɪ]	Zentrum für alternative Technologien
technology [tek'nɒlədʒɪ]	Technik
a world of green living [ə wɜːld əv griːn 'lɪvɪŋ]	*etwa:* eine Welt grünen Lebens

7B
programme ['prəʊgræm]	Programm
areas of interest ['eərɪəz əv 'ɪntrest]	Interessensgebiete
indicate ['ɪndɪkeɪt]	zeigen, hinweisen auf
community organisations [kə'mjuːnətɪ ˌɔːgənaɪ'zeɪʃnz]	Gemeindeorganisationen, Gemeindeeinrichtungen
culture ['kʌltʃə]	Kultur
education [ˌedʒʊ'keɪʃn]	Erziehung, Bildungswesen
environment [ɪn'vaɪrənmənt]	Umwelt
health [helθ]	Gesundheit, Gesundheitswesen
commerce ['kɒmɜːs]	Handel
legal system ['liːgl 'sɪstəm]	Rechtssystem
government ['gʌvnmənt]	Regierung

8
sightseeing ['saɪtˌsiːɪŋ]	Besichtigung v. Sehenswürdigkeiten

8A
none [nʌn]	keine, keiner, keins

9A
suggestion [sə'dʒestʃn]	Vorschlag, Anregung
cultural ['kʌltʃərəl]	kulturell
ecological [ˌiːkə'lɒdʒɪkl]	ökologisch
activity [æk'tɪvətɪ]	Tätigkeit, Aktivität

9B
react [rɪ'ækt]	reagieren

Unit 3

instead [ɪnˈsted]	stattdessen	
I'd prefer to ... [aɪd prɪˈfɜː tʊ]	Ich würde es vorziehen, ...	
prefer [prɪˈfɜː]	vorziehen, bevorzugen	

9 C
show around [ʃəʊ əˈraʊnd] — umherführen
category [ˈkætəɡərɪ] — Kategorie

10 A
beginning [bɪˈɡɪnɪŋ] — Anfang, Beginn

Preview A

3
in the midnight hour [ɪn ðə ˈmɪdnaɪt ˈaʊə] — um Mitternacht, zu mitternächtlicher Stunde
hour [ˈaʊə] — Stunde

4
crazy comparisons [ˈkreɪzɪ kəmˈpærɪsnz] — verrückte Vergleiche

5
winner [ˈwɪnə] — Gewinner, Sieger

5 A
free [friː] — *hier:* kostenlos
bring back [brɪŋ bæk] — *hier:* mit nach Hause nehmen

6
the human body [ðə ˈhjuːmən ˈbɒdɪ] — der menschliche Körper
feeling [ˈfiːlɪŋ] — Gefühl
burglar [ˈbɜːɡlə] — Einbrecher
electrical equipment [ɪˈlektrɪkl ɪˈkwɪpmənt] — Elektrogerät/e
equipment [ɪˈkwɪpmənt] — Geräte, Ausrüstung

Unit 4

around the house [əˈraʊnd ðə haʊs] — im Haus

1 A
freezer [ˈfriːzə] — Tiefkühltruhe, Gefrierfach
fridge [frɪdʒ] — Kühlschrank
toaster [ˈtəʊstə] — Toaster
dishwasher [ˈdɪʃˌwɒʃə] — Geschirrspülmaschine
food processor [fuːd ˈprəʊsesə] — Küchenmaschine
coffee machine [ˈkɒfɪ məˈʃiːn] — Kaffemaschine
microwave [ˈmaɪkrəʊweɪv] — Mikrowelle
hoover [ˈhuːvə] — Staubsauger
iron [ˈaɪən] — *hier:* Bügeleisen
kettle [ˈketl] — Wasserkessel, Kessel

1 C
everyone [ˈevrɪwʌn] — jede/r, jedermann
So have I. [ˌsəʊ hæv ˈaɪ] — Ich auch. *(als Reaktion auf: I've got ...)*
I haven't. [ˈaɪ ˌhævnt] — Ich nicht. *(als Reaktion auf: I've got ...)*
Nor have I. [ˌnɔː hæv ˈaɪ] — Ich auch nicht. *(als Reaktion auf: I haven't got ...)*
I have. [ˈaɪ ˌhæv] — Ich aber. *(als Reaktion auf: I haven't got ...)*

2
shop window [ʃɒp ˈwɪndəʊ] — Schaufenster

2 A
item [ˈaɪtəm] — *hier:* Gegenstand
at the back [ət ðə bæk] — hinten, im hinteren Teil
on the left [ɒn ðə left] — links, auf der linken Seite
in the middle [ɪn ðə mɪdl] — in der Mitte
on the right [ɒn ðə raɪt] — rechts, auf der rechten Seite
at the front [ət ðə frʌnt] — vorne, im vorderen Teil

3 A
Listen and note her answers. — Hören Sie zu und notieren Sie ihre Antworten.
note [nəʊt] — notieren, aufschreiben
most useful [məʊst ˈjuːsfʊl] — am nützlichsten

V

UNIT 4

least useful [liːst ˈjuːsfʊl]	am wenigsten nützlich	improve [ɪmˈpruːv]	verbessern
frustrating [frʌˈstreɪtɪŋ]	frustrierend	taste [teɪst]	Geschmack
annoying [əˈnɔɪɪŋ]	lästig, ärgerlich	CD player [ˌsiː ˈdiː ˈpleɪə]	CD-Spieler
soon [suːn]	bald		
colour printer [ˈkʌlə ˈprɪntə]	Farbdrucker		
electric guitar [ɪˈlektrɪk gɪˈtɑː]	elektrische Gitarre		

5

agreeing and disagreeing [əˈgriːɪŋ ənd ˌdɪsəˈgriːɪŋ]	zustimmen und ablehnen

gameboy [ˈgeɪmbɔɪ]	Gameboy (tragbares Computerspiel)
video recorder [ˈvɪdɪəʊ rɪˈkɔːdə]	Videorecorder
walkman [ˈwɔːkmən]	Walkman (tragbarer Kassettenrecorder)

5B

That's true. [ðæts truː]	Das stimmt.
I think so, too. [aɪ θɪŋk səʊ ˈtuː]	Das glaube ich auch.
I don't think so. [aɪ ˈdəʊnt θɪŋk səʊ]	Ich glaube nicht.
Nor do I. [ˌnɔː duː ˈaɪ]	Ich auch nicht.
I wouldn't say that. [aɪ ˈwʊdnt seɪ ðæt]	Ich würde das nicht sagen.
Nor would I. [ˌnɔː wʊd ˈaɪ]	Ich auch nicht.
It depends what you mean by … [ɪt dɪˈpendz wɒt juː miːn baɪ]	Es kommt darauf an, was du mit … meinst.
Nowadays computer games carry health warnings!	Neuerdings wird auf Computerspielen vor möglichen Gesundheitsrisiken gewarnt!
Do you think they can do any harm?	Glaubst du denn, daß sie schädlich sind?
Only if you eat them!	Nur wenn man sie ißt!

3 C

Look at this! [lʊk ət ðɪs]	Sieh dir das an!
surprising [səˈpraɪzɪŋ]	überraschend
lifestyle [ˈlaɪfstaɪl]	Lebensstandard, Lebensstil
microwave oven [ˌmaɪkrəweɪv ˈʌvn]	Mikrowellenherd
TV set [ˌtiːˈviː set]	Fernsehgerät
credit card [ˈkredɪt kɑːd]	Kreditkarte
Professor Schnabel's cleaning lady mistakes his time machine for a new dryer.	Professor Schnabels Putzfrau verwechselt seine Zeitmaschine mit einem neuen Wäschetrockner.
cleaning lady [ˈkliːnɪŋ ˈleɪdɪ]	Putzfrau
mistake somthing for [mɪˈsteɪk ˈsʌmθɪŋ fɔː]	etwas verwechseln mit
dryer [ˈdraɪə]	Wäschetrockner

6

everyday stories [ˈevrɪdeɪ ˈstɔːrɪz]	Alltagsgeschichten

6A

minisaga [ˈmɪnɪˌsɑːgə]	kurze Geschichte von exakt 50 Wörtern
love among the laundry [lʌv əˈmʌŋ ðə ˈlɔːndrɪ]	Liebe inmitten der Wäsche
among [əˈmʌŋ]	unter, zwischen
laundry [ˈlɔːndrɪ]	Wäsche (Kleidungsstücke usw.)
striped [straɪpt]	gestreift
sock [sɒk]	Socke
curled [kɜːld]	hier: aufgerollt
laund(e)rette [ˌlɔːndəˈret]	Waschsalon
return [rɪˈtɜːn]	hier: zurückgeben
smile [smaɪl]	Lächeln

4

inventions and their results [ɪnˈvenʃnz ənd ðeə rɪˈzʌlts]	Erfindungen und ihre Auswirkungen
invention [ɪnˈvenʃn]	Erfindung
result [rɪˈzʌlt]	hier: Auswirkung

4A

make something easy [meɪk ˈsʌmθɪŋ ˈiːzɪ]	etwas leicht machen
change [tʃeɪndʒ]	verändern, ändern
millions of jobs [ˈmɪljənz əv dʒɒbz]	Millionen von Arbeitsplätzen
spoil [spɔɪl]	verderben, ruinieren
family life [ˈfæməlɪ laɪf]	Familienleben
enjoyable [ɪnˈdʒɔɪəbl]	angenehm, erfreulich

UNIT 4

once a week [wʌns ə wiːk]	einmal pro Woche
... were seen no more [wə siːn nəʊ mɔː]	... wurden nie wieder gesehen
wedding present ['wedɪŋ 'preznt]	Hochzeitsgeschenk
wedding ['wedɪŋ]	Hochzeit

7
burglar ['bɜːglə]	Einbrecher

7 A
What have the burglars done? [wɒt hæv ðə 'bɜːgləz dʌn]	Was haben die Einbrecher getan?
done [dʌn]	Partizip Perfekt v. *do:* tun, machen

7 B
taken ['teɪkn]	Partizip Perfekt v. *take:* nehmen; *hier:* stehlen, mitnehmen
broken ['brəʊkn]	Partizip Perfekt v. *break:* (zer)brechen
damage ['dæmɪdʒ]	beschädigen
drunk [drʌŋk]	Partizip Perfekt v. *drink:* trinken

8
burglary ['bɜːgləri]	Einbruch

8 A
last summer [lɑːst 'sʌmə]	im letzten Sommer
What do you think happened? [wɒt dʊ jʊ θɪŋk 'hæpnd]	Was ist Ihrer Meinung nach geschehen?
happen ['hæpn]	sich ereignen, geschehen
at work [ət wɜːk]	bei/auf der Arbeit
out shopping [aʊt 'ʃɒpɪŋ]	zum Einkaufen ausgegangen
get in [get ɪn]	*hier:* herein-, hineingelangen
back door [bæk dɔː]	Hintertür, Hintereingang
front door [frʌnt dɔː]	Vordertür, Vordereingang
kitchen window ['kɪtʃɪn 'wɪndəʊ]	Küchenfenster
police [pə'liːs]	Polizei
identify [aɪ'dentɪfaɪ]	identifizieren
stolen ['stəʊlən]	Partizip Perfekt v. *steal:* stehlen

insurance company [ɪn'ʃɔːrəns 'kʌmpəni]	Versicherungsgesellschaft
cash [kæʃ]	Bargeld
foreign ['fɒrən]	fremd, ausländisch
coin [kɔɪn]	Münze
jewellery ['dʒuːəlri]	Schmuck, Juwelen
watch [wɒtʃ]	Uhr, Armbanduhr
in the end [ɪn ðɪ end]	schließlich, am Ende
caught [kɔːt]	Partizip Perfekt v. *catch:* fangen; *hier:* ergreifen
unsafe [ˌʌn'seɪf]	unsicher
quite a long time [kwaɪt ə lɒŋ taɪm]	eine recht lange Zeit

9
mystery crimes ['mɪstəri kraɪmz]	rätselhafte Verbrechen
mystery ['mɪstəri]	Geheimnis, Rätsel
crime [kraɪm]	Verbrechen

9 A
a young couple [ə jʌŋ 'kʌpl]	ein junges Paar
couple ['kʌpl]	Paar, Ehepaar
left [left]	Verg.-Form v. *leave:* verlassen; *hier:* abstellen
shocked [ʃɒkt]	schockiert
police station [pə'liːs ˌsteɪʃn]	Polizeiwache
theft [θeft]	Diebstahl
they came back home [ðeɪ keɪm bæk həʊm]	sie kamen nach Hause zurück
amazed [ə'meɪzd]	erstaunt, verblüfft
seat [siːt]	Sitz
champagne [ˌʃæm'peɪn]	Champagner, Sekt
the letter said [ðə 'letə sed]	in dem Brief stand
borrow ['bɒrəʊ]	sich (etwas) borgen, leihen
emergency [ɪ'mɜːdʒənsi]	Notfall, Notlage
ticket ['tɪkɪt]	*hier:* Eintrittskarte
enjoy oneself [ɪn'dʒɔɪ wʌn'self]	sich amüsieren, gut unterhalten
on their way home [ɒn ðeə weɪ həʊm]	auf ihrem Heimweg
suddenly ['sʌdnli]	plötzlich
began [bɪ'gæn]	Verg.-Form v. *begin:* anfangen, beginnen

V

UNIT 4

9 B
Find a title for the story and explain the crime. — Überlegen Sie sich eine Überschrift für die Geschichte und erklären Sie das Verbrechen.

explain [ɪkˈspleɪn] — erklären

9 D
retired [rɪˈtaɪəd] — pensioniert, im Ruhestand lebend

10
What have we taken? [wɒt hæv wiː teɪkn] — Was haben wir genommen?

10 A
sack [sæk] — Sack

10 B
special occasion [ˈspeʃl əˈkeɪʒn] — besonderer Anlaß
occasion [əˈkeɪʒn] — Gelegenheit, Anlaß

13 B
Go ahead. [gəʊ əˈhed] — Nur zu!

UNIT 5

body and soul [ˈbɒdɪ ənd ˈsəʊl] — Körper und Seele

1
Don't worry, be happy! [dəʊnt ˈwʌrɪ biː ˈhæpɪ] — Sorg dich nicht, sei glücklich!

1 B
bored [bɔːd] — gelangweilt
marry [ˈmærɪ] — heiraten
someone else [ˈsʌmwʌn els] — jemand anderes/anderen
manic [ˈmænɪk] — manisch
depressant [dɪˈpresnt] — Beruhigungsmittel
lonely [ˈləʊnlɪ] — einsam
They say that men suffer, as badly, as long. [ðeɪ seɪ ðət men ˈsʌfər əz ˈbædlɪ əz lɒŋ] — Es heißt, daß Männer ebenso schlimm und lange leiden.
suffer [ˈsʌfə] — leiden
badly [ˈbædlɪ] — schlimm, schlecht

in case they are wrong [ɪŋ keɪs ðeɪ ə rɒŋ] — falls sie unrecht haben
in case [ɪŋ keɪs] — Im Falle, daß, falls
angry [ˈæŋgrɪ] — wütend, verärgert
laughter [ˈlɑːftə] — Lächeln, Gelächter
medicine [ˈmedsɪn] — Medizin
tired [ˈtaɪəd] — müde
yawn [jɔːn] — gähnen
Poor tired Tim! [pɔː ˈtaɪəd tɪm] — Armer, müder Tim!
nervous breakdown [ˌnɜːvəs ˈbreɪkdaʊn] — Nervenzusammenbruch
It takes a worried man to sing a worried song. [ɪt teɪks ə ˈwʌrɪd mæn tu sɪŋ ə ˈwʌrɪd sɒŋ] — Nur wer besorgt ist, kann ein besorgtes Lied singen.
Don't worry. He's in a good mood. — Keine Sorge. Er ist gut gelaunt.
mood [muːd] — Laune, Stimmung

1 D
Mime a mood. — Stellen Sie eine Laune pantomimisch dar.
mime [maɪm] — als Pantomime darstellen

2 A
annoyed [əˈnɔɪd] — verärgert, ärgerlich
makes me laugh [meɪks mi lɑːf] — bringt mich zum Lachen
laugh [lɑːf] — lachen

3 A
news [njuːz] — Nachricht/en
Congratulations! [kənˌgrætʃʊˈleɪʃnz] — Herzlichen Glückwunsch!
How disappointing! [haʊ ˌdɪsəˈpɔɪntɪŋ] — Wie enttäuschend!
upset [ʌpˈset] — erschüttert, bestürzt
Oh dear! [əʊ dɪə] — Du liebe Zeit! Ach herrje!
That's great! [ðæts greɪt] — Das ist toll/super!
Well done! [wel dʌn] — Gut gemacht!
What a pity! [ˌwɒt ə ˈpɪtɪ] — Wie schade!

3 C
found out [faʊnd aʊt] — Partizip Perfekt v. *find out:* herausfinden, feststellen
have a baby [hæv ə ˈbeɪbɪ] — ein Baby bekommen

196 one hundred and ninety-six

Unit 5

rain [reɪn]	regnen
awful [ˈɔːfʊl]	schrecklich, furchtbar
brochure [ˈbrəʊʃə]	Broschüre, Prospekt
insured [ɪnˈʃɔːd]	versichert
pass [pɑːs]	*hier:* (eine Prüfung) bestehen
driving test [ˈdraɪvɪŋ test]	Führerscheinprüfung
I'm afraid not. [aɪm əˈfreɪd nɒt]	Leider nicht.
What's the matter? [wɒts ðə ˈmætə]	Was ist los?

3D

shuffle [ˈʃʌfl]	(Karten) mischen
hand out [hænd aʊt]	ausgeben, verteilen

4

How would you feel? [haʊ wʊd ju fiːl]	Wie würden Sie sich fühlen?

4A

respond [rɪˈspɒnd]	*hier:* reagieren
polite [pəˈlaɪt]	höflich
embarrassed [ɪmˈbærəst]	verlegen, peinlich berührt
arrange to meet [əˈreɪndʒ tʊ miːt]	sich verabreden, ein Treffen vereinbaren
arrange [əˈreɪndʒ]	arrangieren, vereinbaren
on time [ɒn taɪm]	rechtzeitig
unreliable [ˌʌnrɪˈlaɪəbl]	unzuverlässig
sort of person [sɔːt əv ˈpɜːsn]	Art Mensch
sort [sɔːt]	Art, Typ
ring someone up [rɪŋ ˈsʌmwʌn ʌp]	jdn. anrufen
asleep [əˈsliːp]	schlafend
call back [kɔːl bæk]	zurückrufen *(Telefon)*
perfectly normal [ˈpɜːfɪktli ˈnɔːməl]	völlig normal

5A

Label the parts and say what is missing.	Beschriften Sie die Teile und sagen Sie, was fehlt.
label [ˈleɪbl]	beschriften, etikettieren
miss [mɪs]	*hier:* fehlen
chin [tʃɪn]	Kinn
ear [ɪə]	Ohr
face [feɪs]	Gesicht
finger [ˈfɪŋɡə]	Finger
foot [fʊt]	Fuß
hand [hænd]	Hand
head [hed]	Kopf
knee [niː]	Knie
mouth [maʊθ]	Mund
nose [nəʊz]	Nase
toe [təʊ]	Zehe
shoulder [ˈʃəʊldə]	Schulter
arm [ɑːm]	Arm

6

keep fit [kiːp fɪt]	sich in Form halten, fit bleiben

6A

instruction [ɪnˈstrʌkʃn]	Anweisung, Instruktion
bend [bend]	beugen, sich beugen
press [pres]	drücken
lift [lɪft]	heben, hochheben
stand [stænd]	stehen
touch [tʌtʃ]	berühren
30 cm apart [ˈθɜːti ˈsentɪˌmiːtəz əˈpɑːt]	30 cm auseinander
above [əˈbʌv]	über
forward [ˈfɔːwəd]	*hier:* nach vorne
put your hands on the floor [pʊt jɔː hændz ɒn ðə flɔː]	*hier:* berühren Sie mit den Händen den Boden
floor [flɔː]	Boden, Fußboden
starting position [ˈstɑːtɪŋ pəˈzɪʃn]	Ausgangsposition, Startposition
three more, two more [θriː mɔː tuː mɔː]	noch drei, noch zwei
ready, set [ˈredi set]	auf die Plätze, fertig
hell [hel]	Hölle

7A

game [ɡeɪm]	Spiel
rule [ruːl]	Regel, Spielregel
out of the game [aʊt əv ðə ɡeɪm]	aus dem Spiel ausgeschieden
attack [əˈtæk]	Angriff
Ivan! You're out! [ˈaɪvən jɔːr aʊt]	Ivan! Du bist draußen!

8

count your blessings [kaʊnt jɔː ˈblesɪŋz]	*etwa:* Sei dankbar für das, was du hast.

8A

seriously [ˈsɪərɪəsli]	ernsthaft
ill [ɪl]	krank
been [biːn]	Partizip Perfekt v. *be*: sein

V

UNIT 5

cold [kəʊld]	Erkältung
flu [flu:]	Grippe
hangover ['hæŋəʊvə]	Kater, Katzenjammer
since [sɪns]	seit *(bei Angabe eines Zeitpunktes)*
Touch wood! [ˌtʌtʃ 'wʊd]	Toi, toi, toi!

9
Make as many lines as you can.	Schreiben Sie so viele Zeilen wie möglich.

UNIT 6

1
Who goes where? [hu: gəʊz weə]	Wer fährt wohin?

1 A
Where do you think most Germans go on holiday?	Wohin, glauben Sie, fahren die meisten Deutschen in Urlaub?
German ['dʒɜ:mən]	*hier:* Deutscher, Deutsche
go on holiday [gəʊ ɒn 'hɒlɪdeɪ]	in die Ferien fahren
Name the top three countries.	Nennen Sie die drei führenden Länder.
top three [tɒp θri:]	die drei wichtigsten, die drei Haupt-

1 B
spent [spent]	Partizip Perfekt v. *spend:* verbringen
eastern Länder [ˌi:stən 'lendə]	östliche Bundesländer
in what used to be Czechoslovakia [ɪn wɒt ju:st tʊ bɪ ˌtʃekəsləʊ'vækɪə]	in der ehemaligen Tschechoslowakei
Hungary ['hʌŋgərɪ]	Ungarn
Russia ['rʌʃə]	Rußland
nearly ['nɪəlɪ]	beinahe, fast
altogether [ˌɔ:ltə'geðə]	insgesamt, im ganzen
the second largest group [ðə 'seknd 'lɑ:dʒɪst gru:p]	die zweitgrößte Gruppe
Sweden ['swi:dn]	Schweden
Portugal ['pɔ:tʃʊgl]	Portugal

apart from the Germans themselves [ə'pɑ:t frəm ðə 'dʒɜ:mənz ðəm'selvz]	außer den Deutschen selbst
apart from [ə'pɑ:t frɒm]	außer
Dutch [dʌtʃ]	*hier:* Niederländer/in

2
Which European countries have you been to? [wɪtʃ ˌjʊərə'pi:ən 'kʌntrɪz hæv ju bɪn tu:]	In welchen europäischen Ländern waren Sie schon einmal?
have been to [hæv bi:n tu:]	gewesen sein *(Land, Stadt usw.)*

2 A
driven ['drɪvn]	Partizip Perfekt v. *drive:* fahren
drive through [draɪv θru:]	durch (ein Land usw.) fahren
flown [fləʊn]	Partizip Perfekt v. *fly:* fliegen
fly over [flaɪ 'əʊvə]	überfliegen *(im Flugzeug)*

3
Has anybody ever been to Australia? [hæz 'enɪˌbɒdɪ 'evə bɪn tʊ ɒ'streɪljə]	Ist jemand schon einmal in Australien gewesen?
ever ['evə]	jemals, je

3 A
all of us [ɔ:l əv ʌs]	wir alle, jeder von uns
a lot of us [ə lɒt əv ʌs]	viele von uns
several of us ['sevrəl əv ʌs]	einige von uns
none of us [nʌn əv ʌs]	niemand/keiner von uns

4
Where and when? [weər ənd wen]	Wo und wann?

4 A
take a trip [teɪk ə trɪp]	auf Reise gehen
travel through ['trævl θru:]	durch (ein Land usw.) reisen

4 B
Normandy ['nɔ:məndɪ]	Normandie

Unit 6

Easter ['iːstə]	Ostern

5

Africa ['æfrɪkə]	Afrika
camping safari ['kæmpɪŋ sə'fɑːri]	Camping-Safari
adventure [əd'ventʃə]	Abenteuer
Egypt ['iːdʒɪpt]	Ägypten
Morocco [mə'rɒkəʊ]	Marokko
East African [ˌiːst 'æfrɪkən]	ostafrikanisch
wildlife ['waɪldlaɪf]	wildlebende Tiere
tour [tʊə]	Reise, Rundreise
farmhouse ['fɑːmhaʊs]	Bauernhaus
villa ['vɪlə]	Villa
apartment [ə'pɑːtmənt]	Apartment
pretty ['prɪti]	schön, reizvoll
region ['riːdʒən]	Region, Gegend
pool [puːl]	Schwimmbad, Pool
just [dʒʌst]	hier: nur, bloß
discover [dɪs'kʌvə]	entdecken
holiday package ['hɒlɪdeɪ 'pækɪdʒ]	Pauschalurlaub, Pauschalreise
less [les]	weniger
normal ['nɔːml]	normal, üblich
air fare ['eə ˌfeə]	Flugpreis
bargain ['bɑːgɪn]	Schnäppchen, gutes Geschäft
save [seɪv]	sparen
fully inclusive ['fʊli ɪŋ'kluːsɪv]	alles inklusive
provide [prə'vaɪd]	bieten, besorgen
unforgettable [ˌʌnfə'getəbl]	unvergeßlich
break [breɪk]	hier: Abwechslung
whether ['weðə]	ob
watersports facilities ['wɔːtəˌspɔːts fə'sɪlətiz]	Wassersporteinrichtungen
chef-prepared ['ʃef prɪ'peəd]	v. Küchenchef zubereitet
discount ['dɪskaʊnt]	Rabatt
booking ['bʊkɪŋ]	Buchung
secluded [sɪ'kluːdɪd]	abgelegen, einsam
beachside ['biːtʃsaɪd]	am Strand gelegen
superb [suː'pɜːb]	hervorragend
unlimited [ʌn'lɪmɪtɪd]	unbegrenzt
windsurfing ['wɪndsɜːfɪŋ]	Windsurfen
sailing ['seɪlɪŋ]	Segeln
waterskiing ['wɔːtəskiːɪŋ]	Wasserski
expert tuition ['ekspɜːt tjuː'ɪʃn]	fachliche Anleitung, fachmännischer Unterricht
children's creche ['tʃɪldrənz kreʃ]	Kinderkrippe
Sardinia [sɑː'dɪnjə]	Sardinien
Corsica ['kɔːsɪkə]	Korsika
mile [maɪl]	Meile
up the Nile [ʌp ðə naɪl]	den Nil herauf
leisurely ['leʒəli]	gemächlich
cruise [kruːz]	Schiffsreise, Kreuzfahrt
accompany [ə'kʌmpəni]	begleiten
guest lecturer [gest 'lektʃərə]	Gastdozent/in
self-catering [ˌself'keɪtərɪŋ]	Selbstverpflegung
Pembrokeshire ['pembrʊkʃə]	Grafschaft in Wales
coast [kəʊst]	Küste
cottage ['kɒtɪdʒ]	kleines Landhaus
available [ə'veɪləbl]	vorhanden, verfügbar
peacefully ['piːsfʊli]	friedlich
located [ləʊ'keɪtɪd]	gelegen
close to ['kləʊs tʊ]	in der Nähe von
sandy ['sændi]	sandig
excellent ['eksələnt]	ausgezeichnet, hervorragend
alpine skiing ['ælpaɪn 'skiːɪŋ]	alpiner Skilauf (Abfahrt, Slalom usw.)
nordic skiing ['nɔːdɪk 'skiːɪŋ]	nordischer Skilauf (Langlauf usw.)
choice [tʃɔɪs]	Auswahl, Wahl
unspoilt [ˌʌn'spɔɪlt]	unberührt, unverdorben
option ['ɒpʃn]	Alternative, Wahl
beginner [bɪ'gɪnə]	Anfänger
expert ['ekspɜːt]	Fachmann/frau, Experte, Expertin
crowd [kraʊd]	Menge, Masse
lift queue [lɪft kjuː]	Schlange vor dem Skilift
tropical ['trɒpɪkl]	tropisch
paradise ['pærədaɪs]	Paradies
explore [ɪk'splɔː]	erforschen
character hotel ['kærəktə həʊ'tel]	etwa: Hotel mit persönlicher Note
tailor-made [ˌteɪlə'meɪd]	speziell zugeschnitten
Greenland ['griːnlənd]	Grönland
Iceland ['aɪslənd]	Island
South Africa [ˌsaʊθ 'æfrɪkə]	Südafrika
reservation [ˌrezə'veɪʃn]	Reservierung

V

Unit 6

5 A
sun [sʌn]	Sonne
active ['æktɪv]	aktiv
travel around ['trævəl ə'raʊnd]	umherreisen

5 B
What about you?	Wie steht's mit Ihnen?, Wie ist es bei Ihnen?
preference ['prefərəns]	Vorliebe

5 B
I can't stand ... [aɪ kɑːnt stænd]	Ich kann ... nicht ausstehen.

5 C
customer ['kʌstəmə]	Kunde
suitable ['sjuːtəbl]	passend, geeignet
change [tʃeɪndʒ]	*hier:* tauschen
role [rəʊl]	Rolle *(in Rollenspielen usw.)*

6 A
ocean view ['əʊʃn vjuː]	Seeblick
B & B (= bed and breakfast) [ˌbiː ənd 'biː]	Pension
vacancy ['veɪkənsɪ]	*hier:* freies Zimmer

7 A
manager ['mænɪdʒə]	Geschäftsführer, Manager
insect ['ɪnsekt]	Insekt
outside my window [ˌaʊt'saɪd maɪ 'wɪndəʊ]	(draußen) vor meinem Fenster
water ['wɔːtə]	Wasser
workman ['wɜːkmən]	Arbeiter
do something about [duː 'sʌmθɪŋ ə'baʊt]	etwas daran machen, etwas dagegen tun
fill up [fɪl ʌp]	auffüllen
bathwater ['bɑːθwɔːtə]	Badewasser

7 C
immediately [ɪ'miːdʒətlɪ]	sofort, unmittelbar
deal with [diːl wɪð]	sich kümmern um, sich beschäftigen mit

8 B
sort out [sɔːt aʊt]	klären, in Ordnung bringen

8 C
letter of complaint ['letər əv kəm'pleɪnt]	Beschwerdebrief
complaint [kəm'pleɪnt]	Beschwerde, Klage
travel company ['trævl 'kʌmpənɪ]	Reisegesellschaft
complain [kəm'pleɪn]	sich beklagen, beschweren
in fact [ɪn fækt]	tatsächlich, in der Tat
in addition [ɪn ə'dɪʃn]	außerdem
therefore ['ðeəfɔː]	deshalb, aus diesem Grunde
Yours faithfully, [ˌjɔːz 'feɪθfʊlɪ]	Mit freundlichen Grüßen *(Briefschluß)*

9
getting tired ['getɪŋ 'taɪəd]	müde werden

9 A
New Zealand [ˌnjuː 'ziːlənd]	Neuseeland
great time guide [greɪt taɪm gaɪd]	*Name eines Freizeitkalenders*
published quarterly ['pʌblɪʃt 'kwɔːtəlɪ]	erscheint vierteljährlich
publish ['pʌblɪʃ]	veröffentlichen, herausgeben
bus terminal ['bʌs ˌtɜːmɪnl]	Busbahnhof, Endstation
airport ['eəpɔːt]	Flughafen
waiting room ['weɪtɪŋ ruːm]	Wartesaal
form [fɔːm]	Formular
guide book [gaɪd bʊk]	Reiseführer *(Buch)*
struggle ['strʌgl]	Kampf, Ringen
timetable ['taɪmˌteɪbl]	Fahrplan
haste [heɪst]	Hast, Eile
tiring ['taɪərɪŋ]	ermüdend, anstrengend

10
roses on Mount Vesuvius ['rəʊzɪz ɒn maʊnt vɪ'suːvjəs]	Rosen auf dem Vesuv

10 A
conference ['kɒnfərəns]	Tagung, Konferenz
association [əˌsəʊsɪ'eɪʃn]	Verband
annual ['ænjʊəl]	jährlich, Jahres-
delegate ['delɪgət]	Abgeordnete/r, Delegierte/r

UNIT 6

miss [mɪs]	*hier:* verpassen
delayed [dɪˈleɪd]	verspätet
fog [fɒg]	Nebel
food-poisoning [ˈfuːdˌpɔɪznɪŋ]	Lebensmittelvergiftung
fall down [fɔːl daʊn]	herab-, hinunterfallen
fell [fel]	Verg.-Form v. *fall:* fallen
stairs [steəz]	Treppe
marketing director [ˈmɑːkɪtɪŋ dɪˈrektə]	Leiter der Marketingabteilung
bitten [ˈbɪtn]	Partizip Perfekt v. *bite:* beißen
snake [sneɪk]	Schlange
develop blood-poisoning [dɪˈveləp ˈblʌdˌpɔɪznɪŋ]	sich eine Blutvergiftung zuziehen
develop [dɪˈveləp]	entwickeln, erschließen
blood-poisoning [ˈblʌdˌpɔɪznɪŋ]	Blutvergiftung
organiser [ˈɔːgənaɪzə]	Organisator/in
golf competition [gɒlf ˌkɒmpəˈtɪʃn]	Golfturnier
competition [ˌkɒmpəˈtɪʃn]	Wettbewerb, Konkurrenz
move [muːv]	*hier:* verlegen, verschieben
high point [haɪ pɔɪnt]	Höhepunkt
Minister of Development [ˈmɪnɪstər ɒv dɪˈveləpmənt]	Minister für (wirtschaftliche) Entwicklung
address [əˈdres]	*hier:* ansprechen, (Worte) richten
Forum [ˈfɔːrəm]	*Versammlungsort und Marktplatz in Städten des römischen Reiches*
drop [drɒp]	*hier:* abwerfen
ceremony [ˈserəmənɪ]	Feier
low-flying [ˌləʊˈflaɪɪŋ]	tieffliegend
appear [əˈpɪə]	erscheinen, auftauchen
completely [kəmˈpliːtlɪ]	vollständig
drown [draʊn]	*hier:* übertönen
speech [spiːtʃ]	Rede, Ansprache
unfortunately [ʌnˈfɔːtʃnətlɪ]	unglücklicherweise, leider
five times [faɪv taɪmz]	fünf Mal
not a single flower [nɒt ə ˈsɪŋgl ˈflaʊə]	nicht eine einzige Blume
single [ˈsɪŋgl]	einzig, einzeln
land [lænd]	landen
all over Mount Vesuvius [ɔːl ˈəʊvə maʊnt vɪˈsuːvjəs]	überall auf dem Vesuv

11
away or at home [əˈweɪ ɔːr ət həʊm]	*hier:* im Urlaub oder daheim
away [əˈweɪ]	weg, fort

11 A
argument [ˈɑːgjʊmənt]	Argument

PREVIEW B

1
race round Europe [reɪs əˈraʊnd ˈjʊərəp]	Wettrennen durch Europa
race [reɪs]	Rennen, Wettrennen
starting point [ˈstɑːtɪŋ pɔɪnt]	Ausgangspunkt
Move by throwing a dice.	Würfeln Sie, um vorzuziehen.
throw [θrəʊ]	werfen
dice [daɪs]	Würfel
task [tɑːsk]	Aufgabe

2A
bought [bɔːt]	Partizip Perfekt v. *buy:* kaufen
recently [ˈriːsəntlɪ]	kürzlich, vor kurzem
in the last year [ɪn ðə lɑːst ˈjɪə]	während des letzten Jahres

3
when the doorbell rang [wen ðə ˈdɔːbel ræŋ]	als es an der Türe läutete
doorbell [ˈdɔːbel]	Türklingel
rang [ræŋ]	Verg.-Form v. *ring:* läuten

4
These questions are related to the topics of the next three units.	Diese Fragen stehen in Verbindung mit den Themen der nächsten drei Lektionen.
related to [rɪˈleɪtɪd tuː]	*hier:* in Verbindung stehen mit
present [ˈpreznt]	*hier:* gegenwärtig, augenblicklich
had [hæd]	Partizip Perfekt v. *have:* haben
carry [ˈkærɪ]	tragen, bei sich haben

V

UNIT 7

1A

the Gents (= Gentlemens' toilet) [ðə dʒents]	Herrentoilette
canary [kəˈneərɪ]	Kanarienvogel
escape [ɪˈskeɪp]	entkommen; *hier:* entfliegen
need [niːd]	*hier:* müssen
fax [fæks]	Fax
wide [waɪd]	breit, weit
Can I get a coffee around here? [kən aɪ get ə ˈkɒfɪ əˈraʊnd hɪə]	Kann ich hier irgendwo eine Tasse Kaffee bekommen?
around here [əˈraʊnd hɪə]	in der Nähe, in dieser Gegend

2A

have a job [hæv ə dʒɒb]	eine Arbeitsstelle/einen Job haben
Write down three words you associate with it.	Schreiben Sie drei Wörter auf, die Ihnen dazu einfallen.
associate [əˈsəʊʃɪeɪt]	in Verbindung bringen, assoziieren

3B

comment [ˈkɒment]	Kommentar, Bemerkung
librarian [laɪˈbreərɪən]	Bibliothekar/in
vineyard [ˈvɪnjɑːd]	Weinberg
builder [ˈbɪldə]	Bauunternehmer/in
battery [ˈbætərɪ]	Batterie
sales assistant [seɪlz əˈsɪstənt]	Verkäufer/in
tourist guide [ˈtʊərɪst gaɪd]	Fremdenführer/in
disc jockey [ˈdɪsk ˌdʒɒkɪ]	Discjockey
good fun [gʊd fʌn]	macht Spaß
fun [fʌn]	Spaß, Scherz
unhealthy [ʌnˈhelθɪ]	ungesund

3C

became [bɪˈkeɪm]	Verg.-Form v. *become:* werden
he decided to train as a librarian [hɪ dɪˈsaɪdɪd tʊ treɪn əz ə laɪˈbreərɪən]	er entschloß sich, eine Ausbildung zum Bibliothekar zu beginnen
train [treɪn]	sich ausbilden
antique dealer [ænˈtiːk ˈdiːlə]	Antiquitätenhändler/in
for a while [fər ə waɪl]	eine Zeitlang
at that point [ət ðæt pɔɪnt]	*hier:* zu jener Zeit, zu diesem Zeitpunkt
proper job [ˈprɒpə dʒɒb]	feste/passende Arbeitsstelle
qualified librarian [ˈkwɒlɪfaɪd laɪˈbreərɪən]	ausgebildeter Bibliothekar
work out [wɜːk aʊt]	*hier:* funktionieren, klappen
department manager [dɪˈpɑːtmənt ˈmænɪdʒə]	Abteilungsleiter
after a while [ˈɑːftər ə waɪl]	einige Zeit später

3E

anything [ˈenɪθɪŋ]	*hier:* irgendetwas
professional Western movie background street crosser	von Beruf: Straßenüberquerer in der Kulisse von Westernfilmen
professional [prəˈfeʃnl]	beruflich, professionell

4A

cook [kʊk]	kochen
brush up [brʌʃ ʌp]	auffrischen
apply for [əˈplaɪ fɔː]	*hier:* sich bewerben um/für
look for [lʊk fɔː]	suchen
get bored [get bɔːd]	sich langweilen
get rid of [get rɪd ɒv]	loswerden, sich entledigen
staff [stɑːf]	Mitarbeiter, Belegschaft
last in, first out [lɑːst ɪn fɜːst aʊt]	wer zuletzt gekommen ist, muß als erster gehen
finish [ˈfɪnɪʃ]	*hier:* beenden, abschließen
studies [ˈstʌdɪz]	Studium
prepared [prɪˈpeəd]	bereit, willig
anywhere [ˈenɪweə]	*hier:* irgendwohin
at home on our own [ət həʊm ɒn aʊər əʊn]	alleine zu Hause
on one's own [ɒn wʌnz əʊn]	alleine
do business [duː ˈbɪznɪs]	Geschäfte machen

Unit 7

export ['ekspɔːt]	Ausfuhr, Export
might [maɪt]	kann/könnte vielleicht
forgotten [fə'gɒtn]	Partizip Perfekt v. *forget:* vergessen
at last [ət lɑːst]	schließlich, endlich
advanced cookery course [əd'vɑːnst 'kʊkəri kɔːs]	Kochkurs für Fortgeschrittene
advanced [əd'vɑːnst]	fortgeschritten

5A

kitchen equipment ['kɪtʃɪn ɪ'kwɪpmənt]	Kücheneinrichtung
at the moment [ət ðə 'məʊmənt]	zur Zeit, momentan
expand [ɪk'spænd]	expandieren, (sich) ausdehnen
sales department [seɪlz dɪ'pɑːtmənt]	Verkaufsabteilung
department [dɪ'pɑːtmənt]	Abteilung
just now [dʒʌst naʊ]	zur Zeit
prepare [prɪ'peə]	vorbereiten
information material [ˌɪnfə'meɪʃn mə'tɪərɪəl]	Informationsmaterial
agent ['eɪdʒənt]	Vertreter/in, Agent/in
help out [help aʊt]	aushelfen
give trouble [gɪv 'trʌbl]	Scherereien/Ärger bereiten
trouble ['trʌbl]	Scherereien, Ärger
trainee [treɪ'niː]	Auszubildende/r

6

Can I take a message? [kən aɪ teɪk ə 'mesɪdʒ]	Kann ich etwas ausrichten?, Möchten Sie eine Nachricht hinterlassen?
message ['mesɪdʒ]	Mitteilung, Botschaft

6A

plc = public limited company [ˌpiːel'siː] ['pʌblɪk 'lɪmɪtɪd 'kʌmpəni]	Aktiengesellschaft
I'll tell her. [aɪl tel hɜː]	Ich sage ihr Bescheid.
call [kɔːl]	*hier:* anrufen
order ['ɔːdə]	Auftrag, Bestellung
Hold on, Mr. Taylor. [həʊld ɒn 'mɪstə 'teɪlə]	Bleiben Sie bitte am Apparat, Herr Taylor.
I'll put you through. [aɪl pʊt jʊ θruː]	Ich verbinde Sie.

the line's busy [ðə laɪnz 'bɪzi]	der Anschluß ist besetzt
leave a message [liːv ə 'mesɪdʒ]	eine Nachricht hinterlassen
he's not in this morning [hiːz nɒt ɪn ðɪs 'mɔːnɪŋ]	er ist heute vormittag nicht da
phone back [fəʊn bæk]	zurückrufen *(Telefon)*
as soon as possible [əz suːn əz 'pɒsəbl]	so bald wie möglich
possible ['pɒsəbl]	möglich
about [ə'baʊt]	*hier:* wegen, über

6B

Speaking. ['spiːkɪŋ]	Am Apparat.

7

on the phone [ɒn ðə fəʊn]	*hier:* am Telefon

7A

caller ['kɔːlə]	Anrufer/in
receptionist [rɪ'sepʃənɪst]	*hier:* Person an der Telefonzentrale

8A

driver ['draɪvə]	Fahrer/in
wait [weɪt]	warten
hide [haɪd]	(sich) verstecken
cigarette [ˌsɪgə'ret]	Zigarette
iron ['aɪən]	bügeln
washing ['wɒʃɪŋ]	*hier:* Wäsche
dig [dɪg]	graben
hole [həʊl]	Loch
bark [bɑːk]	bellen
postman ['pəʊstmən]	Briefträger
dress up [dres ʌp]	sich schick/fein machen
baby ['beɪbi]	Baby
nappy ['næpi]	Windel
build [bɪld]	bauen
nest [nest]	Nest

8B

situation [ˌsɪtjʊ'eɪʃn]	Situation

9

job satisfaction [dʒɒb ˌsætɪs'fækʃn]	Zufriedenheit am Arbeitsplatz

9A

nature warden ['neɪtʃə ˌwɔːdn]	Aufseher/in in einem Naturschutzgebiet

V

UNIT 7

nature ['neɪtʃə]	Natur
hospital helper ['hɒspɪtl 'helpə]	Hilfskraft in einem Krankenhaus
traffic warden ['træfɪk ˌwɔːdn]	Politesse *(weiblich und männlich)*

9 B

accountant [ə'kaʊntənt]	Buchhalter/in
a number of other jobs [ə 'nʌmbər əv 'ʌðə dʒɒbz]	eine ganze Reihe anderer Stellen
earn [ɜːn]	verdienen
confrontation [ˌkɒnfrʌn'teɪʃn]	Konfrontation
rubbish ['rʌbɪʃ]	Abfall; *hier:* Unsinn, Mist
woken ['wəʊkn]	Partizip Perfekt v. *wake:* wecken, aufwecken, aufwachen
sunrise ['sʌnraɪz]	Sonnenaufgang
nature reserve ['neɪtʃə rɪ'zɜːv]	Naturschutzgebiet
make sure [meɪk ʃɔː]	sich überzeugen, sicherstellen
keep out of danger [kiːp aʊt əv 'deɪndʒə]	von Gefahren fernhalten
danger ['deɪndʒə]	Gefahr
practical ['præktɪkl]	praktisch
erosion [ɪ'rəʊʒn]	Erosion
cause [kɔːz]	verursachen
walker ['wɔːkə]	Spaziergänger/in, Wanderer
wave action [weɪv 'ækʃn]	Wellentätigkeit, Seegang
paperwork ['peɪpəwɜːk]	Papierarbeit, Papierkram
public enquiries ['pʌblɪk ɪn'kwaɪərɪz]	Anfragen aus der Bevölkerung
zoology [zʊ'ɒlədʒɪ]	Zoologie
mixed recipe [mɪkst 'resɪpɪ]	*etwa:* bunte Mischung
recipe ['resɪpɪ]	Rezept, Rezeptur
inner ['ɪnə]	innerlich, innerer, innere/inneres/verborgen
fight [faɪt]	sich streiten, kämpfen
parking space ['pɑːkɪŋ speɪs]	Parklücke
each other [iːtʃ 'ʌðə]	einander, sich *(gegenseitig)*
humanity [hjuː'mænɪtɪ]	Menschlichkeit, Menschheit
chance [tʃɑːns]	Gelegenheit, Möglichkeit, Chance
appreciate [ə'priːʃɪeɪt]	schätzen, würdigen
reflect on [rɪ'flekt ɒn]	nachdenken über

9 C

amusing [ə'mjuːzɪŋ]	amüsant, unterhaltsam
plenty of ['plentɪ əv]	reichlich, viel
variety [və'raɪətɪ]	Abwechslung

10

exchange [ɪks'tʃeɪndʒ]	tauschen, austauschen
as necessary [æz 'nesəsərɪ]	bei Bedarf

UNIT 8

1

be merry [bɪ 'merɪ]	sei fröhlich *(altmodisch)*
samples of heritage recipes ['sɑːmplz əv 'herɪtɪdʒ 'resɪpiːz]	*etwa:* Auswahl traditioneller Rezepte
vegetarian meals [ˌvedʒɪ'teərɪən miːlz]	vegetarische Mahlzeiten
Indian cookery ['ɪndjən 'kʊkərɪ]	Indische Küche
cookery ['kʊkərɪ]	Kochkunst, Küche
glorious ['glɔːrɪəs]	herrlich, glorreich

1 B

ingredient [ɪn'griːdɪənt]	Zutat, Bestandteil
dictionary ['dɪkʃənərɪ]	Wörterbuch, Lexikon

2

curry ['kʌrɪ]	Currygericht
serves 4 [sɜːvz fɔː]	*hier:* für 4 Personen
mixed [mɪkst]	gemischt, vermischt
aubergine ['əʊbəʒiːn]	Aubergine
pepper ['pepə]	*hier:* Paprikaschote
courgette [kɔː'ʒet]	Zucchini
leek [liːk]	Porree, Lauch
cauliflower ['kɒlɪˌflaʊə]	Blumenkohl
tin [tɪn]	Dose, Büchse
tablespoon ['teɪblspuːn]	Eßlöffel
juice [dʒuːs]	Saft
ginger ['dʒɪndʒə]	Ingwer

Unit 8

clove of garlic [kləʊv əv 'gɑːlɪk]	Knoblauchzehe
garlic ['gɑːlɪk]	Knoblauch
oil [ɔɪl]	Öl; *hier:* Speiseöl
teaspoon ['tiːspuːn]	Teelöffel
ground [graʊnd]	Partizip Perfekt v. *grind:* mahlen, reiben
coriander [ˌkɒrɪ'ændə]	Koriander
cinnamon ['sɪnəmən]	Zimt
turmeric ['tɜːmərɪk]	Kurkuma, Gelbwurzel
cumin ['kʌmɪn]	Kreuzkümmel
chil(l)i powder ['tʃɪlɪ ˌpaʊdə]	Chilipulver
salt to taste [sɔːlt tʊ teɪst]	Salz zum Abschmecken

2A

bring to the boil [brɪŋ tʊ ðə bɔɪl]	zum Kochen bringen
cook gently [kʊk 'dʒentlɪ]	köcheln
stir [stɜː]	rühren
occasionally [ə'keɪʒənlɪ]	gelegentlich
heat [hiːt]	erhitzen
saucepan ['sɔːspən]	Kochtopf
chopped [tʃɒpt]	gehackt, zerhackt
spice [spaɪs]	Gewürz
fry [fraɪ]	braten
peel [piːl]	schälen
chop finely [tʃɒp 'faɪnlɪ]	feinschneiden, feinhacken
sharp [ʃɑːp]	scharf
knife [naɪf]	Messer
cut into pieces [kʌt 'ɪntʊ 'piːsɪz]	in Stücke schneiden
cut [kʌt]	schneiden
serve [sɜːv]	servieren
tinned tomatoes [tɪnd tə'mɑːtəʊz]	Tomaten in der Dose

3

favourite recipes ['feɪvərɪt 'resɪpɪz]	Lieblingsrezepte

3A

local speciality ['ləʊkl ˌspeʃɪ'ælətɪ]	örtliche/regionale Spezialität
you must let us have the recipe [jʊ mʌst let ʌs hæv ðə 'resɪpɪ]	Sie müssen uns unbedingt das Rezept geben
a pinch of salt [ə pɪntʃ əv sɔːlt]	eine Prise Salz

fork [fɔːk]	Gabel
procedure [prə'siːdʒə]	Verfahren; *hier:* Zubereitung
arrange [ə'reɪndʒ]	*hier:* anrichten, garnieren
cover ['kʌvə]	zudecken, abdecken
grate [greɪt]	reiben, raspeln
pour [pɔː]	gießen, einschenken
roast [rəʊst]	rösten, braten
season [siːzn]	würzen
slice [slaɪs]	in Scheiben schneiden
spread [spred]	ausbreiten

3B

Compile a class recipe book.	Stellen Sie ein Kochbuch Ihres Kurses zusammen.
compile [kəm'paɪl]	zusammenstellen

4

get together [get tə'geðə]	sich treffen, zusammenfinden

5

wild weekend [waɪld 'wiːkend]	wildes Wochende

5B

invite [ɪn'vaɪt]	einladen
arrangement [ə'reɪndʒmənt]	Vereinbarung, Verabredung
put it in the diary [pʊt ɪt ɪn ðə 'daɪərɪ]	tragen Sie sie in Ihren Terminkalender ein
diary ['daɪərɪ]	Tagebuch, Terminkalender

6

celebration [ˌselɪ'breɪʃn]	Feier

6A

Mother's Day ['mʌðəz deɪ]	Muttertag
New Year [ˌnjuː 'jɪə]	Neujahr
Valentine's Day ['væləntaɪnz deɪ]	Valentinstag
wedding anniversary ['wedɪŋ ˌænɪ'vɜːsərɪ]	Hochzeitstag
film [fɪlm]	Film
valentine ['væləntaɪn]	Valentinsgruß, Valentinskarte
whisper ['wɪspə]	flüstern
soft [sɒft]	weich, sanft

V

UNIT 8

I am mine. [aɪ æm maɪn]	Ich gehöre mir.	raise a loving cup [reɪz ə ˈlʌvɪŋ kʌp]	einen Pokal heben, anstoßen
Merry Christmas [ˌmeri ˈkrɪsməs]	Frohe Weihnachten	raise [reɪz]	heben, hochheben
Many happy returns [ˈmeni ˈhæpi rɪˈtɜːnz]	*etwa:* Herzlichen Glückwunsch zum Geburtstag	earth [ɜːθ]	Erde
		goodwill [ˌgʊdˈwɪl]	Wohlwollen
		ritual [ˈrɪtʃʊəl]	Ritual
Happy New Year [ˈhæpi njuː jɪə]	frohes Neues Jahr	**9**	
Happy Anniversary! [ˈhæpi ˌænɪˈvɜːsəri]	Alles Gute zum Hochzeitstag!	special days [ˈspeʃl deɪz]	besondere Tage
anniversary [ˌænɪˈvɜːseri]	Jahrestag; *hier:* Hochzeitstag	raise money for charity [reɪz ˈmʌni fə ˈtʃærəti]	Geld für wohltätige Zwecke sammeln
Here's to another wonderful year with you. [hɪəz tʊ əˈnʌðə ˈwʌndəfʊl jɪə wɪð juː]	Auf ein weiteres wunderbares Jahr mit dir.	charity [ˈtʃærəti]	Wohltätigkeit, Nächstenliebe
		support [səˈpɔːt]	Unterstützung
Best wishes on your retirement [best ˈwɪʃɪz ɒn jɔː rɪˈtaɪəmənt]	Alles Gute zur Pensionierung	**9A**	
		solid food [ˈsɒlɪd fuːd]	feste Nahrung
		let oneself go [let wʌnself ˈgəʊ]	sich gehen/treiben lassen
For the best Mum in the world [fə ðə best mʌm ɪn ðə wɜːld]	Für die beste Mutti auf der Welt	be allowed to do something [bɪ əˈlaʊd tʊ duː ˈsʌmθɪŋ]	etwas tun dürfen
Just for you on Valentine's Day [dʒʌst fə juː ɒn ˈvæləntaɪnz deɪ]	Nur für dich zum Valentinstag	allow [əˈlaʊ]	erlauben, gestatten
		Invent your own public holiday.	Erfinden Sie Ihren eigenen gesetzlichen Feiertag.
Happy Easter [ˌhæpi ˈiːstə]	Frohe Ostern	invent [ɪnˈvent]	erfinden
All the best! [ɔːl ðə best]	Alles Gute!	public holiday [ˈpʌblɪk ˈhɒlɪdeɪ]	öffentlicher/gesetzlicher Feiertag
Cheers! [tʃɪəz]	Hoch soll er/sie leben!	**9C**	
7		present [prɪˈzent]	*hier:* präsentieren, vorstellen
the born loser [ðə bɔːn ˈluːzə]	der geborene Verlierer	design [dɪˈzaɪn]	Entwurf
7A		**10A**	
forgot [fəˈgɒt]	Verg.-Form v. *forget:* vergessen	*five things you would like to be*	fünf Dinge, die Sie gerne wären
I beg (your) pardon? [aɪ beg jɔː ˈpɑːdn]	Wie bitte?	**10B**	
babysitter [ˈbeɪbiˌsɪtə]	Babysitter	writer [ˈraɪtə]	*hier:* Schreiber, Verfasser
ex-wife [ˈekswaɪf]	Ex-Frau		
7B		**11**	
celebrate [ˈselɪbreɪt]	feiern	association [əˌsəʊsiˈeɪʃn]	*hier:* Assoziation
don't think much of [dəʊnt θɪŋk mʌtʃ ɒv]	nicht viel halten von	swop [swɒp]	tauschen, austauschen
8			
wish [wɪʃ]	wünschen		
bloody [ˈblʌdi]	verflucht, verdammt		

Unit 9

1A
pair of trousers [peər əv ˈtraʊzəz]	Hose
pair of tights [peər əv taɪts]	Strumpfhose
shirt [ʃɜːt]	Hemd
skirt [skɜːt]	Rock
blouse [blaʊz]	Bluse
pair of socks [peər əv sɒks]	Paar Socken
coat [kəʊt]	Mantel
pair of shorts [peər əv ʃɔːts]	kurze Hose, Shorts
tie [taɪ]	Krawatte
underwear [ˈʌndəweə]	Unterwäsche
pullover [ˈpʊlˌəʊvə]	Pullover
jacket [ˈdʒækɪt]	Jacke

1C
wardrobe [ˈwɔːdrəʊb]	Kleiderschrank, Garderobe
hers [hɜːz]	ihre(r/s); (auf Handtüchern usw.: Sie)
his [hɪz]	seine(r/s); (auf Handtüchern usw.: Er)
theirs [ðeəz]	ihre(r/s) (Mehrzahl)

2A
throw off [θrəʊ ɒf]	ablegen, abwerfen
breathe [briːð]	atmen
move [muːv]	(sich) bewegen
I am free to choose [aɪ æm friː tʊ tʃuːz]	Ich habe die Freiheit, zu wählen
light clothes [laɪt kləʊdz]	leichte/luftige Kleidung
none at all [nʌn ət ɔːl]	überhaupt keiner/keine/keins

3B
follow [ˈfɒləʊ]	folgen, be-, verfolgen

4
a question of clothes [ə ˈkwestʃn əv kləʊdz]	eine Frage der Kleidung

4A
piece of clothing [piːs əv ˈkləʊðɪŋ]	Kleidungsstück
comfortable [ˈkʌmftəbl]	bequem
elegant [ˈelɪgənt]	elegant, geschmackvoll
a piece of clothing that holds special memories [ə piːs əv ˈkləʊðɪŋ ðət həʊldz ˈspeʃl ˈmeməriz]	ein Kleidungsstück, mit dem besondere Erinnerungen verbunden sind

4B
remind someone of something [rɪˈmaɪnd ˈsʌmwʌn əv ˈsʌmθɪŋ]	jdn. an etwas erinnern
worn [wɔːn]	Partizip Perfekt v. *wear:* tragen

5
young fashions [jʌŋ ˈfæʃnz]	junge Mode
fashion [ˈfæʃn]	Mode

5A
size [saɪz]	Größe
any time she feels like it [ˈeni taɪm ʃi fiːlz laɪk ɪt]	immer, wenn sie Lust dazu hat
kept [kept]	Verg.-Form v. *keep:* (be)halten
children today are into clothes [ˈtʃɪldrən təˈdeɪ ər ˈɪntʊ kləʊdz]	die heutigen Kinder sind an Kleidung interessiert
generation [ˌdʒenəˈreɪʃn]	Generation
motto [ˈmɒtəʊ]	Motto, Leitspruch
afford [əˈfɔːd]	sich leisten
throw away [θrəʊ əˈweɪ]	wegwerfen, fortwerfen
perfectly good clothes [ˈpɜːfɪktli gʊd kləʊdz]	Kleidungsstücke, die völlig in Ordnung sind
certainly not [ˈsɜːtənli nɒt]	gewiß nicht, auf keinen Fall
the rest of us [ðə rest əv ʌs]	die anderen von uns
anyway [ˈeniweɪ]	*hier:* auf jeden Fall, jedenfalls
mend [mend]	flicken, ausbessern
last [lɑːst]	*hier:* dauern, halten

5C
That sounds familiar! [ðæt saʊndz fəˈmɪljə]	Das klingt vertraut!
sound [saʊnd]	sich anhören
familiar [fəˈmɪljə]	vertraut, gewohnt

UNIT 9

That's just like my daughter! [ðæts dʒʌst laɪk maɪ 'dɔːtə]	Genau wie meine Tochter!	wealthy ['welθɪ]	wohlhabend
		businessman ['bɪznɪsmən]	Geschäftsman
6		demand [dɪ'mɑːnd]	Nachfrage
jeans [dʒiːnz]	Jeans	grow [grəʊ]	*hier:* (an)steigen
		mass production [ˌmæsprə'dʌkʃn]	Massenproduktion
6A		introduce [ˌɪntrə'dʒuːs]	*hier:* einführen
expect [ɪk'spekt]	erwarten	World War 2 [ˌwɜːldwɔː'tuː]	der 2. Weltkrieg
Bavaria [bə'veərɪə]	Bayern		
California [ˌkælɪ'fɔːnjə]	Kalifornien	rise [raɪz]	Anstieg, Aufstieg
canvas ['kænvəs]	Segeltuch, Leinwandstoff	in the late 50s [ɪn ðə leɪt 'fɪftɪz]	Ende der 50er Jahre
cotton ['kɒtn]	Baumwolle	in the early 60s [ɪn ðɪ 'ɜːlɪ 'sɪkstɪz]	Anfang der 60er Jahre
cowboy ['kaʊbɔɪ]	Cowboy		
Genoa ['dʒenəʊə]	Genua	item of clothing ['aɪtəm əv 'kləʊðɪŋ]	Kleidungsstück
gold [gəʊld]	Gold	port [pɔːt]	Hafen
material [mə'tɪərɪəl]	Stoff, Material	export [ɪk'spɔːt]	ausführen, exportieren
miner ['maɪnə]	Bergmann		
rock'n roll [ˌrɒkn 'rəʊl]	Rock 'n Roll	**6E**	
soldier ['səʊldʒə]	Soldat	When are jeans acceptable? [wen ɑː dʒiːnz ək'septəbl]	Bei welchen Gelegenheiten lassen sich Jeans tragen?
tent [tent]	Zelt		
tough [tʌf]	zäh, hart, robust	acceptable [ək'septəbl]	annehmbar, akzeptabel
6B			
gave [geɪv]	Verg.-Form v. *give:* geben	**7A**	
emigrate ['emɪgreɪt]	auswandern	waste [weɪst]	verschwenden
at first [ət 'fɜːst]	zuerst, am Anfang	money ['mʌnɪ]	Geld
travelling salesman [ˌtrævlɪŋ 'seɪlzmən]	Handelsreisender	happiness ['hæpɪnɪs]	Glück
		waste [weɪst]	Verschwendung
household goods [ˌhaʊshəʊld 'gʊdz]	Haushaltswaren	fashionable ['fæʃnəbl]	modern
goods [gʊdz]	Waren, Güter	**8**	
the Gold Rush [ðə gəʊld 'rʌʃ]	der Goldrausch	valuables ['væljʊəbl]	Wertsachen
try one's luck [traɪ wʌnz lʌk]	sein Glück suchen	**8A**	
sail for [seɪl fɔː]	mit dem Schiff nach ... fahren	door key ['dɔː ˌkiː]	Türschlüssel
		car key ['kɑː ˌkiː]	Autoschlüssel
wagon ['wægən]	Wagen; *hier:* Planwagen	wallet ['wɒlɪt]	Brieftasche
		purse [pɜːs]	Geldbörse
farmer ['fɑːmə]	Farmer, Bauer	cheque card [tʃek ˌkɑːd]	Scheckkarte
railroad worker ['reɪlrəʊd 'wɜːkə]	Gleisarbeiter/in	ID card [ˌaɪ'diː kɑːd]	Personalausweis
railroad (AE) ['reɪlrəʊd]	Eisenbahn	driving licence ['draɪvɪŋ ˌlaɪsəns]	Führerschein
lumberjack ['lʌmbədʒæk]	Holzfäller/in	handbag ['hændbæg]	Handtasche
		sunglasses ['sʌnglɑːsɪz]	Sonnenbrille
hardwearing [ˌhɑːd'weərɪŋ]	strapazierfähig	ring [rɪŋ]	Ring
denim ['denɪm]	Jeansstoff, Denim	brooch [brəʊtʃ]	Brosche
prove [pruːv]	*hier:* sich herausstellen, beweisen	necklace ['neklɪs]	Halskette, Halsband
		earring ['ɪərɪŋ]	Ohrring

Unit 9

8C
Clear a table.	Räumen Sie einen Tisch leer.
clear [klɪə]	abräumen, wegräumen
object [ˈɒbdʒekt]	Gegenstand
... study them for a minute or two.	... betrachten Sie sie eine oder zwei Minuten lang.
position [pəˈzɪʃn]	Position
take away [teɪk əˈweɪ]	wegnehmen, fortnehmen
under [ˈʌndə]	unter

9
compliment [ˈkɒmplɪmənt]	Kompliment

9A
glad [glæd]	erfreut, froh
suit someone [sjuːt ˈsʌmwʌn]	jdm. stehen, jdn. gut kleiden

9C
pay each other compliments	sich gegenseitig Komplimente machen
Oh Ginger – you look absolutely stunning ... and whatever you rolled in sure does stink.	Oh Ginger, du siehst absolut umwerfend aus ... und worin du dich auch immer gewälzt haben magst, es stinkt gewaltig.

10
mainly [ˈmeɪnli]	hauptsächlich, zur Hauptsache
leather [ˈleðə]	Leder
metal [ˈmetl]	Metall
paper [ˈpeɪpə]	Papier
plastic [ˈplæstɪk]	Plastik, Kunststoff
wood [wʊd]	Holz
wool [wʊl]	Wolle

11
Odd one out [ɒd wʌn aʊt]	*etwa:* Eins paßt nicht; Einer ist falsch.
fit [fɪt]	*hier:* passen

Preview C

2B
dictate [dɪkˈteɪt]	diktieren

3A
What makes ...? [wɒt meɪks]	Was macht ... aus?
ideal [aɪˈdɪəl]	ideal

4
listen ahead [ˈlɪsn əˈhed]	*etwa:* hören Sie schon einmal zu
extract [ˈekstrækt]	Auszug

Unit 10

1A
have a shower [hæv ə ˈʃaʊə]	duschen
shower [ˈʃaʊə]	Dusche
shave [ʃeɪv]	(sich) rasieren

1B
diagram [ˈdaɪəgræm]	Diagramm, Plan
essential [ɪˈsenʃl]	wichtig, unentbehrlich

2B
flush the toilet [flʌʃ ðə ˈtɔɪlət]	die Toilette spülen
teeth [tiːθ]	Zähne (Mz. v. *tooth*)
wash up [wɒʃ ʌp]	abwaschen, Geschirr spülen
water the garden [ˈwɔːtə ðə ˈgɑːdn]	den Garten bewässern/gießen

2C
on average [ɒn ˈævrɪdʒ]	im Durchschnitt

3
energy price [ˈenədʒi praɪs]	Energiepreis

3A
heating system [ˈhiːtɪŋ ˈsɪstəm]	Heizsystem
heating [ˈhiːtɪŋ]	Heizung
one-person household [ˈwʌnˌpɜːsn ˈhaʊshəʊld]	Einpersonenhaushalt
electricity [ˌɪlekˈtrɪsəti]	Elektrizität
household machines [ˌhaʊshəʊld məˈʃiːnz]	Haushaltsgeräte

V

UNIT 10

electrical [ɪˈlektrɪkl]	elektrisch	soap [səʊp]	Seife
bath [bɑːθ]	Bad	hairbrush [ˈheəbrʌʃ]	Haarbürste
		hairdryer [ˈheəˌdraɪə]	Haartrockner, Föhn
		make-up [ˈmeɪkʌp]	Make-up, Schminke

3 B

insulate [ˈɪnsjəleɪt] — isolieren
efficient [ɪˈfɪʃənt] — leistungsfähig
heat [hiːt] — heizen
heat a greater area [hiːt ə ˈgreɪtər ˈeərɪə] — einen größeren Bereich beheizen
living space [ˈlɪvɪŋ speɪs] — Wohnfläche
double [ˈdʌbl] — verdoppeln
energy-intensive [ˈenədʒɪ ɪnˈtensɪv] — Energie-intensiv
increase [ɪnˈkriːs] — steigen, ansteigen
all the time [ˌɔːl ðə ˈtaɪm] — ständig, die ganze Zeit
a 70% increase [ə ˈsevntɪ pəˌsent ˈɪnkriːs] — ein 70%iger Anstieg
increase [ˈɪnkriːs] — Anstieg
amount [əˈmaʊnt] — Menge, Gesamtsumme
triple [ˈtrɪpl] — verdreifachen
not to mention [ˌnɒt tʊ ˈmenʃn] — ganz zu schweigen von
mention [ˈmenʃn] — erwähnen
hifi [ˈhaɪfaɪ] — Stereoanlage, Hi-Fi-Anlage
consumption [kənˈsʌmʃn] — Verbrauch, Konsum
risen [ˈrɪzn] — Partizip Perfekt v. *rise:* ansteigen
kilowatt hour [ˌkɪləwɒt ˈaʊə] — Kilowattstunde
shower [ˈʃaʊə] — *hier:* duschen
frequently [ˈfriːkwəntlɪ] — häufig
all in all [ˌɔːl ɪn ˈɔːl] — alles in allem, insgesamt

3 C

I didn't realize that ... [aɪ ˌdɪdnt ˈrɪəlaɪz ðət] — mir war nicht klar/bewußt, daß ...
realize [ˈrɪəlaɪz] — sich klarmachen, begreifen, erkennen
I was surprised that ... [aɪ wəz səˈpraɪzd ðət] — Ich war überrascht, daß ...
surprise [səˈpraɪz] — überraschen
believe [bɪˈliːv] — glauben

4 A

aspirin [ˈæsprɪn] [ˈæspərɪn] — Aspirin
comb [kəʊm] — Kamm
mirror [ˈmɪrə] — Spiegel
perfume [ˈpɜːfjuːm] — Parfüm
razor [ˈreɪzə] — Rasiermesser, Rasierapparat
shampoo [ʃæmˈpuː] — Shampoo
toothbrush [ˈtuːθbrʌʃ] — Zahnbürste
toothpaste [ˈtuːθpeɪst] — Zahnpasta, Zahncreme
towel [ˈtaʊəl] — Handtuch
aftershave [ˈɑːftəʃeɪv] — Aftershave, Rasierwasser
nail file [neɪl faɪl] — Nagelfeile
scissors [ˈsɪzəz] — Schere
electric shaver [ɪˌlektrɪk ˈʃeɪvə] — elektrischer Rasierapparat
common [ˈkɒmən] — gewöhnlich
cause [kɔːz] — Ursache
skin [skɪn] — Haut

4 B

hardly ever [ˌhɑːdlɪ ˈevə] — fast nie, kaum einmal

5

luxury [ˈlʌkʃərɪ] — Luxus, Luxusartikel
essentials [ɪˈsenʃlz] — Wesentliches, Unentbehrliches

5 B

in your opinion — Ihrer/deiner Meinung nach
opinion [əˈpɪnjən] — Meinung
household equipment [ˌhaʊshəʊld ɪˈkwɪpmənt] — Haushaltsgegenstände
electric kettle [ɪˌlektrɪk ˈketl] — elektrischer Wasserkessel
found [faʊnd] — Partizip Perfekt v. *find:* finden
instant coffee [ˌɪnstənt ˈkɒfɪ] — löslicher Kaffee
on the other hand [ɒn ðɪ ˈʌðə hænd] — andererseits
seem [siːm] — scheinen
dental floss [ˈdentl flɒs] — Zahnseide

5 C

turn up [tɜːn ˈʌp] — aufdrehen, höherstellen
instead of [ɪnˈsted əv] — an Stelle von, anstatt

Unit 10

put on [pʊt ɒn]	anziehen
shelter [ˈʃeltə]	Schutz, Obdach

6
wishful thinking [ˌwɪʃfʊl ˈθɪŋkɪŋ]	Wunschdenken
I wish I had ... [aɪ wɪʃ aɪ hæd]	Wie gerne hätte ich ...; Hätte ich doch nur ...
ground floor [graʊnd flɔː]	Parterre, Erdgeschoß
sauna [ˈsɔːnə]	Sauna

7
domestic disasters [dəˈmestɪk dɪˈzɑːstəz]	häusliche Katastrophen
domestic [dəˈmestɪk]	häuslich
disaster [dɪˈzɑːstə]	Unglück, Katastrophe

7 A
father-in-law [ˈfɑːðərɪnlɔː]	Schwiegervater
paint [peɪnt]	*hier:* (an)streichen
boil [bɔɪl]	kochen
cry [kraɪ]	schreien, weinen
run a bath [rʌn ə ˈbɑːθ]	ein Bad einlaufen lassen
knock [nɒk]	klopfen, anklopfen

7 B
all of a sudden [ˌɔːl əv ə ˈsʌdn]	plötzlich
work [wɜːk]	*hier:* funktionieren

8
ache [eɪk]	Schmerz
pain [peɪn]	Schmerz

8 A
complaint [kəmˈpleɪnt]	Beschwerde; *hier:* Leiden, Gebrechen
backache [ˈbækeɪk]	Rückenschmerzen
insomnia [ɪnˈsɒmnɪə]	Schlaflosigkeit
stiff [stɪf]	steif
neck [nek]	Nacken
stomachache [ˈstʌməkeɪk]	Magenschmerzen
sore throat [sɔː θrəʊt]	Halsschmerzen
throat [θrəʊt]	Kehle, Hals
toothache [ˈtuːθeɪk]	Zahnschmerzen

8 B
remedy [ˈremədɪ]	Heilmittel, Gegenmittel
fresh [freʃ]	frisch
get up [get ʌp]	aufstehen, sich erheben
Keep moving. [kiːp ˈmuːvɪŋ]	Bleib in Bewegung.
open [ˈəʊpn]	*hier:* öffnen
sheep [ʃiːp]	Schaf, Schafe
relaxation [ˌriːlækˈseɪʃn]	Entspannung
brandy [ˈbrændɪ]	Weinbrand, Kognak
sleeping pill [ˈsliːpɪŋpɪl]	Schlaftablette
quite a lot [ˌkwaɪt ə ˈlɒt]	eine ganze Menge, viel, viele
advice [ədˈvaɪs]	Rat, Ratschlag

8 C
tip [tɪp]	Tip, Hinweis, Ratschlag

8 D
ignore [ɪgˈnɔː]	ignorieren
wisdom [ˈwɪzdəm]	Weisheit

9 A
fool [fuːl]	Narr
been [biːn]	Partizip Perfekt v. *be:* sein
tranquiliser [ˈtræŋkwɪlaɪzə]	Beruhigungsmittel
wake [weɪk]	aufwachen, wecken
in case this should let you down [ɪn keɪs ðɪs ʃʊd let jʊ daʊn]	*etwa:* und wenn das alles nichts nützt
smile [smaɪl]	lächeln

Unit 11

1 C
chart [tʃɑːt]	Liste, Tabelle; *hier:* Diagramm
Take turns.	Wechseln Sie sich ab.

2 A
reunite [ˌriːjuːˈnaɪt]	vereinigen, sich wiedertreffen
identical twins [aɪˈdentɪkl twɪnz]	eineiige Zwillinge
identical [aɪˈdentɪkl]	identisch
adopt [əˈdɒpt]	adoptieren
finally [ˈfaɪnəlɪ]	schließlich, endlich
apart [əˈpɑːt]	entfernt, getrennt

V

UNIT 11

just like [dʒʌst laɪk]	genauso wie
left behind [left bɪˈhaɪnd]	Verg.-Form v. *leave behind:* zurücklassen
stop someone [stɒp ˈsʌmwʌn]	jdn. anhalten
strangely [ˈstreɪndʒlɪ]	seltsamerweise, merkwürdigerweise

2 C
similarity [ˌsɪmɪˈlærətɪ]	Ähnlichkeit

3 A
roots map [ruːts mæp]	*etwa:* Ursprungskarte
root [ruːt]	Wurzel
birthplace [ˈbɜːθpleɪs]	Geburtsort

4 A
once upon a time [wʌns əˈpɒn ə ˈtaɪm]	vor langer Zeit; es war einmal *(Anfang v. Erzählungen)*
gradually [ˈgrædʒʊlɪ]	allmählich
all at once [ˌɔːl ət ˈwʌns]	urplötzlich, ganz plötzlich
at once [ət ˈwʌns]	sofort, sogleich

4 B
househusband [ˈhaʊsˌhʌzbənd]	Hausmann
single parent [ˌsɪŋgl ˈpeərənt]	Alleinerziehende/r
lesbian [ˈlezbɪən]	lesbisch
gay [geɪ]	homosexuell, schwul
stepfamily [ˈstepˌfæməlɪ]	Stieffamilie
extend [ɪkˈstend]	ausdehnen, erweitern
yard (AE) (BE: garden) [jɑːd]	Garten
maybe [ˈmeɪbɪ]	vielleicht
fascinating [ˈfæsɪneɪtɪŋ]	faszinierend
life in the city [laɪf ɪn ðə ˈsɪtɪ]	das Stadtleben

4 C
Put these three models in order of popularity.	Ordnen Sie diese drei Modelle nach ihrer Beliebtheit.
model [ˈmɒdl]	Modell
popularity [ˌpɒpjʊˈlærətɪ]	Popularität, Beliebtheit
look after [lʊk ˈɑːftə]	aufpassen auf, sich kümmern um
take care of [teɪk keər ɒv]	aufpassen auf, sich kümmern um

5
future [ˈfjuːtʃə]	Zukunft

5 A
prediction [prɪˈdɪkʃn]	Vorhersage, Prophezeiung
lesbian [ˈlezbɪən]	Lesbierin
gay [geɪ]	Homosexuelle/r, Schwule/r
bring up [brɪŋ ʌp]	aufziehen, großziehen
will [wɪl]	werden *(Zukunft)*

5 B
likely [ˈlaɪklɪ]	wahrscheinlich

6
future prospects [ˈfjuːtʃə ˈprɒspekts]	Zukunftsaussichten
census [ˈsensəs]	Volkszählung
wish [wɪʃ]	Wunsch
hope [həʊp]	hoffen
won't = will not [wəʊnt] [wɪl nɒt]	*hier:* wirst nicht
be able to [bɪ ˈeɪbl tuː]	imstande sein zu, können
unemployed [ˌʌnɪmˈplɔɪd]	arbeitslos
facts [fækts]	*hier:* Informationen
fact [fækt]	Tatsache

7 A
teenage daughter [ˈtiːneɪdʒ ˈdɔːtə]	Tochter im Teenageralter
generally [ˈdʒenərəlɪ]	im allgemeinen
habit [ˈhæbɪt]	Gewohnheit, Angewohnheit

7 C
get on well together [get ɒn wel tə geðə]	sich gut miteinander verstehen

8
parental wisdom [pəˈrentl ˈwɪzdəm]	elterliche Weisheit
parental [pəˈrentl]	elterlich

8 A
Viking [ˈvaɪkɪŋ]	Wikinger
watch out for [wɒtʃ aʊt fɔː]	aufpassen auf, achtgeben auf
pass along (AE) (BE: pass on) [pɑːs əˈlɒŋ] [pɑːs ɒn]	weitergeben

Unit 11

the wit and wisdom it took me a lifetime to gather [ðə wɪt ənd 'wɪzdəm ɪt tʊk mi ə 'laɪftaɪm tʊ 'gæðə]	der Verstand und die Weisheit, die ich während meines ganzen Lebens gesammelt habe	harmonist ['hɑːmənɪst]	Harmoniebedürftige/r
hard [hɑːd]	hart, schwer	rather than ['rɑːðə ðæn]	anstatt, anstelle von
left-handed [ˌleft 'hændɪd]	linkshändig	granny ['grænɪ]	Oma
one-legged [ˌwʌn'legɪd]	einbeinig		
red-headed [ˌred'hedɪd]	rothaarig	**9 B**	
cousin ['kʌzn]	Kusine, Vetter	If I were you [ɪf aɪ wə 'juː]	An deiner Stelle; Wenn ich Du wäre
steel [stiːl]	Stahl		
swordsman ['sɔːdzmən]	Schwertkämpfer		
natural ['nætʃrəl]	natürlich	## Unit 12	
pay attention [peɪ ə'tenʃən]	aufpassen		
diet ['daɪət]	Diät halten	on the road again [ɒn ðə rəʊd ə'gen]	wieder unterwegs
bathe [beɪð]	baden		
to excess [tʊ ɪk'ses]	im Übermaß	**1**	
add [æd]	addieren	means of transport [ˌmiːnz əv 'trænspɔːt]	Transportmittel
subtract [səb'trækt]	subtrahieren	means [miːnz]	Mittel, Hilfsmittel
Sorry, kid – some things a boy's gotta learn on his own.	Tut mir leid Kind – manche Dinge muß ein Junge selber lernen.	**1 A**	
		characteristic [ˌkærəktə'rɪstɪk]	Merkmal, Eigenschaft
8 C			
eat up [iːt ʌp]	aufessen	**1 B**	
		convenient [kən'viːnɪənt]	praktisch, günstig
9 A		uncomfortable [ʌn'kʌmftəbl]	ungemütlich, unbequem
read [red]	Partizp Perfekt v. *read*: lesen	inconvenient [ˌɪnkən'viːnɪənt]	unpraktisch, ungünstig
stay overnight [steɪ əʊvə'naɪt]	übernachten	reliable [rɪ'laɪəbl]	zuverlässig
place [pleɪs]	*hier:* Wohnung	**1 D**	
anxious ['æŋkʃəs]	besorgt, beunruhigt	taxi ['tæksɪ]	Taxi
non-smoking family [ˌnɒn 'sməʊkɪŋ 'fæməlɪ]	Nichtraucherfamilie	**2 A**	
		British Rail [ˌbrɪtɪʃ 'reɪl]	*britische Eisenbahngesellschaft*
widower ['wɪdəʊə]	Witwer	advertisement [əd'vɜːtɪsmənt]	Annonce, Anzeige
move in with someone [muːv ɪn wɪð 'sʌmwʌn]	bei jdm. einziehen	journey ['dʒɜːnɪ]	Reise, Fahrt
		steering wheel ['stɪərɪŋwiːl]	Lenkrad, Steuer
reluctant [rɪ'lʌktənt]	widerwillig	hold one's breath [həʊld wʌnz breθ]	seinen Atem anhalten
daughter-in-law ['dɔːtərɪnlɔː]	Schwiegertochter	breath [breθ]	Atem
parents-in-law ['peərəntsɪnlɔː]	Schwiegereltern	business report ['bɪznɪs rɪ'pɔːt]	Geschäftsbericht
space [speɪs]	Raum, Platz	intellectual [ˌɪntə'lektjʊəl]	intellektuell
get away from [get ə'weɪ frɒm]	entkommen, flüchten vor	Times Crossword [taɪmz 'krɒswɜːd]	*Kreuzworträtsel in der 'Times'*
compromiser ['kɒmprəmaɪzə]	Kompromißbereite/r		

V

UNIT 12

Quick Crossword [kwɪk 'krɒswɜːd]	Kreuzworträtsel für Schnellrater
memorize ['meməraɪz]	auswendig lernen, sich einprägen
try and work out [traɪ ənd wɜːk aʊt]	versuchen Sie festzustellen
fellow traveller ['feləʊ 'trævlə]	Mitreisende/r
do for a living [duː fər ə 'lɪvɪŋ]	den Lebensunterhalt verdienen
persuade [pə'sweɪd]	überreden, überzeugen
a total stranger [ə ˌtəʊtl 'streɪndʒə]	eine völlig fremde Person
life story [laɪf 'stɔːri]	Lebensgeschichte
lost [lɒst]	Verg.-Form v. lose: verlieren
lose touch with someone [luːz tʌtʃ wɪð 'sʌmwʌn]	den Kontakt zu jdm. verlieren

2B

gaze [geɪz]	starren
re-plan [ˌriː'plæn]	neu planen
tricky ['trɪki]	schwierig, heikel
flirt [flɜːt]	flirten
outrageous [aʊt'reɪdʒəsli]	schamlos
the opposite sex [ðɪ 'ɒpəzɪt seks]	das andere Geschlecht
make a fortune [meɪk ə 'fɔːtʃuːn]	ein Vermögen machen
free up the mind [friː ʌp ðə 'maɪnd]	einen klaren Kopf bekommen
interrupt [ˌɪntə'rʌpt]	unterbrechen
indulge oneself [ɪn'dʌldʒ wʌn'self]	sich verwöhnen

2C

advert = advertisement ['ædvɜːt] [əd'vɜːtɪsmənt]	Annonce, Anzeige

3

in ten years' time [ɪn ˌten jɪəz 'taɪm]	in zehn Jahren

3A

lorry ['lɒri]	Lastwagen, Lkw
railway network ['reɪlweɪ ˌnetwɜːk]	Schienennetz
reduce [rɪ'djuːs]	verringern, kürzen
enter ['entə]	betreten, hier: hineinfahren
car-owner [kɑːr 'əʊnə]	Fahrzeugbesitzer/in
park [pɑːk]	parken
prevent [prɪ'vent]	verhindern
traffic jam ['træfɪkdʒæm]	Verkehrsstau
electric car [ɪˌlektrɪk 'kɑː]	Elektroauto
horse [hɔːs]	Pferd
in order to [ɪn 'ɔːdə tuː]	um zu
speed limit ['spiːd ˌlɪmɪt]	Geschwindigkeitsbegrenzung
lower ['ləʊə]	senken, verringern, herabsetzen

3C

solve [sɒlv]	lösen (Problem usw.)

4

announcement [ə'naʊnsmənt]	hier: Durchsage

4A

Geneva [dʒə'niːvə]	Genf
gate [geɪt]	Tor; hier: Flugsteig

4B

platform ['plætfɔːm]	Bahnsteig
get on [get ɒn]	einsteigen (Bahn, Bus, Flugzeug)
come in [kʌm ɪn]	hier: einfahren
sideways ['saɪdweɪz]	seitlich, seitwärts

4C

car park ['kɑːpɑːk]	Parkplatz, Parkhaus
landlord ['lænlɔːd]	hier: Gastwirt

5

giving directions ['gɪvɪŋ daɪ'rekʃnz]	den Weg beschreiben

5A

cross [krɒs]	überqueren
look out for [lʊk aʊt fɔː]	achten auf, Ausschau halten nach
turn [tɜːn]	hier: drehen, umdrehen, abbiegen
motorway ['məʊtəweɪ]	Autobahn
junction ['dʒʌŋkʃn]	Kreuzung, Abfahrt
sign [saɪn]	Schild, Hinweistafel
straight on [streɪt ɒn]	geradeaus weiter
railway bridge ['reɪlweɪ brɪdʒ]	Eisenbahnbrücke
bridge [brɪdʒ]	Brücke

UNIT 12

too far [ˌtuː ˈfɑː]	zu weit
run [rʌn]	*hier:* fahren
change [tʃeɪndʒ]	*hier:* umsteigen
it's the Blackpool line [ɪts ðə ˈblækpuːl ˌlaɪn]	*etwa:* es ist der Zug in Richtung Blackpool
luggage [ˈlʌɡɪdʒ]	Gepäck
Bradford; Leeds [ˈbrædfəd] [liːdz]	*Städte in der engl. Grafschaft Yorkshire*
Temple Meads [ˈtempl miːdz]	*Hauptbahnhof von Bristol*

5 B

plan a route [plæn ə ruːt]	eine Strecke planen
route [ruːt]	Reiseroute, Strecke
necessary [ˈnesəsəri]	notwendig, nötig
bus stop [ˈbʌsstɒp]	Bushaltestelle

6 A

want to [wɒnt tuː]	wollen

6 B

phone box [ˈfəʊnbɒks]	Telefonhäuschen, -zelle

7 A

by rail [baɪ ˈreɪl]	mit der Eisenbahn
shilling [ˈʃɪlɪŋ]	*ehem. englische Münze: Schilling*
pence [pens]	*Mz. v. penny (Münze)*
create [kriːˈeɪt]	schaffen, erschaffen; *hier:* gründen
advertise [ˈædvətaɪz]	Reklame machen für, werben
despite [dɪˈspaɪt]	trotz
problem [ˈprɒbləm]	Problem
promote [prəˈməʊt]	fördern, unterstützen
international [ˌɪntəˈnæʃənl]	international
understanding [ˌʌndəˈstændɪŋ]	Verständnis
hardheaded [ˌhɑːdˈhedɪd]	nüchtern, praktisch denkend
believe in [bɪˈliːv ɪn]	glauben an
Baptist [ˈbæptɪst]	Baptist
horse race [ˈhɔːsreɪs]	Pferderennen
guillotining [ˈɡɪlətiːnɪŋ]	Hinrichtung durch die Guillotine
turn into [tɜːn ˈɪntuː]	verwandeln in/zu
profitable [ˈprɒfɪtəbl]	gewinnbringend, einträglich
commercial organization [kəˈmɜːʃl ˌɔːɡənaɪˈzeɪʃn]	Wirtschaftsunternehmen
success [səkˈses]	Erfolg
negotiate [nɪˈɡəʊʃieɪt]	verhandeln
deal [diːl]	Geschäft, Abmachung
group booking [ɡruːp ˈbʊkɪŋ]	Gruppenbuchung
the English Midlands [ði ˌɪŋglɪʃ ˈmɪdləndz]	*etwa:* Mittelengland
organize [ˈɔːɡənaɪz]	organisieren
mainland Europe [ˌmeɪnlənd ˈjʊərəp]	das europäische Festland
collapse [kəˈlæps]	zusammenbrechen
fall [fɔːl]	Sturz, Fall
traveller [ˈtrævlə]	Reisende/r
the Middle East [ðə ˌmɪdl ˈiːst]	der Nahe Osten
the lucky one [ðə ˈlʌki wʌn]	der/die Glückliche
early [ˈɜːli]	früh
package tour [ˈpækɪdʒ tɔː]	Pauschalreise
a party of 70 tourists [ə ˈpɑːti əv ˈsevnti ˈtɔːrɪsts]	eine 70-köpfige Touristengruppe
head for [hed fɔː]	sich aufmachen nach, unterwegs sein nach
Rome [rəʊm]	Rom
it took [ɪt tʊk]	es wurde/n ... benötigt; man brauchte
stagecoach [ˈsteɪdʒkəʊtʃ]	Postkutsche
numerous [ˈnjuːmərəs]	zahlreiche
bullock [ˈbʊlək]	Ochse
get someone over [ɡet ˈsʌmwʌn ˈəʊvə]	*hier:* jdn. herüber-, hinüberbringen
get into [ɡet ˈɪntuː]	*hier:* hineingeraten
difficulty [ˈdɪfɪkəlti]	Schwierigkeit
forward [ˈfɔːwəd]	nach vorne, vorwärts
jabber [ˈdʒæbə]	plappern
Derbyshire [ˈdɑːbɪʃə]	*Grafschaft Derby*
various [ˈveərɪəs]	verschiedene, mehrere
until [ənˈtɪl]	bis
missionary [ˈmɪʃənəri]	Missionar
teetotaller [tiːˈtəʊtlə]	Abstinenzler/in
aim [eɪm]	Ziel, Absicht
pass into [pɑːs ˈɪntuː]	übergehen in
group [ɡruːp]	*hier:* Konzern

7 B

standard of comfort [ˈstændəd əv ˈkʌmfət]	Komfort
idealist [aɪˈdɪəlɪst]	Idealist
taken over [ˈteɪkn ˈəʊvə]	Partizip Perfekt v. *take over:* übernehmen

V

UNIT 12

8

road accident [rəʊd ˈæksɪdənt]	Verkehrsunfall
accident [ˈæksɪdənt]	Unfall, Unglücksfall
in each case [ɪn iːtʃ keɪs]	in jedem Fall; *hier:* jedesmal
given [ˈɡɪvn]	Partizip Perfekt v. *give:* geben
collide [kəˈlaɪd]	zusammenstoßen
crash [kræʃ]	zusammenstoßen, verunglücken
pedestrian [pəˈdestrɪən]	Fußgänger/in
hit [hɪt]	schlagen, stoßen
run over [rʌn ˈəʊvə]	überfahren
lamp-post [ˈlæmppəʊst]	Laternenpfahl
kill [kɪl]	töten
fly [flaɪ]	Fliege
approach [əˈprəʊtʃ]	sich nähern; *hier:* heranfahren
stop sign [ˈstɒpsaɪn]	Stoppschild
unable [ʌnˈeɪbl]	außerstande, unfähig
in time [ɪn taɪm]	rechtzeitig
avoid [əˈvɔɪd]	vermeiden, ausweichen

9A

got on [gɒt ɒn]	Partizip Perfekt v. *get on:* einsteigen (*Bahn, Bus, Flugzeug*)
got off [gɒt ɒf]	Partizip Perfekt v. *get off:* aussteigen (*Bahn, Bus, Flugzeug*)
for a good reason [fər ə gʊd ˈriːzn]	aus gutem Grund
reason [ˈriːzn]	Grund, Ursache

10

rally [ˈrælɪ]	Rallye

PREVIEW D

2

darts [dɑːts]	Darts (*engl. Pfeilwurfspiel*)
Form teams of three to four players.	Bilden Sie Mannschaften aus drei bis vier Spielern.
form [fɔːm]	bilden, formieren
team [tiːm]	Mannschaft, Team
player [ˈpleɪə]	Spieler/in
dartboard [ˈdɑːtbɔːd]	Zielscheibe, Dartboard
sentence starter [ˈsentəns ˈstɑːtə]	Satzanfang
score double points [skɔː ˈdʌbl pɔɪnts]	doppelte Punktzahl erhalten/erzielen
extra points [ˈekstrə pɔɪnts]	Zusatzpunkte

4A

smell [smel]	riechen
feel [fiːl]	fühlen
taste [teɪst]	schmecken

4B

alarm clock [əˈlɑːm klɒk]	Wecker

5A

entertainment [ˌentəˈteɪnmənt]	Unterhaltung
world language [wɜːld ˈlæŋgwɪdʒ]	Weltsprache

UNIT 13

1

good buy [gʊd baɪ]	günstiger Einkauf

1A

a great deal [ə greɪt ˈdiːl]	sehr viel, eine ganze Menge
surroundings [səˈraʊndɪŋz]	Umgebung
charm [tʃɑːm]	Charme, Reiz
leave [liːv]	*hier:* verlassen
shop for something [ˈʃɒp fə ˈsʌmθɪŋ]	etwas einkaufen
variety [vəˈraɪətɪ]	*hier:* Vielfalt
locally grown [ˈləʊkəlɪ grəʊn]	in der Region erzeugt
plus [plʌs]	plus, und
exotics [ɪgˈzɒtɪks]	Exotisches
photocopy [ˈfəʊtəʊˌkɒpɪ]	Fotokopie
get buried [get ˈberɪd]	beerdigt werden
bury [ˈberɪ]	beerdigen, begraben
event [ɪˈvent]	Ereignis
vet [vet]	Tierarzt
video [ˈvɪdɪəʊ]	Video

UNIT 13

post a parcel [pəʊst ə ˈpɑːsl]	ein Paket aufgeben
post [pəʊst]	abschicken, aufgeben (bei d. Post)
parcel [ˈpɑːsl]	Paket, Päckchen
evening class [ˈiːvnɪŋ klɑːs]	Abendschule
actor [ˈæktə]	Schauspieler
souvenir [ˌsuːvəˈnɪə]	Andenken, Souvenir
carpet [ˈkɑːpɪt]	Teppich
Sunday paper [ˌsʌndɪˈpeɪpə]	Sonntagszeitung
health food [ˈhelθfuːd]	Reformkost
injection [ɪnˈdʒekʃn]	Spritze, Injektion
get something done [get ˈsʌmθɪŋ dʌn]	etwas machen lassen
clean [kliːn]	reinigen, säubern
repair [rɪˈpeə]	reparieren
groceries [ˈgrəʊsərɪz]	Lebensmittel
deliver [dɪˈlɪvə]	liefern, anliefern
fill [fɪl]	füllen
get one's hair done [get wʌnz ˈheə dʌn]	zum Friseur gehen
in many a town [ɪn ˈmenɪ ə taʊn]	in vielen (anderen) Städten (altmodisch)
besides [bɪˈsaɪdz]	außer, abgesehen von
shopping [ˈʃɒpɪŋ]	hier: Einkäufe
ignition [ɪgˈnɪʃn]	Zündung; hier: Zündschloß
while [waɪl]	während
What is the point of this article? [wɒt ɪz ðə ˈpɔɪnt əv ðɪs ˈɑːtɪkl]	Worum geht es bei diesem Artikel eigentlich?
article [ˈɑːtɪkl]	Artikel, Zeitungsartikel
One should appreciate things while one has them. [wʌn ʃʊd əˈpriːʃieɪt θɪŋz waɪl wʌn ˈhæz ðəm]	Man sollte die Dinge zu schätzen wissen, solange man sie noch hat.
sincerely [sɪnˈsɪəlɪ]	ernsthaft, aufrichtig
almost certainly [ˈɔːlməʊst ˈsɜːtənlɪ]	fast sicher/gewiß
gone for ever [gɒn fər ˈevə]	für immer verschwunden
gone [gɒn]	Partizip Perfekt v. go: gehen
may be [meɪ biː]	ist/sind vielleicht
survive [səˈvaɪv]	überleben
what about ...? [wɒt əˈbaʊt]	wie steht's mit ...?

1B

Have you been to the hairdresser's recently? [hæv ju bɪn tʊ ðə ˈheəˌdresəz ˈriːsntlɪ]	Warst du in der letzten Zeit beim Friseur?
hairdresser [ˈheəˌdresə]	Friseur, Friseuse
Neither have I. [ˌnaɪðə həv ˈaɪ]	Ich auch nicht.
library [ˈlaɪbrərɪ]	Bücherei, Bibliothek

1C

dry cleaner's [ˌdraɪˈkliːnəz]	chemische Reinigung
florist's [ˈflɒrɪsts]	Blumengeschäft
off licence [ˈɒfˌlaɪsəns]	Wein- und Spirituosengeschäft
stationer's [ˈsteɪʃənəz]	Schreibwarenhandlung

1D

author	Autor, Verfasser

2

Help! [help]	Hilfe!

2B

I'm afraid [aɪm əˈfreɪd]	Ich fürchte, ... / Leider ...
there's something wrong with [ðeəz ˈsʌmθɪŋ rɒŋ wɪθ]	irgendetwas stimmt nicht mit
sandals [ˈsændlz]	Sandalen
video camera [ˈvɪdɪəʊ ˌkæmərə]	Videokamera
rotten [ˈrɒtn]	faul, verfault
recommend [ˌrekəˈmend]	empfehlen

3

class shopping survey [klɑːs ˈʃɒpɪŋ ˌsɜːveɪ]	Kursumfrage über Einkaufsgewohnheiten
survey [ˈsɜːveɪ]	Umfrage, Gutachten, Überblick

4

the shopping game [ðə ˈʃɒpɪŋ geɪm]	das Einkaufsspiel
follow the instructions in the square you land on	befolgen Sie die Anweisungen auf den Feldern, auf denen Sie auskommen
type of shop	Art v. Laden

UNIT 13

make up an appropriate dialogue	führen Sie ein entsprechendes Gespräch
study the board	schauen Sie sich den Spielplan an
a guide to camping in Britain [ə ˌgaɪd tʊ ˈkæmpɪŋ ɪn ˈbrɪtən]	ein Campingführer für Großbritannien
sunburn [ˈsʌnbɜːn]	Sonnenbrand
Take in a coat for cleaning. [teɪk ɪn ə ˈkəʊt fə ˈkliːnɪŋ]	Bringen Sie einen Mantel zur Reinigung.
pick up [pɪk ˈʌp]	*hier:* abholen
hire [ˈhaɪə]	mieten; *hier:* ausleihen
whole [həʊl]	ganze/r/s
radio alarm clock [ˌreɪdɪəʊ əˈlɑːm klɒk]	Radiowecker
writing paper [ˈraɪtɪŋ ˌpeɪpə]	Schreibpapier
You can move in any direction along the paths.	Sie dürfen auf den vorgegebenen Wegen in beliebiger Richtung ziehen.
Start/Finish square	Start- und Zielfeld
queue [kjuː]	Warteschlange
Miss a turn. [mɪs ə ˈtɜːn]	Einmal aussetzen.
Go straight to the clothes shop. [ɡəʊ ˈstreɪt tʊ ðə ˈkləʊðz ʃɒp]	Gehen Sie auf direktem Weg zum Bekleidungsgeschäft.
umbrella [ʌmˈbrelə]	Regenschirm
special offer [ˌspeʃl ˈɒfə]	Sonderangebot
electrical goods [ɪˈlektrɪkl ɡʊdz]	Elektroartikel
No money left! [nəʊ ˈmʌnɪ left]	Sie haben kein Geld mehr übrig!

5 C

Check with the picture to see how well you did.	Überprüfen Sie anhand des Bildes, wie Sie abgeschnitten haben.

6

babies [ˈbeɪbɪz]	*hier:* Minipackung
Brie [briː]	Brie *(Käse)*
cream [kriːm]	Sahne
jar [dʒɑː]	Glas, Glasbehälter
gin [dʒɪn]	Gin *(alk. Getränk)*
pot [pɒt]	Topf; *hier:* Becher
sweet (wine) [swiːt]	lieblich *(Wein)*
sweets [swiːts]	Bonbons, Süßigkeiten
wrap [ræp]	einwickeln, einpacken
packet [ˈpækɪt]	Päckchen
dozen [ˈdʌzn]	Dutzend
chocolate bar [ˈtʃɒklət bɑː]	Schokoladenriegel
type [taɪp]	Art, Typ
biscuit [ˈbɪskɪt]	Plätzchen, Keks
shake [ʃeɪk]	*hier:* zittern
all this here stuff [ɔːl ðɪs hɪə ˈstʌf]	all dieses Zeug hier
an awful lot less [ən ˌɔːfl lɒt ˈles]	*etwa:* viel weniger
more than enough [ˌmɔː ðən ɪˈnʌf]	mehr als genug
rot [rɒt]	verfaulen lassen
Cheddar, Stilton, Chester [ˈtʃedə] [ˈstɪltən] [ˈtʃestə]	*engl. Käsesorten*
How shall I choose? [ˌhaʊ ʃəl aɪ ˈtʃuːz]	*etwa:* Wie soll ich mich bloß entscheiden?
Which cheese shall it be? [wɪtʃ ˈtʃiːz ʃəl ɪt ˈbiː]	Welcher Käse soll es sein?
Trying to pick one brings me out in spots. [ˌtraɪɪŋ tʊ ˈpɪk wʌn ˈbrɪŋz mɪ aʊt ɪn ˈspɒts]	*etwa:* Die Qual der Wahl macht mich ganz krank.
spot [spɒt]	*hier:* Pickel
animal fat [ˈænɪml fæt]	tierisches Fett
heart attack [ˈhɑːt əˌtæk]	Herzinfarkt
jumbo [ˈdʒʌmbəʊ]	*hier:* Riesenpackung
cornflake variety [ˈkɔːnfleɪk vəˈraɪətɪ]	die Vielfalt an Cornflakes
amaze [əˈmeɪz]	verblüffen
ninety-five p (p = pence) [ˈnaɪntɪˌfaɪv piː] [pens]	95 Pence
I silently scream! [aɪ ˈsaɪləntlɪ skriːm]	*etwa:* Ich schreie in mich hinein!
peace of mind [ˌpiːs əv ˈmaɪnd]	Seelenfrieden
port [pɔːt]	Port(wein)
kiwi-fruit cocktail [ˈkiːwiːˌfruːt ˈkɒkteɪl]	Kiwi-Fruchtcocktail
vodka [ˈvɒdkə]	Wodka
total confusion [ˌtəʊtl kənˈfjuːʒn]	völlige Verwirrung
the state that I'm in [ðə ˈsteɪt ðət aɪm ɪn]	der Zustand, in dem ich mich zur Zeit befinde

UNIT 13

state [steɪt]	hier: Zustand
medium dry [ˌmiːdɪəm 'draɪ]	halbtrocken
I'm dead on my feet [aɪm 'ded ɒn maɪ 'fiːt]	etwa: Ich bin völlig erschlagen

7A

basement ['beɪsmənt]	Keller, Untergeschoß
computer equipment [kəm'pjuːtər ɪ'kwɪpmənt]	Computerzubehör
sports clothes and equipment ['spɔːts ˌkləʊðz and ɪ'kwɪpmənt]	Sportbekleidung und Ausrüstung
travel agency ['trævl ˌeɪdʒənsɪ]	Reisebüro

7B

toiletries ['tɔɪlətrɪz]	Toilettenartikel

7D

shopping centre ['ʃɒpɪŋˌsentə]	Einkaufszentrum
upper floor [ˌʌpə 'flɔː]	Obergeschoß
lower floor [ˌləʊə 'flɔː]	Untergeschoß

8

store manager [stɔː 'mænədʒə]	Geschäftsführer eines Kaufhauses, Filialleiter

8A

sell quickly/slowly [sel 'kwɪklɪ/sel 'sləʊlɪ]	sich gut/schlecht verkaufen
make a good profit [meɪk ə gʊd 'prɒfɪt]	einen guten Profit erzielen

8C

according to Peter Willems [ə'kɔːdɪŋ tʊ 'piːtə 'wɪləmz]	Laut Peter Willems
at the front of the store [ət ðə 'frʌnt əv ðə 'stɔː]	vorne im Geschäft
at the back of the store [ət ðə 'bæk əv ðə 'stɔː]	hinten im Geschäft
at the top of the store [ət ðə 'tɒp əv ðə 'stɔː]	im oberen Stockwerk des Geschäfts

9

service ['sɜːvɪs]	hier: Dienstleistung, Kundendienst

9A

brought [brɔːt]	Verg.-Form v. bring: bringen
counter ['kaʊntə]	Schalter, Theke
shorten ['ʃɔːtn]	kürzen, verkürzen
delivery [dɪ'lɪvərɪ]	Lieferung, Anlieferung
oil [ɔɪl]	hier: Motoröl
tyre ['taɪə]	Reifen
windscreen ['wɪndskriːn]	Windschutzscheibe
give someone a funny look [gɪv 'sʌmwʌn ə 'fʌnɪ lʊk]	jdn. verblüfft/merkwürdig anschauen
funny ['fʌnɪ]	lustig, komisch

9B

service economy	Dienstleistungsgesellschaft
put something to the test	etwas auf die Probe stellen
the customer is always right [ðə 'kʌstəmər ɪz 'ɔːlweɪz raɪt]	der Kunde hat immer recht
in theory at least [ɪn 'θɪərɪ ət liːst]	zumindest in der Theorie
reporter [rɪ'pɔːtə]	Reporter/in, Berichterstatter/in
typical ['tɪpɪkl]	typisch
entire [ɪn'taɪə]	ganz, vollständig
even if [ˌiːvn 'ɪf]	selbst wenn
waitress ['weɪtrɪs]	Kellnerin
not at all [nɒt ət 'ɔːl]	überhaupt nicht, keineswegs
joke [dʒəʊk]	Witz, Scherz
fresh order [freʃ 'ɔːdə]	neue Bestellung
queue [kjuː]	sich anstellen, Schlange stehen
discover [dɪ'skʌvə]	hier: feststellen, bemerken
put something back [pʊt 'sʌmθɪŋ bæk]	hier: etwas zurückgeben
cashier [kæ'ʃɪə]	Kassierer/in
Von's Supermarket [vɒnz 'suːpəˌmɑːkɪt]	Supermarktkette in den USA
till [tɪl]	Kasse, Schalter
whenever [wen'evə]	immer wenn, sobald
eye contact ['aɪ kɒntækt]	Augenkontakt
petrol station attendant ['petrəl ˌsteɪʃn ə'tendənt]	Tankwart

V

empty ['emtɪ]	leeren
ashtray ['æʃtreɪ]	Aschenbecher
efficiently [ɪ'fɪʃəntlɪ]	*hier:* sorgfältig
jokingly ['dʒəʊkɪŋlɪ]	scherzhaft
disabled [dɪs'eɪbld]	behindert, invalide
Wells Fargo [ˌwelz 'fɑːgəʊ]	*Bankgesellschaft in den USA*
promise ['prɒmɪs]	versprechen
credit ['kredɪt]	gutschreiben, vergüten
account [ə'kaʊnt]	*hier:* Bankkonto
quick service counter [kwɪk 'sɜːvɪs 'kaʊntə]	Schnellkasse
response [rɪ'spɒns]	Antwort, Reaktion
request [rɪ'kwest]	Bitte, Anfrage
simple ['sɪmpl]	einfach, simpel
transaction [træn'zækʃn]	Geschäftsvorgang, Transaktion
present ['preznt]	*hier:* anwesend, gegenwärtig
treated poorly by Western standards ['triːtɪd 'pɔːlɪ baɪ 'westən 'stændədz]	nach westlichen Maßstäben schlecht behandelt
treat [triːt]	behandeln
poorly ['pɔːlɪ]	*hier:* armselig
standard ['stændəd]	Maßstab, Norm
be questioned [biː 'kwestʃnd]	be-, gefragt werden
neither ... nor ['naɪðə nɔː]	weder ... noch
noon [nuːn]	Mittag (12 Uhr)
opening hours [ˌəʊpnɪŋ 'aʊəz]	Öffnungszeit(en)
guaranteed [ˌgærən'tiːd]	garantiert; *hier:* festgelegt
delivery time [dɪ'lɪvərɪ taɪm]	Lieferzeit

9 C

salesperson ['seɪlzˌpɜːsn]	Verkäufer/in
unfriendly [ʌn'frendlɪ]	unfreundlich

10 A

puzzle ['pʌzl]	Puzzle, Rätsel
clues [kluːz]	*hier:* Beschreibungen für das Worträtsel

Unit 14

preview ['priːvjuː]	Vorschau
documentary [ˌdɒkjʊ'mentərɪ]	Dokumentarfilm
DNA [ˌdiːen'eɪ]	DNS (*Erbgut*)
drama ['drɑːmə]	Drama, Schauspiel
star [stɑː]	Hauptrolle spielen
follow up ['fɒləʊ ʌp]	*hier:* Nachfolgestück
Presumed Innocent [prɪ'zjuːmd 'ɪnəsənt]	*etwa:* Für unschuldig befunden (*Titel*)
comedy ['kɒmədɪ]	Komödie, Kabarett
the Edinburgh Fringe [ðɪ 'edɪnbərə frɪndʒ]	*Alternativprogramm zum Edinburgh Festival*
pick of the week [pɪk əv ðə 'wiːk]	*etwa:* Höhepunkt der Woche
fixture ['fɪkstʃə]	*hier:* Spielplan
award-winner [ə'wɔːd ˌwɪnə]	Preisträger
pop [pɒp]	Popmusik
Proms [prɒmz]	Promenadenkonzerte
far flung recipe [ˌfɑː'flʌŋ 'resɪpɪ]	*etwa:* exotisches Rezept
guide [gaɪd]	*hier:* Programmzeitschrift
satellite ['sætəlaɪt]	Satellit
regulars ['regjʊləz]	*hier:* regelmäßige Programme
strawberry ['strɔːbərɪ]	Erdbeere
plant [plɑːnt]	Pflanze
infertility treatment [ˌɪnfə'tɪlətɪ 'triːtmənt]	Behandlung von Unfruchtbarkeit
rank [ræŋk]	rangieren
medical ['medɪkl]	medizinisch
priority [praɪ'ɒrətɪ]	Vorrang, Priorität
star [stɑː]	Stern
the week ahead [ðə wiːk ə'hed]	die kommende Woche

2

Square-eyed Europe ['skweəraɪd 'jʊərəp]	*etwa:* Europa mit dem Fernsehblick

2A

series ['sɪərɪz]	Serie
game show ['geɪmʃəʊ]	Spielshow, Gameshow
everywhere ['evrɪweə]	überall
attract [ə'trækt]	anziehen
viewer ['vjuːə]	Zuschauer/in

UNIT 14

football match ['fʊtbɔːl mætʃ]	Fußballspiel
soap (opera) [səʊp 'ɒpərə]	Seifenoper, Fernsehserie
go for [gəʊ fɔː]	*hier:* bevorzugen, stehen auf
whereas [weər'æz]	wohingegen, während
week for week [wiːk fə wiːk]	Woche für Woche
guarantee [ˌgærən'tiː]	Garantie
family saga ['fæməlɪ 'sɑːgə]	Familiensaga
anywhere else ['enɪweər els]	irgendwo sonst

3A

you own your own European TV station	Sie besitzen Ihren eigenen europäischen Fernsehsender
own [əʊn]	besitzen
one's own [wʌnz əʊn]	jemandes eigene/s/r
charge [tʃɑːdʒ]	*hier:* berechnen
maximum ['mæksɪməm]	Maximum; *hier:* Höchstbetrag
advertising time ['ædvətaɪzɪŋ taɪm]	Werbezeit
work out [wɜːk aʊt]	*hier:* erarbeiten
below [bɪ'ləʊ]	unten, untenstehend
commission [kə'mɪʃn]	in Auftrag geben
definitely ['defɪnɪtlɪ]	ganz sicher/gewiß
couch [kaʊtʃ]	Couch, Sofa
president ['prezɪdənt]	Präsident
European Commission [ˌjʊərə'pɪən kə'mɪʃn]	Europäische Kommission
cardboard ['kɑːdbɔːd]	Pappe, Karton
homelessness ['həʊmləsnəs]	Obdachlosigkeit
News Nuggets ['njuːz ˌnʌgɪts]	*etwa:* die wichtigsten Nachrichten in Kürze
nugget ['nʌgɪt]	(Gold) Klumpen
highlight ['haɪlaɪt]	Höhepunkt, Highlight
regional ['riːdʒənəl]	regional
Black Forest [blæk 'fɒrɪst]	Schwarzwald
featuring ... ['fiːtʃərɪŋ]	in der Hauptrolle mit ...
long-distance lorry driver [ˌlɒŋ 'dɪstəns 'lɒrɪ ˌdraɪvə]	Fernfahrer/in
baldy ['bɔːldɪ]	Glatzkopf
share a flat [ʃeər ə 'flæt]	zusammen wohnen
on the ball [ɒn ðə 'bɔːl]	am Ball
hit [hɪt]	Hit (*Schlager usw.*)
blackbird ['blækbɜːd]	Amsel
based on [beɪst ɒn]	basierend auf, nach
best-selling romantic novel ['bestˌselɪŋ rəʊ'mæntɪk 'nɒvl]	Romanbestseller
classic ['klæsɪk]	Klassiker
re-run ['riːrʌn]	Wiederholung
Ecu (=European Currency Unit) ['ekjuː] [ˌjʊərə'pɪən 'kʌrənsɪ 'juːnɪt]	Ecu (*europ. Währungseinheit*)

3B

schedule ['ʃedjuːl]	*hier:* Sendeplan

4A

warn about [wɔːn ə'baʊt]	warnen vor
rhyme [raɪm]	Reim
so far as children are concerned [səʊ fɑːr əz 'tʃɪldrən ə kən'sɜːnd]	wenn es um Kinder geht
concerned [kən'sɜːnd]	betroffen
television set [ˌtelɪ'vɪʒn set]	Fernseher, Fernsehapparat
idiotic [ɪdɪ'ɒtɪk]	idiotisch, blödsinnig
almost ['ɔːlməʊst]	beinahe, fast
gape [geɪp]	gähnen
screen [skriːn]	*hier:* Bildschirm, Glotze
stare [steə]	starren
hypnotize ['hɪpnətaɪz]	hypnotisieren
climb [klaɪm]	klettern
window sill ['wɪndəʊsɪl]	Fensterbrett, Fensterbank
kick [kɪk]	treten
punch [pʌntʃ]	schlagen
sink [sɪŋk]	Spüle
beloved tot [bɪ'lʌvɪd tɒt]	geliebter Knirps
install [ɪn'stɔːl]	einrichten, installieren
still [stɪl]	*hier:* still, ruhig

4C

educational [ˌedʒʊ'keɪʃnəl]	erzieherisch
value ['væljuː]	Wert

5

mood music ['muːd ˌmjuːsɪk]	stimmungsvolle Musik

V

UNIT 14

5A
imagine [ɪˈmædʒɪn]	sich vorstellen
scene [siːn]	Szene; *hier:* Bild

5B
peaceful [ˈpiːsfʊl]	friedlich

6
slogan [ˈsləʊgən]	Werbespruch, Slogan

7A
grid	Gitter, Netz; *hier:* Tabelle
collection [kəˈlekʃn]	Sammlung, Kollektion
blues [bluːz]	Blues
cassette [kəˈset]	*hier:* Musikkassette
violin player [ˌvaɪəˈlɪn ˈpleɪə]	Geigenspieler/in
guitarist [gɪˈtɑːrɪst]	Gitarrist/in
pianist [ˈpɪənɪst]	Pianist/in
clarinet [ˌklærəˈnet]	Klarinette
My baby's left my lily pad –	Mein Baby hat meine Seerose verlassen –
my legs were both deep fried	meine Schenkel waren in Fett gebraten
I eat flies all day and when I'm gone they'll stick me in formaldehyde.	Ich esse Fliegen den ganzen Tag lang und wenn ich sterbe bettet man mich in Formaldehyd.
I got the greens real bad	Ich fühle mich richtig mies (*'the greens'* = *Anspielung auf 'the blues'*)

7C
choir [ˈkwaɪə]	Chor
dislike [dɪsˈlaɪk]	nicht mögen
local radio station [ˈləʊkl ˈreɪdɪəʊ ˌsteɪʃn]	lokale Radiostation
Number One [ˌnʌmbə ˈwʌn]	*hier:* Nummer eins in der Hitparade

8
talent show [ˈtælənt ʃəʊ]	Talentshow
perform [pəˈfɔːm]	aufführen, vortragen, spielen
recite [rɪˈsaɪt]	aufsagen, vortragen
arrogantly [ˈærəgəntlɪ]	arrogant
carefully [ˈkeəfʊlɪ]	sorgfältig

UNIT 15

1
God [gɒd]	Gott

1B
translation [trænsˈleɪʃn]	Übersetzung

1C
acrostic	Akrostichon (*Vers, bei dem die Anfangsbuchstaben der einzelnen Zeilen einen Begriff ergeben*)
native speaker [ˌneɪtɪv ˈspiːkə]	Muttersprachler/in
go crazy [gəʊ ˈkreɪzɪ]	verrückt werden, durchdrehen

1D
stop [stɒp]	aufhören

2
Sorry? [ˈsɒrɪ]	*hier:* Wie bitte? Verzeihung?
What was that again? [wɒt wəz ðæt əˈgen]	*etwa:* Was haben Sie da gesagt? Würden Sie das bitte noch einmal sagen?

2A
I'm afraid I didn't get that. [aɪm əˈfreɪd aɪ ˈdɪdnt ˈget ðæt]	*etwa:* Ich habe Sie leider nicht verstanden.
a three-hour drive [ə ˈθriː aʊə draɪv]	eine dreistündige Autofahrt
get in [get ɪn]	*hier:* eintreffen, ankommen
you'd better … [jʊd ˈbetə]	es wäre/ist besser, wenn du/Sie …
in that case [ɪn ˈðæt keɪs]	in diesem Fall
order number [ˈɔːdə ˈnʌmbə]	Bestellnummer

2B
motorway junction [ˌməʊtəweɪ ˈdʒʌŋkʃn]	Autobahnkreuz, -dreieck
by how much exactly [baɪ haʊ ˈmʌtʃ ɪgˈzæktlɪ]	um wieviel genau

UNIT 15

present price ['preznt praɪs]	aktueller Preis, derzeitiger Preis
place an order [pleɪs ˯ ɒn ˯ 'ɔːdə]	eine Bestellung aufgeben

3A
reader ['riːdə]	Leser/in
ghost [gəʊst]	Gespenst, Geist
melody ['melədɪ]	Melodie
queen [kwiːn]	Königin

3C
class vote	Abstimmung in der Klasse

4A
Germanic [dʒɜːˈmænɪk]	germanisch
Latin ['lætɪn]	lateinisch
North America [nɔːθ ˯ əˈmerɪkə]	Nordamerika
basis ['beɪsɪs]	Basis, Grundlage
spoken ['spəʊkn]	Partizip Perfekt v. *speak:* sprechen
tribe [traɪb]	(Volks)Stamm
everyday ['evrɪdeɪ]	alltäglich
Old English [əʊld 'ɪŋglɪʃ]	Altenglisch (*etwa 7.–11. Jhd.*)
Christianity [ˌkrɪstɪˈænətɪ]	Christentum
monk [mʌŋk]	Mönch
nun [nʌn]	Nonne
bishop ['bɪʃəp]	Bischof
Dane [deɪn]	Däne, Dänin
Norwegian [nɔːˈwiːdʒən]	Norweger/in
Norman ['nɔːmən]	Normanne
conquer ['kɒŋkə]	erobern
court [kɔːt]	Hof
law [lɔː]	Recht, Gesetz
Middle English ['mɪdl 'ɪŋglɪʃ]	Mittelenglisch
period ['pɪərɪəd]	Zeitraum, Periode
it is only in the last 150 years [ɪt ˯ ɪz ˯ 'əʊnlɪ ˯ ɪn ðə lɑːst ˯ ˌwʌnˈhʌndrəd ˯ ənd 'fɪftɪ 'jɪəz]	erst in den letzten 150 Jahren
growth [grəʊθ]	Anwachsen, Wachstum
the British Empire [ðə ˌbrɪtɪʃ ˯ 'empaɪə]	das britische Weltreich
India ['ɪndɪə]	Indien
settler ['setlə]	Siedler/in
factor ['fæktə]	Faktor
arrival [əˈraɪvl]	Ankunft, Eintreffen
Atlantic coast [ətˈlæntɪk ˯ kəʊst]	Atlantikküste
economic [ˌiːkəˈnɒmɪk]	wirtschaftlich
influence ['ɪnfluəns]	Einfluß

5A
play for time [pleɪ fə ˯ 'taɪm]	auf Zeit spielen, Zeit schinden

5C
hairstyle ['heəstaɪl]	Frisur

6
riddle ['rɪdl]	Rätsel

6A
palace ['pælɪs]	Palast
core [kɔː]	Kern
wherein she may be [weərˈɪn ʃɪ meɪ 'biː]	worin sie wohnen darf
unlock [ˌʌnˈlɒk]	aufschließen

7
definition [ˌdefɪˈnɪʃn]	Definition, Erklärung
stuff [stʌf]	Zeug, Stoff

8A
hardly ['hɑːdlɪ]	kaum, kaum noch
employer [ɪmˈplɔɪə]	Arbeitgeber/in
primary school ['praɪmərɪ skuːl]	Grundschule
official European language [əˈfɪʃl ˌjʊərəˈpɪən 'læŋgwɪdʒ]	europäische Amtssprache
official [əˈfɪʃl]	offiziell

8C
foreign language ['fɒrən 'læŋgwɪdʒ]	Fremdsprache
taught [tɔːt]	Partizip Perfekt v. *teach:* lehren
multilingual [ˌmʌltɪˈlɪŋgwəl]	mehrsprachig, multilingual

10
accent ['æksent]	Akzent

PREVIEW E

1
connection [kəˈnekʃn]	Verbindung
left [left]	Partizip Perfekt v. *leave:* verlassen

V

PREVIEW E

logical explanation ['lɒdʒɪkl ˌekspləˈneɪʃn] — logische Erklärung
logical ['lɒdʒɪkl] — logisch
make up [ˌmeɪk ˈʌp] — *hier:* erfinden

2
Truth or lies? [truːθ ɔː laɪz] — Wahrheit oder Lügen?

3
cartoon [kɑːˈtuːn] — Kartoon, Zeichnung
hang up [hæŋ ʌp] — *hier:* aufhängen

4
course project [kɔːs ˈprɒdʒekt] — Kursprojekt
opinion poll [əˈpɪnjən pəʊl] — Meinungsumfrage
review [rɪˈvjuː] — *hier:* Rezension, Kritik
hunt [hʌnt] — jagen; *hier:* aufspüren
drawing [ˈdrɔːɪŋ] — Zeichnung

5
diploma [dɪˈpləʊmə] — Diplom
pretend [prɪˈtend] — vortäuschen
somewhere [ˈsʌmweə] — irgendwo

Personal and place names — Personennamen und Ortsnamen

Dieses Verzeichnis enthält alle englischen Namen, die in BRIDGES 2 vorkommen und die nicht schon auf der Cassette oder im Kapitel-Verzeichnis erwähnt werden. Hier finden Sie auch einige Namen, die in Englisch anders ausgesprochen werden.

1/4B	Rusty [ˈrʌstɪ]	
	the Caldwells [ðə ˈkɔːldwelz]	
1/9	The Beatles [ðə ˈbiːtlz]	
2/1B	Iris Clark [ˈaɪrɪs klɑːk]	
	Ann Holden [æn ˈhəʊldən]	
	Tony Nicholls [ˈtəʊnɪ ˈnɪklz]	
	Jenny Robinson [ˈdʒenɪ ˈrɒbɪnsən]	
	George Small [ˈdʒɔːdʒ smɔːl]	
	Kevin Wall [ˈkevɪn wɔːl]	
2/2C	Smith [smɪθ]	
	Jones [dʒəʊnz]	
	Diane [daɪˈæn]	
	Peter [ˈpiːtə]	
	David [ˈdeɪvɪd]	
2/8D	Bob Dylan [bɒb ˈdɪlən]	
2/9B	John Keats [dʒɒn kiːts]	
2/9C	George Bernard Shaw [dʒɔːdʒ ˈbɜːnəd ʃɔː]	
3/3A	Bridget [ˈbrɪdʒɪt]	
	Jim [dʒɪm]	
	Graham [ˈgreɪəm]	
	Sue [suː]	
	Eric [ˈerɪk]	
	Shirley [ˈʃɜːlɪ]	
3/3E	Wilson [ˈwɪlsn]	
3/4A	Christine [ˈkrɪstiːn]	
	Carol [ˈkærəl]	
3/4A	Edinburgh [ˈedɪnbərə]	
	York [jɔːk]	
3/7B	Sophie Bernstein [ˈsəʊfɪ ˈbɜːnstiːn]	
Pr.A/6	Four Seasons [fɔː ˈsiːznz]	
4/3A	Carole McKendrick [ˈkærəl məˈkendrɪk]	
4/3C	Professor Schnabel [prəˈfesə ˈʃnɑːbl]	
4/5B	Joy Stick [dʒɔɪ stɪk]	
4/6A	Sally [ˈsælɪ]	
	Molly Burnett [ˈmɒlɪ bɜːˈnet]	
4/9D	Amsterdam [ˈæmstəˌdæm]	
5/1B	David Pryce-Jones [ˈdeɪvɪd ˌpraɪs ˈdʒəʊnz]	
	Wendy Cope [ˈwendɪ kəʊp]	
	Walter de la Mare [ˈwɔːltə dəlæˈmeə]	
	Rolling Stones [ˈrəʊlɪŋ stəʊnz]	
	Kim Dammers [kɪm ˈdæməz]	
	Bob Marley [bɒb ˈmɑːlɪ]	
5/3B	Queen's Court [kwiːnz kɔːt]	
5/7A	Simon [ˈsaɪmən]	
5/8C	Maria [məˈrɪə]	
	Robert [ˈrɒbət]	
6/1B	Czechoslovakia [ˌtʃekəsləʊˈvækɪə]	
	Hungary [ˈhʌŋgərɪ]	
	Russia [ˈrʌʃə]	
6/4B	Mannheim [ˈmænhaɪm]	
	Zurich [ˈzjʊərɪk]	
	Prague [prɑːg]	
	Venice [ˈvenɪs]	
6/5	Botswana [bɒˈtswɑːnə]	
	Zimbabwe [zɪmˈbɑːbwɪ]	
	Amberley Road [ˈæmbəlɪ ˈrəʊd]	
	Westbury [ˈwestbərɪ]	
	Bignor [ˈbɪgnə]	
	Pulborough [ˈpʊlbərə]	
	Perth [pɜːθ]	
	Sussex [ˈsʌsɪks]	
	Nile [naɪl]	

Names

	Cairo [ˈkaɪrəʊ]	10/5B	Atlantic [ətˈlæntɪk]
	Aswan [ˈæsˈwɑːn]	11/2A	Carole Wood [ˈkærəl wʊd]
	Wallace [ˈwɒlɪs]		Portsmouth [ˈpɔːtsməθ]
	Dorking [ˈdɔːkɪŋ]		Valerie White [ˈvælərɪ waɪt]
	Surrey [ˈsʌrɪ]	11/4A	Frances Politzer [ˈfrɑːnsɪs ˈpɒlɪtsə]
	Egypt Air [ˈiːdʒɪpt eə]	11/4B	Susie [ˈsuːzɪ]
	Quebec [kwɪˈbek]		Charlie Brown [ˈtʃɑːlɪ braʊn]
	Headwater [ˈhedwɑːtə]	11/9A	Granny Betty [ˈgrænɪ ˈbetɪ]
	St. Lucia [sənt ˈluːʃə]	12/1D	John Hegley [dʒɒn ˈheglɪ]
	British Airways [ˌbrɪtɪʃ ˈeəweɪz]	12/4A	Frankfurt [ˈfræŋkfət]
	Royal St. Lucian [ˌrɔɪəl sənt ˈluːʃən]	12/4B	Victoria Station [vɪkˌtɔːrɪə ˈsteɪʃn]
	Embassy [ˈembəsɪ]		Brighton [ˈbraɪtən]
	The Himalayas [ðə ˌhɪməˈleɪəz]		Dover [ˈdəʊvə]
	Wiltshire [ˈwɪltʃə]	12/4C	Rover [ˈrəʊvə]
	Hyde Park [ˌhaɪdˈpɑːk]		Metro [ˈmetrəʊ]
	Oxford Street [ˈɒksfəd striːt]		Honda [ˈhɒndə]
	Bayswater [ˈbeɪzwɑːtə]	12/5A	Birmingham [ˈbɜːmɪŋəm]
	Highgrove Hotels [ˈhaɪgrəʊv həʊˈtelz]		The Coach and Horses
6/6A	Brosnans [ˌbrɒzˈnɑːns]		[ðə ˌkəʊtʃ ənd ˈhɔːsɪz]
6/7A	Heartbreak Hotel [ˈhɑːtbreɪk həʊˈtel]		Nelson Drive [ˈnelsən ˈdraɪv]
6/10	Mount Vesuvius [maʊnt vɪˈsuːvjəs]		Euston [ˈjuːstən]
6/10A	Sorrento [səˈrentəʊ]		Preston [ˈprestən]
	Gatwick [ˈgætwɪk]		Chorley [ˈtʃɔːlɪ]
	Kuoni Travel [kjʊˈəʊnɪ ˈtrævl]		Blackpool [ˈblækpuːl]
	Dublin [ˈdʌblɪn]		Southport Road [ˈsaʊθpɔːt ˈrəʊd]
	Pompeii [pɒmˈpeɪiː]		Bradford [ˈbrædfəd]
7/1A	Los Angeles [lɒs ˈændʒɪluːz]	12/7A	Thomas Cook [ˌtɒməs ˈkʊk]
7/3A	Mark Scott [mɑːk skɒt]		Leicester [ˈlestə]
7/3E	Warren Hagstrom [ˈwɒrən ˈhægstrəm]		Loughborough [ˈlʌfbrə]
	Roger Taylor [ˈrɒdʒə ˈteɪlə]		Concorde [ˈkɒŋkɔːd]
	Jenny Faber [ˈdʒenɪ ˈfeɪbə]		Lapland [ˈlæplænd]
	Liz May [lɪz meɪ]		St Gotthard Pass [sənt ˈgɒtɑːd pɑːs]
	Mr Cosby [ˈmɪstə ˈkɒzbɪ]	13/1	Beaminster [ˈbiːmɪnstə]
7/6A	Truman [ˈtruːmən]	13/1A	Dorset [ˈdɔːsɪt]
7/6B	Ms Burton [mɪz ˈbɜːtən]	13/6	Madeira [məˈdɪərə]
7/9B	Linda Goodison [ˈlɪndə ˈgʊdɪsən]	13/7D	St Lukes [sənt ˈluːks]
	Vicky Seager [ˈvɪkɪ ˈsiːgə]		Auckland [ˈɔːklənd]
	Hilbre Island [ˈhɪlbrə ˈaɪlənd]	13/8C	Peter Willems [ˈpiːtə ˈwɪləmz]
	Bangor University [ˈbæŋgə ˌjuːnɪˈvɜːsətɪ]	13/9B	Tokyo [ˈtəʊkɪəʊ]
8/1	Betty Crocker [ˈbetɪ ˈkrɒkə]	14	Victoria Principal [vɪkˈtɔːrɪə ˈprɪnsəpl]
	Rosamond Richardson		Ned Sherrin [ned ˈʃerɪn]
	[ˈrɒzəmənd ˈrɪtʃədsən]		Esther Rantzen [ˈestə ˈrænsən]
8/5C	Susan [suːzn]		Andrew Davis [ˈændruː ˈdeɪvɪs]
	Paul [pɔːl]		Keith Floyd [kiːθ flɔɪd]
8/6A	Louise Hudson [luːˈiːz ˈhʌdsən]		Malaysia [məˈleɪzɪə]
8/10B	Malta [ˈmɔːltə]		Lord Healey [lɔːd ˈhiːlɪ]
9/2A	Vicky Feaver [ˈvɪkɪ ˈfiːvə]		Geoff Hamilton [dʒef ˈhæməltən]
9/4B	Tim [tɪm]		Polly Toynbee [ˈpɒlɪ ˈtɔɪnbiː]
	Jane [dʒeɪn]		Patric Walker [ˈpætrɪk ˈwɔːkə]
9/6A	Nimes [niːm]	14/3A	Eurown TV [ˈjʊərəʊn ˌtiːˈviː]
9/6B	Levi Strauss [ˈliːvaɪ straʊs]		Strasbourg [ˈstræzbɜːg]
	New York City [ˌnjuː jɔːk ˈsɪtɪ]		Eurcity [ˈjʊəsɪtɪ]
	Kentucky [kenˈtʌkɪ]	14/4A	Roald Dahl [rəʊld dɑːl]
9/9A	Ginger [ˈdʒɪndʒə]	14/8	Hamlet [ˈhæmlət]

Alphabetical word list   Alphabetisches Wortregister

Jeder Eintrag ist mit dem Verweis auf die entsprechende Kapitel- und Schrittnummer des ersten Vorkommens versehen.

Wörter bzw. Bedeutungen, die bereits in **BRIDGES 1** vorkamen, werden hier nicht wiederholt.

Wörter und Wendungen, die in der ICC-Liste enthalten sind, sind mit einem Punkt (•) gekennzeichnet.

A
- able to 11/6
- above 5/6A
- absolutely 9/9C
- accent 15/10
- accept 3/6
- acceptable 9/6E
- accident 12/8
- accompany 6/5
- according to 1/3D
- account 13/9B
- accountant 7/9B
- ache 10/8
- acrostic 15/1C
- active 2/6, 6/5A
- activity 3/9A
- actor 13/1A
- actress 2/9C
- actually 3/4D
- address 6/10A
- adopt 11/2A
- advanced 7/4A
- adventure 6/5
- advert(isement) 12/2A
- advertise 12/7A
- advertising time 14/3A
- advice 10/8B
- aerobics 2/6
- afford 9/5A
- afraid 5/2C
- Africa 6/5
- after a while 7/3C
- aftershave 10/4A
- agent 7/5A
- ahead 4/13A
- aim 12/7A
- air fare 6/5
- airport 6/9A
- alarm clock Pr.D/4B
- alcohol 12/7C
- all at once 11/4A
- all day 3/4E

- all in all 10/3B
- all of a sudden 10/7B
- all of us 6/3A
- all right 3/3C
- All the best! 8/6A
- all the time 10/3B
- allow 8/9A
- almost 14/4A
- almost certainly 13/1A
- alpine 6/5
- alternative 3/7A
- although 2/2A
- altogether 6/1B, 9/6B
- amaze 13/6A
- amazed 4/9A
- among 4/6
- amount 10/3B
- amusing 7/9C
- angry 5/1B
- animal fat 13/6A
- anniversary 8/6A
- announcement 12/4
- annoyed 5/2A
- annoying 4/3A
- annual 6/10A
- antique dealer 7/3C
- anxious 11/9A
- any time 1/8A
- anybody 1/9
- anyway 9/5A
- anywhere 7/4A
- anywhere else 14/2A
- apart 5/6A, 11/2A
- apart from 6/1B
- apartment 6/5
- appear 6/10A
- appearance 2
- apply for 7/4A
- appreciate 7/9B
- approach 12/8
- appropriate 3/1B
- area 3/7B

- argument 6/11A
- arm 5/5A
- around 4, 7/1A
- arrange 5/4A, 8/3A
- arrangement 8/5B
- arrogantly 14/8
- article 13/1A
- arts 2/6
- as necessary 7/10
- as soon as possible 7/6A
- ashtray 13/9B
- ask permission 3/3A
- asleep 5/4A
- aspirin 10/4A
- assistant 7/3B
- associate 7/2A
- association 6/10A, 8/11
- at first 9/6B
- at home 6/11
- at last 7/4A
- at least 2/10A
- at once 11/4A
- at that point 7/3C
- at the moment 7/5A
- at the same time 3/1B
- at work 4/8A
- athletic 2/6
- Atlantic 15/4A
- attack 5/7A
- attendant 13/9B
- attract 14/2A
- aubergine 8/2
- Australia 6/3
- author 13/1D
- available 6/5
- average 2/2A
- avoid 12/8
- award-winner 14
- away 6/11
- awful 5/3C

B
- B & B (= bed and breakfast) 6/6A
- baby 7/8A, 13/6
- babysitter 8/7A
- back 4/2A, 13/8C
- back door 4/8A
- backache 10/8A
- background 7/3E
- badly 5/1B
- bald 2/1
- baldy 14/3A
- ball 14/3A
- bar 1/7
- bargain 6/5
- bark 7/8A
- based on 14/3A
- basement 13/7A
- basis 15/4A
- bath 10/3A
- bathe 11/8B
- bathwater 6/7A
- battery 7/3B
- Bavaria 9/6A
- be able to 11/6
- be merry 8
- beachside 6/5
- beard 2/1
- beauty 2/9C
- became 7/3C
- been 5/8A, 10/9A
- beg someone's pardon 8/7A
- began 4/9A
- beginner 6/5
- beginning 1/1B, 3/10A
- believe 10/3C
- believe in 12/7A
- beloved 14/4A
- below 14/3A
- bend 5/6A
- besides 13/1A
- best-selling 14/3A

birthplace 11/3A
- biscuit 13/6
bishop 15/4A
- bitten 6/10A
Black Forest 14/3A
blackbird 14/3A
blessing 5/8
- blonde 2/6
blood-poisoning 6/10A
- bloody 8/8
- blouse 9/1A
blueish 2/2A
blues 14/7A
- body Pr.A/6A
- boil 10/7A, 13/9A
booking 6/5
- bored 5/1B
born loser 8/7
- borrow 4/9A
- bottle 1/8A
- bought Pr.B/2A
- box 2/6
boxing 2/6
- boy 2/2C
boyfriend 1/2
brandy 10/8B
- break 6/5
breakdown 5/1B
breath 12/2A
breathe 9/2A
- bridge 12/5
- bring 3/1B
- bring back Pr.A/5A
bring to the boil 8/2A
- bring up 11/5A
British Rail 12/2A
- brochure 5/3C
broke down 4/13B
- broken 4/7B
brooch 9/8A
- brought 13/9A
brush up 7/4A
- build 7/8A
builder 7/3B
bullock 12/7A
burglar Pr.A/6
burglary 4/8
bury 13/1A
- bus stop 12/5B
bus terminal 6/9A
- business 1/2
- business people 1/2
- businessman 9/6B

- busy 7/6A

C
California 9/6A
- call 7/6A
call about 7/6A
call back 5/4A
- call each other 1/3D
caller 7/7A
- came back 4/1A
camping safari 6/5
canary 7/1A
- can't say 1/1B
- can't stand 6/5B
canvas 9/6A
- car key 9/8A
- car park 12/4C
- car-owner 12/3A
cardboard 14/3A
- carefully 14/8
carpet 13/1A
- carry Pr.B/4
- cash 4/8A
cashier 13/9B
- cassette 14/7A
- castle 3/7A
category 3/9C
- caught 4/8A
cauliflower 8/2
- cause 7/9B, 10/4A
CD Player 4/4A
celebrate 8/7B
celebration 8/6
census 11/6A
- centre 3/7A
ceremony 6/10A
- certainly not 9/5A
champagne 4/9A
- chance 7/9B
- change 4/4A, 6/5C, 12/5
character hotel 6/5
characteristic 12/1A
- charge 14/3A
charity 8/9
charm 13/1A
chart 11/1C
- Cheers! 8/6A
chef-prepared 6/5
- cheque card 9/8A
cherry 2/9B
children's creche 6/5
chil(l)i powder 8/2
chin 5/5A
chocolate bar 13/6A

- choice 6/5
choir 14/7C
chop finely 8/2A
chopped 8/2A
Christianity 15/4A
- cigarette 7/8A
cinnamon 8/2
circle 3/1B
clarinet 14/7A
class reunion 2
class shopping survey 13/3
classic 14/3A
- clean 13/1A
cleaning lady 4/3C
- clear 9/8C
- clever 2/5B
- climb 14/4A
- close 1/3A, 2/3A, 6/5
clothing 9/4A
clove of garlic 8/2
clue 13/10A, Pr.E/4
- coast 6/5
- coat 9/1A
cocktail 13/6A
- coffee machine 4/1A
- coin 4/8A
- cold 5/8A
collapse 12/7A
collection 14/7A
collide 12/8
colour printer 4/3A
column 2/5B
- comb 10/4A
comfort 12/7B
- comfortable 9/4A
- come in 12/4B
comedy 14
- comfortable 9/4A
comment 7/3B
commerce 3/7B
commercial organization 12/7A
commission 14/3A
- common 10/4A
community organisation 3/7B
- company 4/8A
comparison Pr.A/4
competition 6/10A
compile 8/3B
- complain 6/8C
complaint 6/8C, 10/8A

- complete 1/4C
- completely 6/10A
compliment 9/9
compromiser 11/9A
computer equipment 13/7A
concerned 14/4A
conference 6/10A
confrontation 7/9B
confusion 13/6A
- Congratulations! 5/3A
- connection Pr.E/1
conquer 15/4A
consequence 2/7
consumption 10/3B
convenient 12/1B
- cook 2/6, 7/4A
cookery 7/4B
cooking 3/1B
core 15/6A
coriander 8/2
cottage 6/5
- cotton 9/6A
couch 14/3A
counter 13/9A
- couple 4/9A
courgette 8/2
- course 3/4A
court 15/4A
cousin 11/8A
cover 8/3A
cowboy 9/6A
crash 12/8
crazy Pr.A/4
- cream 13/6A
create 12/7A
credit 13/9B
credit card 4/3C
- crime 4/9
criticize 1/4C
- cross 12/5
crossword 12/2A
- crowd 6/5
cruise 6/5
- cry 10/7A
cultural 3/9A
culture 3/7B
cumin 8/2
curled 4/6
curly 2/2A
current 1/4C
curry 8/2
- customer 6/5C
- cut 8/2A

D

- damage 4/7B
- Dane 15/4A
- danger 7/9B
- dangerous 1/4B
- dark 2/1
- dartboard Pr.D/2
- darts Pr.D/2
- daughter-in-law 11/9A
- day-trip 3/4A
- dead on one's feet 13/6A
- deal 12/7A
- deal with 6/7C
- definitely 14/3A
- definition 15/7
- delay 6/10A
- delegate 6/10A
- deliver 13/1A
- delivery 13/9A
- demand 9/6B
- denim 9/6B
- dental floss 10/5B
- department 7/3C, 7/5A
- depend 2/5B
- depressant 5/1B
- description 2/3B
- design 8/9C
- despite 12/7A
- detail 1/7A
- develop 6/10A
- development 6/10A
- diagram 10/1B
- diary 8/5B
- dice Pr.B/1
- dictate Pr.C/2B
- dictionary 8/1B
- diet 11/8b
- difficulty 12/7A
- dig 7/8A
- diploma Pr.E/5
- director 6/10A
- disabled 13/9B
- disagree 1/4A
- disappoint 5/3C
- disaster 10/7
- disc jockey 7/3B
- discount 6/5
- discover 6/5, 13/9B
- dishwasher 4/1A
- dislike 14/7C
- DNA 14
- do aerobics 3/3A

do business 7/4A
- do for a living 12/2A
do something about something 6/7A
- do the shopping 3/2B
documentary 14
domestic 10/7
- done 4/7
- door key 9/8A
doorbell Pr.B/3
- double 10/3B
dozen 13/6
drama 14
drawing Pr.E/4
- dress 1/8A
dress up 7/8A
- drinks 13/6A
- drive through 6/2A
- driven 6/2A
driver 7/8A
- driving licence 9/8A
driving test 5/3C
- drop 3/3A, 6/10A
drown 6/10A
- drunk 4/7B
dry cleaner's 13/1C
dryer 4/3C
- during 3/4C

E

- each other 1/3D
- ear 5/5A
- early 9/6B
- earn 7/9B
earring 9/8A
- earth 8/8
- east 6/5
- Easter 6/4B
- eastern 6/1B
eat out 2/6
eat up 11/8C
- ecological 3/9A
- economic 15/4A
economy 1/4C
Ecu (= European Currency Unit) 14/3A
educated 2/6
- education 3/7B
educational 14/4C
efficient 10/3B
Egypt 6/5
election 1/4C
- electrical Pr.A/6

- electricity 10/3A
elegant 9/4A
- embarrassed 5/4A
emergency 4/9A
emigrate 9/6B
empire 15/4A
- employer 15/8A
- empty 13/9B
- end 1/1B
- energy 10/3
energy-intensive 10/3B
- enjoy oneself 4/9A
enjoyable 4/4A
- enormous 3/3A
enquiry 7/9B
- enter 12/3A
entertain 3/1B
entertainment Pr.D/5A
entire 13/9B
- entrance 2/9E
- environment 3/7B
- equal 2/9E
equipment Pr.A/6
erosion 7/9B
escape 7/1A
- especially 1/4C
essential 10/1B, 10/5
etiquette 1/8
European Commission 14/3A
- even 3/3A
- even if 13/9B
- evening class 13/1A
- event 13/1A
- ever 6/3
- everyday 4/6
- everyone 4/1C
- everywhere 14/2A
ex-wife 8/7A
- exactly Pr.B/3
- excellent 6/5
- excess 11/8B
- exchange 7/10A
exotics 13/1A
- expand 7/5A
- expect 9/6A
- expert 6/5
- explain 4/9B
- explanation Pr.E/1
explore 6/5
- export 7/4A, 9/6B
extended 11/4B
- extra Pr.D/2

extract Pr.C/4
eye contact 13/9B

F

- face 5/5A
facilities 6/5
fact 11/6
factor 15/4A
- fair 2/1
- faithfully 6/8C
- fall 12/7A
- fall down 6/10A
- familiar 9/5C
far flung 14
- farmer 9/6B
farmhouse 6/5
- fascinating 11/4B
fashion 9/5
fashionable 9/7A
- fat 2/1
- father-in-law 10/7A
fax 7/1A
- featuring 14/3A
- feel 5/4A, Pr.D/4A
feel like 9/5A
- feeling Pr.A/6
feet 2/9E
- fell down 6/10A
- fellow student 1/7
fellow traveller 12/2A
- fewer 11/5A
- fight 7/9B
- figure 2/2A
- fill 13/1A
fill up 6/7A
- film 8/6A
- finally 11/2A
- fine 1/1B
- finger 5/5A
- finish 7/4A
- fit 2/4A, 9/11
fixture 14
flirt 12/2B
- floor 5/6A
florist's 13/1C
- flown 6/2A
- flu 5/8A
flush 10/2B
- fly 12/8
- fly over 6/2A
fog 6/10A
- follow 9/3B
follow up 14
food processor 4/1A

food-poisoning 6/10A
- fool 10/9A
- foot 2/6, 5/5A
- football match 14/2A
  for a while 7/3C
- for ever 13/1A
- for the first time 1/2
- foreign 4/8A
- forget 1/1B
- forgot 8/7A
- forgotten 7/4A
- fork 8/3A
- form 6/9A, Pr.D/2
  formal 1/8A
  fortune 12/2B
- forward 5/6A, 12/7A
- found 10/5B
- found out 5/3C
- free Pr.A/5A, 9/2A
  free up 12/2B
  freezer 4/1A
- frequently 10/3B
- fresh 8/2, 10/8B
  fridge 4/1A
  friendship 2/6
- front door 4/8A
  frustrating 4/3A
  fry 8/2A
  full name 2/2C
  fully inclusive 6/5
- fun 7/3B
- funny 13/9A
- future 11/5
  future prospects 11/6

G
- game 4/5B
  game show 14/2A
  gameboy 4/3A
  gape 14/4A
  garlic 8/2
- gate 12/4A
  gather 11/8A
- gave 9/6B
  gay 11/4B, 11/5A
  gaze 12/2B
- generally 11/7A
  generation 9/5A
- generous 2/5B
  Geneva 12/4A
  Genoa 9/6A
- gentleman 2/6
  gently 8/2A
- Gents 7/1A

German 6/1A
- get away from 11/9A
  get bored 7/4A
  get buried 13/1A
- get in 4/8A, 15/2A
- get into 12/7A
- get married 2/7
- get off 12/9A
- get on 12/4B
  get on well together 11/7C
- get one's hair done 13/1A
  get rid of 7/4A
  get someone over something 12/7A
- get something done 13/1A
  get started 3/4D
- get tired 6/9
  get to know someone 0/1
  get together 8/4
- get up 5/1A, 10/8B
  ghost 15/3A
  gin 13/6A
  ginger 8/2
  give trouble 7/5A
- given 12/8
- glad 9/9A
- glasses 2/1
  glorious 8/1
- Go ahead. 4/13B
- go back 0/3
  go crazy 15/1C
- go down 1/11A
  go for 14/2A
- go on holiday 6/1A
- go to bed 3/1B
- go up 1/11A
- God 15/1
- going to do something 3/4C
- gold 9/6A
  Gold Rush 9/6B
  golf 2/6
- gone 13/1A
  good buy 13/1
  good fun 7/3B
- good-looking 2/5B
  goods 9/6B
  goodwill 8/8
- got 12/9A
- government 3/7B
  gradually 11/4A

granny 11/9A
grate 8/3A
- great 1/1B
  great deal 13/1A
  Greenland 6/5
- grey 2/2A
  grid 14/7A
  groceries 13/1A
- ground 2/9B, 8/2
- ground floor 10/6
- group 12/7A
- grow 2/9E, 9/6B
  growth 15/4A
  guarantee 14/2A
  guaranteed 13/9B
- guide 14
  guide book 6/9A
  guillotining 12/7A
  guitar 4/3A
  guitarist 14/7A

H
- habit 11/7A
  had Pr.B/4
  hairbrush 10/4A
- hairdresser 13/1B
  hairdryer 10/4A
  hairstyle 15/5C
- half of it 3/3A
- hand 5/5A
  hand out 5/3D
  handbag 9/8A
  handshake 1/3A
  hang up Pr.E/3
  hangover 5/8A
- happen 4/8A
  happiness 9/7A
- hard 11/8A
  hard-wearing 9/6B
- hard work 2/8A
  hard-working 2/5B
  hardheaded 12/7A
- hardly 15/8A
- hardly ever 10/4B
  harmonist 11/9A
  harm 4/5B
  haste 6/9A
- have a baby 5/3C
- have a job 7/2A
- have a shower 10/1A
- have been to 6/2
- have children 2/9C
- have to 1/8B
- head 5/5A
- headache 10/8A

head for 12/7A
- health 3/7B
  health food 13/1A
  health warning 4/5B
- heart 2/6
  heart attack 13/6A
- heat 8/2A, 10/3B
- heating 10/3A
- heating system 10/3A
  height 2/2A
- hell 5/6A
- Help! 13/2
- help oneself to something 3/3A
  help out 7/5A
  heritage 8/1
- hers 9/1C
- herself 3/2A
  hide 7/8A
  hifi 10/3B
  high point 6/10A
  highlight 14/3A
- hill 2/9A
- himself 3/2A
- hire 13/4
- his 9/1C
- hit 12/8, 14/3A
- hobby 1/4C
- hold on 7/6A
  hold one's breath 12/2A
- hole 7/8A
  homelessness 14/3A
  honest 2/5B
  hoover 4/1A
- hope 11/6
  horrible 1/4A
- horse 12/3A
- hospital 3/7A
  hospital helper 7/9A
  host/hostess 3/3A
  household 9/6B, 10/3A
  househusband 11/4B
  housewarming party 1/8A
- however 1/4C
- human Pr.A/6A
  humanity 7/9B
- humo(u)r 2/6
  Hungary 6/1B
  hunt Pr.E/4
  hypnotize 14/4A

I

Iceland 6/5
ID card 9/8A
- ideal Pr.C/3B
  idealist 12/7B
  identical 11/2A
  identify 4/8A
  identity 1/7
  idiotic 14/4A
  ignition 13/1A
  ignore 10/8D
- ill 5/8A
- illness 1/4A
- imagine 14/5A
- immediately 6/7C
- improve 4/4A
  in addition 6/8C
- in case 5/1B
- in each case 12/8
  in fact 6/8C
- in order to 12/3A
  in reply to 1/8A
  in the end 4/8A
  in time 12/8
- inch 2/6
- include 1/4C
  inconvenient 12/1B
- increase 10/3B
  indeed 1/4C
  India 15/4A
  indicate 3/7B
  indulge 12/2B
  infertility treatment 14
- influence 15/4A
  informant 1/4C
  ingredient 8/1B
  injection 13/1A
  inner 7/9B
  innocent 14
  insect 6/7A
  insomnia 10/8A
  install 14/4A
  instant coffee 10/5B
- instead 3/9B
- instead of 10/5C
  instruction 5/6A
  insulate 10/3B
- insurance 4/8A
  insured 5/3C
  intellectual 12/2A
  intelligence 2/9C
- intelligent 2/5B
  intensive course 1/7A

- interest 1/7A
- international 12/7A
- interrupt 12/1B
- into something 9/5A
- introduce 9/6B
  invent 8/9B
  invention 4/4
- invite 8/5B
- iron 4/1A, 7/8A
  item 4/2A, 9/6B

J

jabber 12/7A
- jacket 9/1A
  jar 13/6A
  jeans 9/6
  jewellery 4/8A
  job satisfaction 7/9
- joke 13/9B
  jokingly 13/9B
  journey 12/2A
- juice 8/2
  jumbo 13/6A
  junction 12/5
- just 6/5
  just like 11/2A
- just now 7/5A

K

- keep fit 5/6
  keep moving 10/8B
  keep out of danger 7/9B
  keep talking 1/6
- kept 9/5A
  kettle 4/1A
  kick 14/4A
  kid 11/8B
- kill 12/8
  kilowatt hour 10/3B
  kindness 3/6
- kiss 1/3D
  kiwi-fruit 13/6
- knife 8/2A
  knock 10/7A

L

label 5/5A
lamp-post 12/8
- land 6/10A
  landlord 12/4C
- language school 1/7A
- last 9/5A

- late 9/6B
  Latin 15/4A
- laugh 5/2A
  laughter 5/1B
  laund(e)rette 4/6
  laundry 4/6
- law 15/4A
- lazy 2/5A
- leather 9/10
- leave 13/1A
- leave a message 7/6A
  leaving school 2/8A
  lecturer 6/5
  leek 8/2
- left 4/9A
- left behind 11/2A
  left-handed 11/8A
- leg 2/2A
  legal system 3/7B
  leisurely 6/5
  lesbian 11/4B, 11/5A
- less 6/5
  let oneself go 8/9A
  let someone down 10/9A
  librarian 7/3B
- library 13/1B
- licence 9/8A
  lie Pr.E/2
  life story 12/2A
  lifestyle 4/3C
  lifetime 11/8A
- lift 5/6A
- light 1/8A, 9/2A
- like 1/8A
  likely 11/5B
  likeness 2/2
- line 7/6A, 12/5A
- listen ahead Pr.C/4
  living space 10/3B
  local radio station 14/7C
  local speciality 8/3A
  locally grown 13/1A
  located 6/5
  logical Pr.E/1
- lonely 2/6, 5/1B
  long distance 14/3A
- look after 11/4C
- look for 7/4A
- look like 2/1
  look out for 12/5
- lorry 12/3A
  lorry driver 14/3A
- lose 2/2A

- lose touch with someone 12/2A
- lost 12/2A
- loud 3/3A
- lounge 1/7
- lovely 1/1B
  lover 1/4C
  loving 8/8
  low-flying 6/10A
  lower 12/3A
  lower floor 13/7B
- luggage 12/5
  lumberjack 9/6B
  luxury 10/5, 10/5C

M

- made 4/4A
- magazine 0/2A
  mainland Europe 12/7A
  mainly 9/10
- make sure 7/9B
  make up 13/4
  make-up 10/4A
  make someone happy 5/1A
- manager 6/7A
  manic 5/1B
  many a town 13/1A
  marketing director 6/10A
- marry 5/1B
  mass production 9/6B
- material 7/5A, 9/6A
- matter 5/3C
  maximum 14/3A
- may 13/1A
- maybe 11/4B
- means 12/1
  means of transport 12/1
- medical 14
- medicine 5/1B
  medium dry 13/6A
  melody 15/3A
- member 2/2B
  memorise 12/2A
  memory 3/3E
  mend 9/5A
- mention 10/3B
- merry 2/9B
- message 7/6
- metal 9/10
- metre 2/9E

microwave 4/1A
- middle 4/2A
Middle East 12/7A
Midlands 12/7A
- midnight 1/7
- might 7/4A
- mile 6/5
mime 5/1D
- mind 12/2B
- mine 8/6A
miner 9/6A
minisaga 4/6
minister 6/10A
- mirror 10/4A
- miss 6/10A
- missing 5/5A
missionary 12/7A
- mistake 4/3C
- mixed 7/9B
model 11/4C
- money 8/9A
monk 15/4A
- mood 5/1B
mood music 14/5
more than enough 13/6
Morocco 6/5
Mother's Day 8/6A
- motorway 12/5
motto 9/5A
moustache 2/1
- mouth 5/5A
- move 6/10A, 9/2A
- move house 3/5A
- move in with someone 11/9A
movie 2/6
- multilingual 15/8C
- musician 2/6
- myself 3/2B
mystery 4/9

N
nail file 10/4A
- name 1/4C
nappy 7/8A
- nasty 2/5A
native speaker 15/1C
- natural 11/8B
- nature 7/9A
nature reserve 7/9B
nature warden 7/9A
naughty 2/9B
- nearly 6/1B
- necessary 7/10B

- neck 10/8A
necklace 9/8A
- need 7/1A
negative 2/5B
negotiate 12/7A
- neither 13/1B
- neither ... nor 13/9B
- nervous 5/1B
nest 7/8A
New Zealand 6/9A
- news 5/3A
- noise 1/4C
non-drinker 2/6
non-smoker 2/6
- non-smoking family 11/9A
- none 3/8A
- none at all 9/2A
noon 13/9B
- nor 2/8C
nordic 6/5
- normal 6/5
Norwegian 15/4A
- nose 5/5A
not a single flower 6/10A
- not at all 13/9B
not ... at all 3/1C
not ... either 2/2A
not to mention 10/3B
- note 4/3A
novel 14/3A
nowadays 4/5B
no more 4/6
nugget 14/3A
number 7/9B
Number One 14/7C
numerous 12/7A
nun 15/4A

O
- object 9/8C
- occasion 4/10B
occasionally 8/2A
- ocean 6/6A
odd one out 9/11
- offer 13/4
off-licence 13/1C
- official 15/8A
- Oh dear! 5/3A
- oil 8/2, 13/9A
on average 10/2C
- on business 1/6
- on holiday 1/6

on one's own 7/4A
on one's way home 4/9A
on the ball 14/3A
on the other hand 10/5B
- on the phone 7/7
- on time 5/4A
- once 2/9C
- once a week 4/6A
once upon a time 11/4A
one's own 14/3A
one-legged 11/8A
one-person household 10/3A
oneself 12/2B
- open 10/8B
opening hours 13/9B
operation 5/8A
- opinion 10/5B
opinion poll Pr.E/4
- opposite 12/2B
option 6/5
- order 7/6A
- order number 15/2A
- ordinary 1/8A
- organize 12/7A
organizer 6/10A
- ourselves 3/2B
outdoors 7/9B
outrageously 12/2B
- outside 3/3A
oven 4/3C
- own 14/3A

P
package 6/5
package tour 12/7A
- packet 13/6
- pain 10/8
- paint 10/7A
- pair 9/1A
palace 15/6A
- paper 9/10
paperwork 7/9B
paradise 6/5
- parcel 13/1A
- pardon 8/7A
- parental 11/8
- parents-in-law 11/9A
- park 12/3A
- parking space 7/9B
- particularly 1/8A
- party 1/8

- pass 5/3C
pass along/pass on 11/8A
pass into 12/7A
path 13/4
- pay 1/4A
- pay attention 11/8B
pay someone a compliment 9/9C
- peace 3/3A
peace of mind 13/6A
- peaceful 14/5B
- peacefully 6/5
- pedestrian 12/8
peel 8/2A
- pence 12/7A
pepper 8/2
- perfect 2/9C
- perfectly 5/4A
perform 14/8
perfume 10/4A
period 15/4A
permission 3/3A
- personal 2/6
persuade 12/2A
pet 1/4B
petrol station 13/9B
- phone 1/8A
- phone back 7/6A
- phone box 12/6B
photocopy 13/1A
pianist 14/7A
- pick 13/6A
pick of the week 14
- pick up 13/4
picnic 2/6
- piece of 9/4A
pinch of 8/3A
- pipe 3/3A
- pity 5/3A
- place 11/9A
place an order 15/2B
- plan 12/5B
- plastic 9/10
- platform 12/4B
- play 2/2C
play for time 15/5A
player Pr. D/2
plc (public limited company) 7/6A
- pleased 1/1B
- plenty of 7/9C
plus 13/1A
poetry 2/9E
- point Pr.B/1, 13/1A

- police 4/8A
- police station 4/9A
- polite 5/4A
- politician 2/5B
- politics 1/4A
- pool 6/5
- poor 5/1B
- poorly 13/9B
- pop 14
- popularity 11/4C
- port 9/6B, 13/6
- portrait 2/3
- position 5/6A
- positive 2/5B
- possible 7/6A
- post 13/1A
- post a parcel 13/1A
- postman 7/8A
- pot 13/6A
- pour 8/3A
- power station 3/7A
- practical 7/9B
- prediction 11/5A
- prefer 3/9B
- preference 6/5B
- prepare 7/4A
- present 1/8A, Pr.B/4, 8/9C, 13/9B
- president 14/3A
- press 5/6A
- presumed 14
- pretend Pr. E/5
- pretty 6/5
- prevent 12/3A
- primary school 15/8A
- priority 14
- problem 1/1B, 12/7A
- procedure 8/3A
- profession 1/7A
- professional 2/6, 7/3E
- profit 13/8A
- profitable 12/7A
- programme 3/7B
- project 1/4C
- promise 13/9B
- promote 12/7A
- Proms 14
- proper job 7/3C
- prove 9/6B
- provide 6/5
- public enquiry 7/9B
- public holiday 8/9A
- publish 6/9A
- published 6/9A
- pullover 9/1A
- punch 14/4A
- purse 9/8A
- put on 10/5C
- put something back 13/9B
- put something to the test 13/9B
- put through 7/6A
- puzzle 13/10A

Q
- qualified 7/3C
- quarterly 6/9A
- queen 15/3A
- question 13/9B
- questionnaire 1/8A
- queue 6/5, 13/9B
- quick service counter 13/9B
- quiet 3/3A
- quote 2/8A

R
- race Pr.B/1
- radio alarm clock 13/4
- rail 12/7A
- railroad 9/6B
- railroad worker 9/6B
- railway network 12/3A
- rain 5/3C
- raise 8/8
- raise money 8/9
- rally 12/10
- rang Pr.B/3
- rank 14
- rather than 11/9A
- razor 10/4A
- re-plan 12/2B
- re-run 14/3A
- react 3/9B
- read 11/9A
- reader 15/3A
- Ready, set ... 5/6A
- realize 10/3C
- reason 12/9A
- recently Pr.B/2A
- receptionist 7/7A
- recipe 7/9B
- recite 14/8
- recommend 13/2B
- red-headed 11/8A
- reddish 2/2A
- reduce 12/3A
- reflect 7/9B
- region 6/5
- regional 14/3A
- regular 14
- related 2/2C
- related to Pr.B/4
- relationship 2/6
- relative 1/5
- relaxation 10/8B
- reliable 12/1B
- religion 1/4C
- reluctant 11/9A
- remedy 10/8B
- remind someone of something 9/4B
- rent 1/4A
- repair 13/1A
- reply 2/9C
- report 12/2A
- reporter 13/9B
- request 13/9B
- re-run 14/3A
- reservation 6/5
- respond 5/4A
- response 13/9B
- rest 1/1B
- result 4/4
- retire 3/5A
- retired 4/9D
- retirement 2/8A
- return 3/6, 4/6
- reunite 11/2A
- review Pr.E/4
- rhyme 14/4A
- rhythm 1/10A
- riddle 15/6
- ring 9/8A
- ring someone up 5/4A
- rise 9/6B
- risen 10/3B
- ritual 8/8
- roast 8/3A
- rock'n roll 9/6A
- role 6/5C
- roll in 9/9C
- romance 2/6
- romantic 14/3A
- Rome 12/7A
- root 11/3A
- rot 13/6A
- rotten 13/2B
- route 12/5B
- rubbish 7/9B
- rug 3/3E
- rule 5/7A
- run 12/5
- run a bath 10/7A
- run away 2/9B
- run over 12/8
- running 2/6
- Russia 6/1B

S
- sack 4/10A
- safari 6/5
- saga 14/2A
- sail for 9/6B
- sailing 6/5
- salary 1/4A
- sales 7/3B
- salesperson 13/9B
- salt 8/2A
- sample 8/1
- sandals 13/2B
- sandy 6/5
- Sardinia 6/5
- satellite 14
- satisfaction 7/9
- saucepan 8/2A
- sauna 10/6
- save 6/5
- saying 2/9A
- scene 14/5A
- schedule 14/3B
- scissors 10/4A
- score Pr.D/2
- scream 13/6A
- screen 14/4A
- season 8/3A
- seat 4/9A
- secluded 6/5
- second largest 6/1B
- seek 2/6
- seem 10/5B
- self-catering 6/5
- self-employed 2/6
- send 1/1B
- sense 2/6
- sentence starter Pr.D/2
- series 14/2A
- serious 2/6
- seriously 5/8A
- serve 8/2
- service 13/9
- service economy 13/9B

set alight 14
settler 15/4A
- shake 13/6A
- shaking hands 1/3
shampoo 10/4A
- share 3/6
- share a flat 14/3A
- sharp 8/2A
- shave 10/1A
- shaver 10/4A
- sheep 10/8B
shelter 10/5C
shilling 12/7A
- shirt 9/1A
- shocked 4/9A
- shop 13/1A
shop for something 13/1A
- shop window 4/2
- shopping 13/1A
- shopping centre 13/7B
- short 2/1
shorten 13/9A
shortish 2/2A
- shorts 9/1A
- should 1/8B
- shoulder 5/5A
- shouldn't 1/8B
show around 3/9C
- shower 10/1A, 10/3B
shuffle 5/3D
- shy 2/5B
- side 2/9A
sideways 12/4B
- sightseeing 3/8
- sign 12/5
silence 3/6
- silent 3/6
- similar 2/6
similarity 11/2C
- simple 13/9B
- since 5/8A
- sincerely 13/1A
- single 6/10A
- single parent 11/4B
- sink 14/4A
- sit down 3/4E
- situation 7/8B
- size 9/5A
- skin 10/4A
- skirt 9/1A
sleeping pill 10/8B
slice 8/3A

- slim 2/1
slogan 14/6
small talk 1/4
- smell Pr.D/4A
smelly 3/3A
- smile 4/6, 10/9A
snake 6/10A
- so 3/1C, 4/1C
- soap 10/4A
soap (opera) 14/2A
- social event 2/6
- sock 4/6
- softly 8/6A
- soldier 9/6A
solid food 8/9A
- solve 12/3C
- somebody 1/4, 1/9
- someone else 5/1B
- somewhere Pr.E/5
- soon 4/3A
- sore throat 10/8A
- Sorry? 15/2
- sort 3/7A, 5/4A
- sort of person 5/4A
sort out 6/8B
soul 5
- sound 2/11A, 9/5C
South Africa 6/5
souvenir Pr.A/5A
- space 11/9A
speaker 1/3D
Speaking. 7/6B
- special 8/9
- specially 0/2A
speech 6/10A
speed limit 12/3A
- spent 6/1B
spice 8/2A
- spoil 4/4A
- spoken 15/4A
spot 13/6A
- spread 8/3A
square 13/4
staff 7/4A
stagecoach 12/7A
- stairs 6/10A
- stand 5/6A
standard 13/9B
standard of comfort 12/7B
- star 14
stare 14/4A
starting position 5/6A
- state 1/4C, 13/6A

statement 1/3D
stationer's 13/1C
- stay 3/4A, 3/4C
stay overnight 11/9A
- steel 11/8A
steering wheel 12/2A
stepfamily 11/4B
- stiff 10/8A
- still 14/4A
stink 9/9C
- stir 8/2A
- stolen 4/8A
stomachache 10/8A
- stop 15/1D
stop sign 12/8
stop someone 11/2A
store manager 13/8
straight 2/2A
- straight on 12/5
- strange 1/4C
strangely 11/2A
- stranger 1/4C
strawberry 14
stressed 2/12A
striped 4/6
- struggle 6/9A
studies 7/4A
- stuff 13/6A
stunning 9/9C
- stupid 2/5A
- subject 1/4A
- success 12/7A
- suddenly 4/9A
- suffer 5/1B
- suggest 2/9C
- suggestion 3/9A
- suit 1/8A
- suit someone 9/9A
- suitable 6/5C
- sun 6/5A
sunburn 13/4
- Sunday paper 13/1A
sunglasses 9/8A
- sunrise 7/9B
- superb 6/5
- support 8/9
- sure 9/9C
- surprise 1/4C, 10/3C
surprising 4/3C
surroundings 13/1A
survey 13/3
survive 13/1A
Sweden 6/1B
- sweet 13/6A
swop 8/11

swordsman 11/8A
- system 10/3A

T

tablespoon 8/2
taboo 1/4A
tailor-made 6/5
- take 1/8A
- take a trip 6/4A
- take away 9/8C
- take care of 11/4C
- take out 2/3B
take someone out 3/1B
take turns 11/1C
- taken 4/7B
- taken over 12/7B
talent show 14/8
- tall 2/1
task Pr.B/1
- taste 4/4A, Pr.D/4A
- taught 15/8C
- taxi 12/1D
- team Pr.D/2
teaspoon 8/2
technology 3/7A
teenage 11/7A
- teeth 10/2B
teetotaller 12/7A
television set 14/4A
- tent 9/6A
thankyou letter 3/1B
theft 4/9A
- theirs 9/1C
- themselves 3/1B
theory 13/9B
- therefore 6/8C
- these 1/3D
- thin 2/2A
think much of 8/7B
- those 1/4C
- throat 10/8A
- through 1/4C
throw away 9/5A
throw off 9/2A
- throw Pr.B/1
- ticket 4/9A
- tights 9/1A
- till 13/9B
- times 6/10A
- timetable 6/9A
- tin 8/2
- tinned 8/2A
- tip 10/8C
- tired 5/1B

V

tiring 6/9A
to say the least 3/3A
toaster 4/1A
toe 5/5A
toiletries 13/7B
- took 12/7A
- toothache 10/8A
- toothbrush 10/4A
- toothpaste 10/4A
top 13/8C
top three 6/1A
topic 1/4B
tot 14/4A
- total 12/2A
total confusion 13/6
- touch 5/6A
Touch wood! 5/8A
tough 9/6A
- tour 6/5
- tourist guide 7/3B
- towel 10/4A
traffic jam 12/3A
traffic warden 7/9A
- train 7/3C
trainee 7/5A
tranquiliser 10/9A
transaction 13/9B
- translation 15/1B
travel agency 13/7A
- travel around 6/5A
- travel company 6/8C
- travel through 6/4A
traveller 12/7A
- travelling salesman 9/6B
- treat 13/9B
trial 3/3A
tribe 15/4A
tricky 12/2B
triple 10/3B
tropical 6/5
- trouble 7/5A
troubled 3/3A
- trousers 9/1A
truth Pr.E/2
try one's luck 9/6B
tuition 6/5
turmeric 8/2
- turn 12/5
turn into 12/7A

- turn up 10/5C
- TV programme 0/2A
TV set 4/3C
twin 2/2C
- type 13/6
type of shop 13/4
typical 13/9B
- tyre 13/9A

U

- ugly 2/5A
- umbrella 13/4
unable 12/8
unaskable question 1/4C
uncomfortable 12/1B
- under 9/8C
understanding 12/7A
underwear 9/1A
- unemployed 11/6
unforgettable 6/5
unfortunately 6/10A
unfriendly 13/9B
unhappy 2/5B
unhealthy 7/3B
unknown 2/5B
unlimited 6/5
unlock 15/6A
unreliable 5/4A
unsafe 4/8A
unspoilt 6/5
- until 12/7A
unusual 1/3D
- upper floor 13/7B
- upset 5/3A

V

vacancy 6/6A
valentine 8/6A
Valentine's Day 8/6A
valuable 9/8
- value 14/4C
variety 7/9C, 13/1A
- various 12/7A
vegetarian meal 8/1
vet 13/1A
video 13/1A
video camera 13/2B
video recorder 4/3A
- view 6/6A

viewer 14/2A
villa 6/5
vineyard 7/3B
violin player 14/7A
vodka 13/6
- vote 1/4C

W

wagon 9/6B
- wait 7/8A
waiting room 6/9A
- waitress 13/9B
- wake 10/9A
- walk around 3/4E
walker 7/9B
walkman 4/3A
- wall 1/4C 3/4E
- wallet 9/8A
- want to 12/6A
wardrobe 9/1C
- warn 14/4A
wash up 10/2B
washing 7/8A
washing up 3/1B
- waste 9/7A
- watch 4/8A
watch out for 11/8A
- water 6/7A
water the garden 10/2B
waterskiing 6/5
watersports 6/5
wave action 7/9B
- weak 2/5A
wealthy 9/6B
- wear 1/8A
wedding 4/6
wedding anniversary 8/6A
week ahead 14
week for week 14/2A
- weight 1/5A
- Well, ... 3/1C
- Well done! 5/3A
western 7/3E
whatever 9/9C
whenever 13/9B
whereas 14/2A
wherein 15/6A
- whether 6/5

- while 13/1A
whisper 8/6A
- whole 13/4
- wide 7/1A
widow 2/6
widower 11/9A
wild weekend 8/5
wild life 7/9B
- will 11/5A
window sill 14/4A
windscreen 13/9A
windsurfing 6/5
winner Pr.A/5
wisdom 2/9
- wish 8/8, 10/6, 11/6A
wishful thinking 10/6
wit 2/9
- within 1/4C
- without 3/3A
woken 7/9B
- won 4/9D
- won't (will not) 11/6
- wonder 2/9B
- wood 9/10
- wooden 2/9B
- wool 9/10
- work 10/7B
work out 7/3C, 12/2A
- workman 6/7A
- world Pr.D/5A
- World War 2 9/6B
- worn 9/4B
- worried 5/1B
- worry 1/1B, 5/1A
- wrap 13/6
writer 8/10B
writing paper 13/4
- wrong 13/2b

Y

- yard 2/9B, 11/4B
yawn 5/1B
- you'd better ... 15/2A
- young 2/2A
- yours 9/5A
- yourself 1/7A

Z

zoology 7/9B

TAPESCRIPTS

UNIT 1

Step 2

1. ❐ Goodbye, Vicky. Enjoy your trip and don't forget to send a postcard!
   ○ Of course not. Bye, mum.
   ❐ Bye, darling!

2. ❐ It was nice to meet you, Brian. Enjoy the rest of your trip!
   ○ Well, thanks for everything. It was great to be here. I hope we can get together again sometime soon …

3. ❐ Hello, Rosie. How are you?
   ○ Fine, thanks. It's a lovely day, isn't it?
   ❐ Yes, it certainly is. I'm just on my way to the shops.
   ○ Oh, are you? Well, mind how you go now …

4. ❐ Pleased to meet you. I'm Bill Berry.
   ○ Pleased to meet you, Mr Berry. I'm Tess Benson. Did you have a good trip?
   ❐ Yes, thanks. It was fine.
   ○ Great. Well, the car's parked round the corner …

5. ❐ Sorry I'm late.
   ○ Don't worry! No problem. We've got lots of time. The party only started an hour ago!
   ❐ Oh, well, er, …

Step 3 C

❐ Who do I usually shake hands with? Er, well, really only with people I meet for the first time. In my job I meet quite a lot of people, so I have to shake hands quite a lot.
○ What about your boss and other people at work?
❐ Oh, no. When we come in we just say "Hi, everybody!" and get on with the job.
○ And people you know privately? Friends, neighbours?
❐ Again, not really. I mean, the English don't normally shake hands with people they meet regularly, do they? But if there's somebody I haven't seen for a long time, haven't seen them for a year or so, then perhaps I would. But if it's a close friend, I'm more likely to give them a kiss. I suppose men would shake hands then because they don't usually kiss each other. Women kiss and men shake hands more, perhaps. But not every day.
○ And what about first names?

○ Well, I call almost everybody by their first name: family, friends, most of the people I know. A lot of neighbours, too. Of course it's quite easy not to use any names at all. I don't think I say Mr or Mrs to anybody, except perhaps one or two older neighbours. Er, if someone's 40 years older than me and I don't know them very well, I can't just call them Jimmy or Edith or whatever. But, as I said, it's quite easy not to use names at all.
○ And what about people you work with?
❐ At work we're all on first name terms – even the big boss is just "Tony" to everybody. I think that's quite normal; it's like that in a lot of the companies I know.
○ OK. Thanks very much.
❐ You're welcome.

Step 10 B Pronunciation

1. Enjoy the rest of your trip!
2. It was fine.
3. Sorry I'm late.
4. Did you have a good trip?
5. Don't forget to send a postcard!
6. No problem.

Step 11 B Pronunciation

1. Are you here on business?
2. Are you here on holiday?
3. It's a lovely day, isn't it?
4. Did you have a good trip?
5. No problem.
6. It was great to be here.
7. Sorry I'm late.
8. It was nice to meet you.
9. It was fine.

UNIT 2

Step 1 B

❐ By the way, what about those photos of your class reunion? Have you got them yet?
○ Yes, I got them back last week. Now where are they? They must be here somewhere. Just a moment … right, got them. Now, what do you think of this then, eh?
❐ No problem recognizing you, of course! I like your dress. Did you buy it specially?
○ Well, thanks, I did actually. Glad you like it.

- ❏ Well, you certainly look younger than some of these others – and slimmer! Who are they, anyway? I don't recognize any of them.
- ○ Do you remember Jenny Robinson?
- ❏ Yes, of course, the short girl with masses of dark curly hair and a great sense of humour. Played the guitar. She's not on this photo is she?
- ○ She is, you know, but she's had her hair cut. It's very short now, but still dark, and she's not as slim as she used to be – in fact, she's really quite fat.
- ❏ Not this one here?
- ○ That's right, that's Jenny.
- ❏ No, I don't believe it! And who's that man there?
- ○ The tall one with the moustache?
- ❏ Yes.
- ○ Oh, I don't think you ever met him. His name's George Small.
- ❏ George Small? No, I don't know him.
- ○ There are a couple of others you know, though.
- ❏ Are there really? Well, let me have another look. Now the one with the longish fair hair and glasses, she looks a bit familiar. It's not Betty Walker, is it?
- ○ Wrong again! Betty wasn't there, unfortunately. No, that's Iris.
- ❏ Iris?
- ○ Iris Clark.
- ❏ Oh, yes! Iris Clark, of course. Well, well, well. I'm not very good at this, am I?
- ○ Well, people change over the years, you know. I didn't recognize all of them myself.
- ❏ Really?
- ○ No. Tony Nicholls, for example. Do you remember him?
- ❏ Tony Nicholls …
- ○ You know – tall, thin, long curly hair. Bright red, it was; you could see him coming a mile off.
- ❏ Oh, yes. Right!
- ○ Well he's still tall and thin, but he's as bald as a coot now; not a single hair on his head …
- ❏ No, really? That's not him there, is it? With the beard?
- ○ It is, you know.
- ❏ Good heavens! And who's the other man? Do I know him?
- ○ That's Kevin Wall. Er, he was away a lot of the time …

Step 7

Consequences

Take a piece of paper and fold it into nine sections.

At the top of the page, write any adjective: fat, intelligent, rich, ugly, beautiful – anything you like.
Now fold the paper so that you can't see the word. Give your piece of paper to the person on your left.
On your new piece of paper, write the name of a man: a famous man or somebody in your class. Fold the paper again and give it to the person on your left. Now write another adjective: short, happy – anything you like.
Fold the paper again and give it to the person on your left. Now write the name of a woman: a famous woman or somebody in your class.
Fold the paper and pass it to the person on your left. Now write the name of a place: a town, a room, a shop – any place you like.
Fold the paper again and give it to the person on your left. Write a time: in the evening, half past two – anything you like.
Fold the paper and pass it to the person on your left. Write down something the man said.
Fold the paper and pass it to your left. And now write down what the woman said.
Fold the paper and pass it on. Write down the last line of the story: what the man and the woman did.
Pass the paper to your neighbour. Unfold your story and read it. Finally, read it out to the class, like the example in the book.

Step 9 D

There was a naughty boy,
And a naughty boy was he,
He ran away to Scotland
The people for to see -
There he found
That the ground
Was as hard,
That a yard
Was as long,
That a song
Was as merry,
That a cherry
Was as red,
That a door
Was as wooden,
As in England –
So he stood in his shoes
And he wondered,
He wondered,
He stood in his shoes
And he wondered.

The writer George Bernard Shaw was one of the most intelligent men of his time. A beautiful actress once wrote to him and suggested that they should have children together. With her beauty and his intelligence, she said, their children would be perfect. Shaw replied that if the children were as beautiful as her and as intelligent as him, that would be fine, but what if they were as beautiful as him and as intelligent as her?

Step 11 B Pronunciation

George – bald
Martin, Bernard, Mary, John, David
fair, blond, grey, curly, moustache

Step 12 A + B Pronunciation

1. I'm quite tall. I've got fair, curly hair, a reddish beard, and I wear glasses. My eyes are blueish grey.
2. When I was young I was very thin and my legs still are. Now I'd like to lose a few kilos, but I'm not really fat.
3. I'm not very tall, but I'm not really short, either. I've got short, straight, fair hair. My eyes are blueish grey.

UNIT 3

Step 4 B – E

1. ... well, you can stay in a bed and breakfast or with a Scottish family. I'm going to stay with a family because I can talk more English that way. There are lessons most mornings and trips and so on in the afternoon. The course lasts two weeks and I'm going to stay another week with an old friend in Edinburgh afterwards. She says she's really looking forward to seeing me ...

2. ❐ Did you see Bill's note?
   △ The one about Carol's housewarming?
   ❐ That's right. Would you like to go?
   △ Well, I don't know. What about you?
   ❐ Oh, yes. I'd love to go!
   △ I was afraid of that.

   ❐ What are we going to give her?
   △ Do we have to give her a present?
   ❐ Of course we do, but it shouldn't be too difficult. You can always find something for a new house.
   △ I suppose so.

   ❐ What are you going to wear?
   △ What do you mean, what am I going to wear? You don't have to wear anything special for a housewarming, do you?
   ❐ Well, I just thought ...

3. ○ Look, we all said we wanted to go there, so let's get our act together. What are we actually going to do?
   ▽ I don't know. How long are we going to be there?
   ○ That depends what time we get started. We can have the whole day there if you want, but if you stay in bed till ...
   ▽ OK, OK! Well, I'd like to walk round the walls.
   ▷ I'm not going to walk around all day.
   ▽ And I'm not going to sit down all day.
   ❐ I want to see the shops.
   ▷ Do they have bus tours?

Step 7 B

❐ Sophie, you're going to tell us something about your experiences as a student, travelling around the USA.
○ Yes, I went on a special programme called the Host Programme for Travelling Students, or something like that. The idea was that you could travel around the US and stay with families, usually no longer than three days with one family, and the family you stayed with showed you around, arranged a programme for you or whatever.
❐ So what sort of places did you stay in?
○ All sorts; a lot of small places you've probably never heard of. One place in Wisconsin – Eau Claire – was really nice. I rang up the family and they'd forgotten that they were in the programme because they never got any visitors. I was the first guest for years and they were really pleased to have me.
❐ What was their programme like?
○ They took me to an ice cream social, which is like a cocktail party or something, but in the afternoon and with no alcoholic drinks, just lots of ice cream. I was interested in social events because I wanted to meet people. And I visited the school, saw classes and talked to the children. They showed me round the hospital as well.
❐ Oh! What gave them the idea you would want to see the hospital?
○ Ah, well, when you applied for this programme you ticked boxes with your interests and I ticked the box for health. And the education box, which was why I was able to visit the school.
❐ I see. Not the usual things that tourists do.
○ No, certainly not. Another thing I remember – this was a different place now – was a trip round a power station. And in another place there was an election and I went around with one of the candidates and saw how an election campaign worked.

☐ Power stations and politics – sounds an interesting programme!
○ Well, I thought so. A few years later I was organizing a programme for some American teachers over here and we included a lot of things like that in the programme too: school visits, different local organisations, companies and so on. They were very interested in everything.

Step 11 A Pronunciation

are, we, to, be	How long are we going to be there?
there, are	There are lessons most mornings.
do, you	What do you mean?
can, you, a	Can I get you a drink?
and, are	My sister and I are both tall.

Step 11 B + C Pronunciation

1. Are you here on business?
2. Are you here on business?
3. What are you going to wear?
4. How long are we going to be there?
5. You phone to say you can go.
6. Guests should take you out for a meal.
7. It was great to be here.
8. I'm happier than I used to be.

Step 12 B Pronunciation

castle, tourists, next time, next birthday, I just thought, old buildings, they helped themselves, the tallest person

PREVIEW A

Step 3

"In the Midnight Hour"
The lyrics of this song cannot be printed here for copyright reasons.

UNIT 4

Step 3 A

☐ OK, Carole. I'd like to ask you some questions about the equipment you've got in your house.
○ Yes, of course. Go ahead.
☐ Right, well, the first question is: what's the oldest thing you've got?
○ Well, until six months ago it was the freezer, but then it broke down so I had to get a new one. It was about 15 years old, the old one. Now the oldest thing is probably the hoover.
☐ I see. And how old's that?
○ About five years? No, a bit older; maybe six or seven.
☐ Uh huh. And the newest?
○ Er, that must be my microwave.
☐ The microwave, right. And what do you think is the most useful one?
○ The washing machine; no question about it.
☐ And the least useful?
○ Er, the food processor. I've had it at least twelve years and I hardly ever use it. Hang on, that means the processor's the oldest thing I've got, doesn't it? You see, it's so useless I even forgot I had it.
☐ OK, so the food processor is the least useful and the oldest.
○ Well, it makes sense, doesn't it? If you never use something, it lasts forever.
☐ That's right. Now, have you got anything you find frustrating?
○ Oh, I don't know, really ... the video recorder, I suppose. If you try to programme it, it never seems to do what you want. That's pretty frustrating.
☐ Are there any machines in the house which particularly annoy you?
○ My son's gameboy. That annoys me. And his electric guitar. Oh, and his walkman as well.
☐ Yes, I sympathize! Just two more questions. Is there anything you're going to buy soon?
○ Er, I can't think of anything. I've got everything already!
☐ Well, is there anything you'd really like?
○ I don't think so ... oh, there is something, though.
☐ What's that?
○ A colour printer for my computer. That would be really nice.
☐ One colour printer. OK, and thank you very much for answering our questions.
○ Not at all.

Step 4 B

1. Well, I think the CD player's made listening to music more enjoyable. You don't get all those scratchy record noises! And it's easier to use.
2. The coffee machine hasn't improved the taste of coffee – no way! In fact, I think coffee was much better when ...
3. Whether you like it or not, it's a fact: the computer's changed millions of jobs.
4. I don't have much time when I get home and the microwave's made cooking a lot easier, at least for me.
5. I think there's no doubt about it, the television's spoiled family life. Whole families just sit there all day and ...

6. The washing machine has made washing clothes easier. In the old days it was really hard work. When I think of my grandmother ...

Step 5 A + B

1. It's a fact that intelligent people don't watch TV.
2. Everybody should have an electric kettle. They're really useful.
3. CD's aren't as good as LP's. The sound isn't as good.
4. I prefer the radio to the television. I think it's much nicer.
5. I wouldn't buy a microwave. They're bad for you.
6. I don't think anybody needs a dishwasher. I enjoy washing up.
7. Computer games are great. Children play with them happily for hours.
8. Cassette recorders are very useful if you want to learn a foreign language.
9. I hate walkmans. You don't talk to people any more.
10. I don't like the telephone. People always phone at the wrong time.

Step 8 B

You hear about burglaries all the time but you never really think it's going to happen to you. So when it happened, it was a shock. We were on holiday in Scotland at the time. The neighbours had the key and they looked after the place: they turned the lights on in the evening, took the newspaper and the post out of the letter-box and did all the usual things, but in the end it didn't make any difference.
It was two days before the end of our holiday when it happened. Sometime in the middle of the night the burglars tried to get in through the back door, but couldn't. Then they tried to get in through the kitchen window, but they couldn't get in there either, so they tried a third time by breaking open the front door, and that's how they got in.
Fortunately, I suppose, they didn't make much of a mess – in fact, there wasn't much damage at all, apart from the doors. In the living room they opened drawers and cupboards looking for cash, cheques and so on, but we had all our money with us, and all the important papers were at the bank. Upstairs, they went into two of the bedrooms looking for jewellery and so on, but all they found was an old watch and some foreign coins from previous holidays. The main thing they took was CD's, about 80 of them, from the living room and one of the children's bedrooms. Something probably disturbed them because they didn't go into the third bedroom where there were a lot more CD's, and they didn't go into the study where my computer lives. So I suppose we were quite lucky.
The next morning the neighbours saw the damage to the door and called the police station. For the police, this was nothing very serious. They just wrote down a few details and when we got back home two days later we had to go round to the police station, make a list of the stolen things and send everything to the insurance company. About six weeks later we got a letter from the police saying that the case was closed. We sent the letter to the insurance company and some months later we received a cheque.
I think the worst thing was knowing that somebody – a stranger – had got into the house. For a few weeks we wondered whether they would come back again. I put new locks on the windows downstairs, but I suppose if burglars really want to get into your house you can't stop them. If they can get into banks, then private houses and flats are no problem.

Step 9 B

There was a young couple who lived in a nice new house and had a nice new car. Every morning they took the same train to work and left the car outside their house. One morning they opened the front door and were shocked because the car was not there.
They went to the police station and reported the theft. They were very unhappy all day, but of course they went to work, came back home, ate dinner and went to bed as usual. The next morning they left the house at their usual time. They were amazed – the car was there again.
On the seat was a bottle of champagne and a letter. The letter said, "I am sorry that I borrowed your car. I am a doctor and it was an emergency. Please accept this bottle of champagne and these two theatre tickets." The happy couple phoned the police and told them that their car was back. That night they went to the theatre and enjoyed themselves.
On their way home they suddenly began to worry. They ran up to the house, opened the front door and went in. The house was empty.

Step 11 A + B Pronunciation

postcard, welcome party, video recorder, police station, boyfriend, thankyou letter, coffee machine, insurance company, dishwasher, power station, wedding present, credit card

T

Step 12 Pronunciation

The clock's at the back on the left.
The clock's in the middle on the right.
The fridge is at the front on the left.
The fridge is in the middle on the left.
The freezer's at the front on the right.
The microwave's at the back on the left.
The dishwasher's in the middle on the right.
The coffee machine's in the middle on the left.

Step 13 A Pronunciation

1. OK, equipment, yes, course, ahead, right, oldest, freezer, down, new, old, hoover
2. questions, first question is, months ago, now

Step 13 B + C Pronunciation

❐ OK, Carole. I'd like to ask you some questions about the equipment you've got in your house.
○ Yes, of course. Go ahead.
❐ Right, well, the first question is: what's the oldest thing you've got?
○ Well, until six months ago it was the freezer, but then it broke down so I had to get a new one. It was about 15 years old, the old one. Now the oldest thing is probably the hoover.

UNIT 5

Step 1 C

1. ❐ Morning, Sally.
   ○ Morning, Tom. Beautiful day, isn't it?
2. ❐ What's the matter?
   ○ It's my credit card. I know I had it this morning but now I can't find it anywhere! I can't understand it!
   ❐ Oh, dear!
3. Now just you listen to me! We're not interested, we don't want to know and you're going to get out of here now or I'll call the police!
4. Get up, make a cup of tea, wash, get dressed, go to work, look at the post, answer the phone …
5. No, not this evening, I'm afraid … No, we were up all last night with the baby … Yeah, perhaps at the weekend? … OK. Bye.
6. Sorry? Yes, seven, they're arriving at seven! It's already quarter to and Roger still isn't back from the office … oh, I do hope it's going to be all right!

Step 3 C

1. △ Am I pleased to see you! I must tell somebody – I've just found out I'm going to have a baby!
   ○ That's great! Congratulations!
2. △ How was your holiday?
   ○ Don't ask! It rained all week and the food was awful.
   △ Oh, dear! I'm sorry to hear that. And it all looked so good in the brochure, didn't it?
3. ○ Hello, don't usually see you on the bus on a nice day like this.
   △ I know. Somebody's stolen my bike!
   ○ Oh, no! Was it insured?
4. △ Guess what – I've passed my driving test!
   ○ That's great! Well done! You must be really pleased.
   △ I certainly am; the only problem is that I can't afford a car yet.
5. △ Well, did you pass?
   ○ I'm afraid not.
   △ Oh, dear! What a pity! You must be very disappointed!
   ○ You can say that again. I feel really miserable!
6. △ Hello, Jean, you don't look too good. What's the matter?
   ○ We've had burglars!
   △ Oh, no! That's terrible! You must be very upset. When did it happen?

Step 6 B

Stand with your feet about 30 centimetres apart.
Lift your arms above your head.
Bend forward and touch the floor between your feet.
Relax a bit.
Put your hands on the floor again and press.
Return to your starting position.

Step 7 A

Simon says
Stand up.
Sit down.
Simon says stand up.
Touch your right leg.
Touch your left leg.
Simon says touch your left leg.
Simon says sit down.
Relax.
Put your hand on your head.
Stand up.
Simon says put your hand on your head.
Simon says relax.

Simon says lift both your hands.
Put your hands down.
Put your hands down.
Simon says put your left hand down.
Put your right hand down.
Simon says put your right hand down.
Simon says stand up.
Simon says touch your nose.
Now touch your ears.
Simon says touch your right hand with one finger of your left hand.
Touch your left hand with one finger of your right hand.
Now touch it with two fingers.
Simon says lift your left hand.
Put your hand on your head.
Simon says put your hands on your knees.
Press your hands on your knees.
Simon says press.
Simon says relax.
Laugh.
Simon says laugh.
Simon says sit down.

Step 11 A Pronunciation

hangover, angry

Step 11 C Pronunciation

missing, finger, language, things, English, long, longer

Step 12 Pronunciation

△ How was your holiday?
○ Don't ask! It rained all week and the food was awful.
△ Oh, dear! I'm sorry to hear that. And it all looked so good in the brochure, didn't it?

Unit 6

Step 4 A + B

❐ What about you, Bruce? Tell us about the places you've been to.
○ Well, I've lived in two countries, England and Germany. We left England in 1975 and we've been in Germany ever since. We lived in Mannheim for four years, from 1975 to 1979, and then we moved to Nuremberg. I've lived in Nuremberg longer than in any other place, actually.
I haven't travelled to a lot of countries really, because we always go to Britain in the summer – not just to England, though. We've spent several holidays in Wales and we've also been to Scotland two or three times. We visited some friends in Glasgow last year, for example. Glasgow is one of Nuremberg's twin cities and we've met quite a lot of people who live there. I must confess we've never been to Ireland, but I would like to go one day.

Now, where else have we spent holidays? France, of course. We used to live quite close to France so we took short trips there quite often at one time. We also went to Normandy with friends a few years ago. We live closer to Italy now and we've been there on holiday a few times. The last time we went was last Easter, when we spent a few days in Venice. Of course, we're even closer to the Czech Republic, and we have some Czech friends, so we've been there for one or two weekend trips. We spent a nice weekend in Prague last September.
Oh, yes, I've been to Switzerland a few times, mostly on holiday, but not for the last few years. I was in Zürich on business a few months ago, though. I've also been to Hungary on business, and that's about it really. Of course, we've travelled though Austria several times but never stayed for more than a day – which is a pity, because it's a nice country. But you can't go everywhere, unfortunately.

Step 6 B + C

❐ Can I help you?
○ Er, yes, please. We're looking for a room for the night.
❐ What kind of accommodation would you like?
○ Oh, bed and breakfast'll be fine, thanks.
❐ How much would you like to pay?
○ Well, the cheaper the better, really – as long as it's not too far from the town centre.
❐ OK. Is it just for one night?
○ Just tonight, yes.
❐ And would you like no-smoking accommodation?
○ Yes, please.
❐ Right, well, let's see what the computer has to offer … yes, there's a bed and breakfast on Mayfield Road that might be suitable.
○ Uh huh. How far is it from the town centre?
❐ About a mile and a half. There's a bus into the centre.
○ Well, that's fine. Can you tell us how to get there?
❐ Of course. I'll show you on the map.
○ And how much is it per night?
❐ Let me see. With the booking fee included that'll be …

T

Step 7 B + C

1. ❏ Excuse me, there's no water in the swimming pool. When are you going to fill it up?
   ○ I'm very sorry, sir. We had to clean it. We're going to fill it tonight.

2. ❏ Excuse me, there are some workmen playing cards outside my window. Would you please do something about it?
   ○ Of course, madam. I'll speak to them immediately.

3. ❏ Excuse me, there's no furniture in my room. Can you do something about it?
   ○ I'm very sorry, sir. I'll deal with it immediately.

4. ❏ There's an enormous insect in my bed. Will you please do something about it?
   ○ Of course, madam. I'll send someone immediately.

5. ❏ Excuse me, my bathwater's dirty. Could you do something about it?
   ○ I'm very sorry, madam. It happens sometimes. Don't worry about it.

Step 9 C

Railway stations,
bus terminals,
airports.
Hotels
and
waiting rooms.
Forms
to fill in.
Museums
and
art galleries
to see.
And
empty
churches.
Guide books
and
menus
to read.
Struggles with
words.
Timetables
to study.
Haste.
Must holidays
be
so
tiring?

Step 10 A

The British Association of Travel Agents held their annual conference in Sorrento in 1985. Most of the delegates missed the first day - the conference train was late and the flight was delayed because of fog at Gatwick Airport. A large number of delegates got food-poisoning, two delegates fell down stairs and the marketing director of Kuoni travel was bitten by a snake and developed blood-poisoning.
When the organizers of the annual golf competition arrived they found that there was no golf course in Sorrento, so they moved the competition to Dublin.

At the high point of the conference the Italian Minister of Development addressed the delegates in the Forum at Pompeii and a local travel agent decided to fly over the delegates and drop 3,500 roses. The ceremony had just started when a low-flying plane appeared. Its noise completely drowned the minister's speech. It dropped its flowers, but unfortunately missed the Forum. A few minutes later the plane appeared again, flying just over the delegates' heads. Five times the plane flew over and not a single flower landed near the delegates, but there were roses all over Mount Vesuvius.

Step 12 B Pronunciation

Germany, Austria, Russia, Sweden, Italy, Poland
holiday, country, Turkey, flown, Easter, driven

Step 13 B Pronunciation

holiday ads, swimming pool, food-poisoning, travel agent, self-catering, workmen, power station, art galleries, bus terminals, airports, waiting rooms, railway stations, guide books, timetables, an English-speaking country

UNIT 7

Step 1 B

I need an aspirin.
Where do I get a newspaper?
I've just noticed my passport's out of date.
What's for dinner in First Class?
Is it too early for the bar?
Is it are not my wife's ticket here to pick up?
Que?
What's the code for Dayton, Ohio?
Please, somebody.
They've put the wrong name on my ticket.
Where is the Departure Lounge?
Do they take traveller's cheques in duty-free?
Can I choose my seat after I get on board?
Can my son sit in the cockpit?
I think that's my plane taking off.
Where do I check in?

Step 3 A – C

❏ Mark Scott is going to tell us about some of the jobs he's had, and he's certainly had quite a lot. What was your first job, Mark?
○ Well, while I was still at school, I worked as a waiter in a restaurant near the theatre in Bristol. The actors used to come in after the show and so on – it was very interesting. I learned a lot about all sorts of things.

❐ And what about when you left school? You didn't go straight to university, did you?
○ No, I didn't. I worked as a librarian for four years, but the pay wasn't very good so I kept on working as a waiter as well, and for a while I was in the library from nine to five and waiting from six till one. Those were the days! And then I started to move around a bit and had a lot of different jobs. For instance, I worked in a vineyard in France for a while: it was hard work but I've never felt fitter. Oh, and what else did I do? At one time I worked for an antique dealer and then I spent some time working for a builder. Some funny things happened in that job: one of the other workers fell through a roof and landed in the kitchen of this house, and the woman who was in the kitchen at the time said, "Oh, hello my dear, would you like a cup of tea?" So it could be a bit dangerous sometimes, too. Er, then for a while I worked in a factory which made batteries. Now that job was really dirty and unhealthy because of the materials we worked with.
❐ And then?
○ Well, at that point I thought it was time I got a proper job, so I decided to train as a qualified librarian, but it didn't work out and instead of that I got a job as a sales assistant in a department store. That was OK and after a while I became a department manager, but then I finally decided to go to university and study English. I did that, and when I finished I got a job with a language school. I started as a social organizer, which meant I was a tourist guide, a disc jockey and all sorts of other things as well. You work long hours in a job like that but it was good fun. I stayed with the school for nearly five years and by the time I left I knew quite a lot about teaching, too. Then I moved to Germany. I taught Business English for ten years and became a teacher trainer. And now I work for a publisher.

Step 4 B

1. I've been here for two years and I'm thinking about a new job because I'm getting a bit bored. I'd like to work with children.
2. I was really pleased when young John got a job here last year. I've worked here for 20 years and it's a good company, but he's looking for a new job now because they're getting rid of staff, and of course it's last in, first out.
3. We're finishing our studies this year so we're applying for jobs. We'd prefer to stay in this area, but we're prepared to go anywhere.
4. Our children have left home now and we're taking a computer course because we'd like to go out to work again soon. We don't want to spend all day at home on our own.
5. I'm brushing up my English because my company's doing more and more export business, and I might need it. I've forgotten nearly everything I learned at school.
6. My husband retired last month and he's learning to cook at last! When I stop work next year, we want to do an advanced cookery course together in France. He's looking forward to it, and so am I.

Step 6 B

1. △ Truman plc. Good morning.
   ○ Good morning, my name's Roger Taylor. I'd like to speak to Jenny Faber.
   △ Hold on, Mr Taylor, I'll put you through. Oh dear, I'm afraid the line's busy. Would you like to leave a message?
   ○ Yes, please. Would you ask her to phone me back as soon as possible?
   △ Fine, Mr Taylor. I'll tell her you called.
2. ❐ Mr Cosby's office.
   ▽ Hello, this is Liz May. I'm calling about an order. Can I speak to Mr Cosby, please?
   ❐ I'm sorry, he's not in this morning. Can I take a message?
   ▽ Yes, please. Could you tell him I called and that I'll phone back tomorrow?
   ❐ Right, thank you, Ms May. I'll tell him.

Step 11 A + B Pronunciation

I need to send a fax
Is it sunny in Los Angeles?
My canary's escaped.
I'm calling about an order.
I'd like to speak to Jenny Faber.

Step 11 D Pronunciation

Good morning.
I have to phone my wife.
The pay wasn't very good.
I trained as a teacher.
Would you like to leave a message?
He's looking forward to it.
I'm getting a bit bored.

T

Unit 8

Step 2 B

… and here once more is the recipe for that simple but delicious vegetable curry.
First of all, the ingredients. For four or five servings you need: one kilo of mixed vegetables such as aubergines, peppers, potatoes, courgettes, leeks, cauliflowers and carrots; a tin of tomatoes; one tablespoon of lemon juice; a two-centimetre piece of fresh ginger; three or four cloves of garlic; two tablespoons of oil; two teaspoons of ground coriander; one teaspoon of ground cinnamon; half a teaspoon of turmeric; one teaspoon of ground cumin; half a teaspoon of chili powder and a little salt to taste.
And here's what you do. First prepare the vegetables and cut them into pieces of about one or two centimetres. Then peel the ginger and the garlic and chop them finely together. Heat the oil in a heavy saucepan, add the chopped ginger and garlic and the dry spices and fry everything together for a minute or two. Now add the vegetables, the lemon juice and the tinned tomatoes and season with salt. Bring the curry to the boil and cook it gently for 30 – 40 minutes. Stir occasionally. Serve with boiled rice.
Mm, I'm feeling hungry already! And that's all from us today at Studio Five. We hope you'll be with us again tomorrow at the same time for …

Step 4 A

- ❐ Hello?
- ○ Hello, Pat. It's Chris.
- ❐ Oh, hello, Chris. How are you?
- ○ Fine, thanks. Look, the reason I'm calling is I've just seen in the paper that there's a new Indian restaurant in town. Would you like to go there tomorrow?
- ❐ Oh, that would be nice! But I'm afraid I can't go tomorrow - I'm working late. What about Friday?
- ○ Friday's fine, yes. Where shall we meet? At the restaurant? Or I can pick you up at your flat, if you prefer.
- ❐ Well, that would be great, thanks. What time?
- ○ Half past seven?
- ❐ OK, half past seven. I'm looking forward to it.
- ○ Me too. See you Friday, then. Bye.
- ❐ Bye.

Step 6 B

1. ❐ Happy Birthday!
   ○ Happy Birthday to you, Happy Birthday to you, Happy Birthday, dear …

2. Quiet please, everybody! It's time for a little speech, I'm afraid. We're all here today to wish Jim Russell all the best for the future now he's leaving us after no less than 40 years with the firm. Yes, it was 40 years ago – almost to the day – when … and so, Jim, we all wish you all the best!

3. ❐ Hello, there! Nice to see you! Come in, come in!
   ○ Merry Christmas!

4. ❐ Happy New Year everybody!
   ○ Happy New Year!

5. ❐ Well, here's to the happy couple! How many years is it now?
   ○ That's a good question! Let me think … must be 13 years!
   ❐ 13 years! Well, congratulations, and cheers!
   ○ Cheers!

Unit 9

Step 2 B

Coat

Sometimes I have wanted
to throw you off
like a heavy coat.

Sometimes I have said
you would not let me
breathe or move.

But now that I am free
to choose light clothes
or none at all

I feel the cold
and all the time I think
how warm it used to be.

Step 3 A

How many white shirts are there in the room?
How many pairs of brown shoes are there in the room?
How many pairs of red socks are there in the room?
How many pairs of black trousers are there in the room?
How many pink or yellow blouses are there in the room?
How many green skirts or dresses are there in the room?
How many blue pullovers are there in the room?

Step 3 B

If you're wearing jeans today, stand up.
If your neighbour's wearing white socks, stand up.
If you're wearing a suit, stand up.
If any of your neighbour's clothes are blue, stand up.
If you like hats, stand up.

If you often wear shorts in the summer, stand up.
If you like T-shirts, stand up.
If you never wear a tie, stand up.
If your neighbour's shoes are black, stand up.

Step 5 B

1. I'm about the same size as my daughter and she just helps herself to my clothes any time she feels like it. Of course, she only takes the nicest things. She's got more clothes than the rest of us, anyway. And now she's started to borrow my husband's pullovers and shirts as well, and her brother's shirts, and her boyfriend's jackets. Of course, nobody is allowed to wear anything of hers. Her motto seems to be: 'What's mine is mine, and what's yours is mine, too.'

2. Children today are into clothes. I think that's a big difference between my generation and my children's generation. My parents certainly weren't rich, but they weren't poor, either, just sort of average. My brother and I, we only had one of most things – one pair of shoes, one coat, one pullover, one pair of trousers for school, and so on – but it didn't worry us. Most children were in the same situation. Clothes weren't very important to us. Certainly not as important as they are to today's young people. And fashion? We didn't know what it meant.

3. The fashions didn't change every six months like they do today, and we kept the same clothes for years. We couldn't afford to throw away perfectly good skirts or blouses just because we got bored with them, or because the colour wasn't fashionable anymore. We mended them to make them last longer, or we made the dresses a bit longer or a bit shorter. And children's clothes were passed on from one child to the next, so when your big sister's clothes were too small for her, you got them, and when they were too small for you, your little sister got them.

Step 7 B

Happiness is waste

The better you look, the happier you are.
To look good, you need fashionable clothes.
Fashionable clothes are expensive,
Therefore the more money you spend on clothes, the happier you are.

The quicker fashions change, the more clothes you buy
And the more money you spend.

Therefore the quicker fashions change, the happier you are.
The more clothes you buy, the more clothes you throw away.
Therefore the more you waste, the happier you are.
Therefore happiness is waste.

Step 9 B

1. ❐ I like your new glasses.
   ❍ Oh, thank you!

2. ❐ That pullover really suits you.
   ❍ Oh, do you think so? I'm glad you like it.

3. ❐ Those jeans look really great.
   ❍ Thank you!

4. ❐ That's a beautiful ring.
   ❍ Thank you. It was my grandmother's.

5. ❐ That's a new blouse, isn't it?
   ❍ Yes, I got it last week. Do you like it?
   ❐ Mm. It's very nice.

Step 12 A + B Pronunciation

green blouses
green pullovers
green coats

red blouses
red pullovers
red coats

white blouses
white pullovers
white coats
white trousers
white dresses

12 D Pronunciation

favourite clothes
sit down
favourite piece of clothing
one pair
one coat

we got bored
a bit longer
credit card
handbag
sunglasses

PREVIEW C

Step 4

1. Here is an announcement for passengers on Flight BA728 to Geneva. This flight is now boarding at Gate 23. Passengers on Flight BA728 to Geneva, please proceed to Gate 23.

2. ❐ And what do you do if you can't sleep at night?
   ✦ It doesn't happen very often, but I usually try to read till I fall asleep. Either that or I do relaxation exercises.
   ∇ I watch television. It's so boring it's difficult to stay awake, isn't it? If that doesn't work, I take a sleeeping pill.

3. Since my husand and I got divorced, I've brought my son up on my own. He spends every other weekend with his father.
4. Leave the motorway at junction 16 and follow the signs for Birmingham. Go straight on for about, er, three miles till you come to a pub called the Coach and Horses. Turn left there, and after about a mile look out for Nelson Drive.
5. Somebody washing up.
6. ❐ What do you think of your mother, generally?
   △ Well, she's all right.
   ❐ And compared to other people's mothers?
   △ She's different; not as conservative as most of them.

UNIT 10

Step 2 B

1. cleaning teeth
2. flushing the toilet
3. having a shower
4. washing up
5. washing the car
6. drinking
7. watering the garden
8. washing clothes

Step 8 C

❐ Excuse me, I'm from Radio Downtown and we're asking people how they deal with everyday aches and pains. Can I ask you some questions?
○ Well, if you're quick, you can.
❐ Thank you very much. What you do when you have a headache?
○ Well, I usually just take an aspirin.
❐ And toothache?
○ I don't know, really. It doesn't often happen. Go to the dentist if it's really bad, probably. Otherwise, take an aspirin?
❐ And what about you, madam, what do you do for headaches?
△ Open the window if I'm indoors, maybe go for a little walk – get some fresh air, that's the main thing.
❐ And for stomachache?
△ Stomachache? I haven't had stomachache for ages. Let me think … if it were really bad I'd probably go to bed.
❐ Do you ever have backache?
○ Yes, I'm afraid I do.
❐ And what do you do about it?
○ I ignore it.
❐ And stomachache?
○ Stomachache? A small brandy works wonders in my experience.

❐ Excuse me, I'm from Radio Downtown and we're asking people how they deal with everyday aches and pains. Can I ask you some questions?
▽ Go ahead.
❐ Thank you. Do you ever suffer from backache?
▽ Yes. Yes, I do.
❐ And do you do anything about it?
▽ I keep moving as much as possible.
❐ And do you ever have a stiff neck?
▽ In the mornings, yes.
❐ And what do you do about that?
▽ Well, it depends. Sometimes I do some exercises, sometimes I do nothing at all. It often gets better on its own.
❐ And you, sir? What do you do if you've got a sore throat?
✧ Stop talking, that's the first thing. I also drink hot water with honey and lemon and rum.
❐ And what do you do if you can't sleep at night?
✧ It doesn't happen very often, but I usually try to read till I fall asleep. Either that or I do relaxation exercises.
▽ I watch television. It's so boring it's difficult to stay awake, isn't it? If that doesn't work, I take a sleeeping pill.
❐ And what if you have a hangover?
▽ A hangover? Well, I take an aspirin and a long, hot shower, and then I try and get some fresh air.
✧ I don't drink, so I've never had one.
❐ Thank you very much.
✧ You're welcome.

Step 9 B

Remember aspirin

Remember aspirin
when you have a headache.

Take sleeping tablets
if you wake at night.

And if you feel lonely
– take a tranquilizer.

But in case this should let you down
– think of me.
Think what a fool I've been.
And you'll smile
and
it'll help.

Step 11 A + B Pronunciation

1. If I could afford it, I'd have my own sauna.
2. Luxury is living on your own in a big flat.

3. Opening the window could be good for quite a lot of things.
4. Is it sunny in Los Angeles?
5. My father-in-law was painting his front door when it started to rain.
6. At one point …
7. Can I get a coffee round here?
8. If you want to feel happy, just laugh.

Step 11 D Pronunciation

1. I never use a razor; I always use an electric shaver.
2. On the other hand, …
3. Can I speak to Mr. Cosby, please?
4. I wouldn't like to be a traffic warden.
5. Counting sheep's good for insomnia.
6. Speaking.
7. Can I take a message?
8. After a while, …

UNIT 11

Step 4 A

Life and numbers

Once upon a time
there was
just Me.
I soon realized there were
three of us, then gradually
four. At last there were just
the two of us. All at once four
of us. Suddenly just the two
of us again. Now there is
only Me
as in the beginning.

Step 4 B

1. Well, my first marriage broke up when my wife just walked out and left me with the children, and that was hard, very hard, I can tell you, for two or three years or more. It's not always easy now, of course, but what happened was that fairly soon after my divorce came through I met Susan, and we got along so well it was, well, just sort of obvious to both of us that we should get together, and so that's what we did. Susan was on her own after her husband was killed in an accident and left her with three little kids, and for the two of us to deal with five of them was easier for both of us than being on our own, so we got together. Then, nature being the way it is, it wasn't long before the twins joined us and then there were nine of us altogether, and the children aged between three and eleven. Well, it's a bit noisy round here sometimes, but actually it's great. We all love each other so much and enjoy each other's company. And the big ones help look after the little ones. The family almost runs itself.

2. Since my husband and I got divorced, I've brought my son up on my own. He spends every other weekend with his father. Fortunately we haven't got any real financial problems, and I've also managed to keep working, but life as a single parent isn't always easy. His father buys him expensive presents and takes him out, and I have all the daily problems with homework, or persuading him to wash, that kind of thing.

3. We both have good jobs and our careers to think about and we don't really see at the moment how we could find the time for children, or even how we could afford it at the moment, really. I mean, if one of us had to give up our job, we wouldn't be able to afford the house. And we wouldn't really want to pay somebody to look after the children. I think it's something which we'll think seriously about in five years or so – we'll have to see how things are going professionally and financially.

4. When James lost his job he decided to stay at home and look after the children. We thought it would be just temporary, but in fact he really likes it, and we've decided to keep things that way, at least for the next few years.

5. Mother, father: married to each other; two children: one girl, one boy – I suppose we're what you call a traditional family, but we seem to be in a minority these days. We notice that when we look round at the other children's families, the other children our children are at school with. In fact, I read somewhere recently that we only make up about ten or eleven per cent of todays's households.

Step 7 A

❏ What do you think of your daughter, generally?
○ I think she's very nice. She's amusing, friendly, good-looking, fun to have around – I like her.
❏ What is she good at?
○ She dresses well, she's good at art, quite musical, and she's very easy to talk to: she's a natural conversationalist.
❏ What do you think of your mother, generally?
△ Well, she's all right.

❏ And compared to other people's mothers?
△ She's different; not as conservative as most of them.
❏ What do your friends think of her?
△ They think she's nice because she lets me do everything I want.
❏ Has she got any annoying habits?
○ Yes, she doesn't tidy her room; er, leaves shampoo all over the bathroom, and she doesn't hang up her coat when she comes in.
△ Throwing my boyfriend out of the house too early; er, and not giving me enough money.
❏ What sort of things do you talk about with each other?
○ Well, anything and everything, really. I can't think of anything that we specially don't talk about.
△ Er, school, and other people's boyfriends, because that's what she likes to hear about.
❏ Do you have any tastes or interests in common?
○ Well, we both prefer jeans to skirts. We like the same films – some films anyway. Then there's music and food – let's say, she generally eats what I cook, at least.
△ I have nothing in common with my mother at all. I don't like the same clothes as her or the same food as her and we do not have the same taste in music. Er, she doesn't like putting on make-up or going out in the evening to pubs. She hates dancing, and I love it, and when we're on holiday she likes sightseeing and museums, which I think is dead boring.
❏ And in what ways are you like each other?
○ People say we look alike. We both enjoy life. We've got a similar sense of humour, I think.
△ Well, we've got the same colour hair.

Step 11 A + B Pronunciation

My mother's from Leeds but her family came from Ireland. They arrived in Leeds about two or three generations ago. My father comes from Cornwall. Cornwall's in the south-west of England.

Step 11 D Pronunciation

1. ❏ My father's parents were from Scotland.
   ○ I don't know where my grandparents came from.
2. ❏ My parents met in Japan.
   ○ Japan? What were they doing there?
3. ❏ My mother was working for an company in Tokyo.
   ○ What about your father?
4. ❏ My family's been in this area for about a hundred years.
   ○ Oh. We only moved here last June.

Unit 12

Step 1 D

York
I went round the Railway Museum
in York
there were plenty of trains
but it was quicker to walk

Step 4 A

Here is an announcement for passengers on Flight BA728 to Geneva. This flight is now boarding at Gate 23. Passengers on Flight BA728 to Geneva, please proceed to Gate 23.

Lufthansa regret to announce a delay of 45 minutes to Flight LH4029 to Frankfurt. This flight is now scheduled to leave at 13.45. We apologize for any inconvenience.

Final call for Air France Flight AF825 to Paris, departing at 12.40. Will passengers please proceed immediately to Gate 15. Passengers for Paris on Flight AF825, please proceed immediately to Gate 15.

Step 4 B

Attention, please! The train now standing at Platform 3 is the 2.40 Gatwick Express. The 2.36 to Brighton has been delayed and will leave Platform 3 at approximately 2.45. The 2.38 Dover train will be leaving in approximately ten minutes from Platform 5. Customers for Dover, please proceed to Platform 5.

Step 4 C

Does anybody here own a yellow Metro, because I'm afraid it's blocking the exit to the car park. Could you move it a bit? Right, thanks very much. Oh, and there's a policeman outside who'd like a word with the owner of the black Rover. Don't ask me why.

Step 5 A

1. Leave the motorway at junction 16 and follow the signs for Birmingham. Go straight on for about, er, three miles till you come to a pub called the Coach and Horses. Turn left there, and after about a mile look out for Nelson Drive. It's on the right. It's, er, just before a railway bridge, so if you cross a bridge you'll know you've gone too far.

2. Take the train from Euston to Preston and change there for Chorley. I think it's the Blackpool line, but you can check that. If you've got heavy luggage, the best thing is to take a taxi from the station, because it's quite a long walk. There are buses to Southport Road, but I don't know how often they run in the evening.

Bradford to Bristol

from Bradford Yorkshire
to Bristol Temple Meads
you don't have to change your underwear
but you have to change at Leeds

Step 7 B

In July 1841, Thomas Cook offered a day trip by rail from Leicester to Loughborough for one shilling (five pence in today's money). 150 years later, the company he created advertised a day trip by Concorde to Lapland for £1,595.
The man who started it all was born on November 22, 1808 in Derbyshire, England. He left school at the age of ten and worked in various jobs until 1828, when he became a Baptist missionary. He was a teetotaller and the aim of the Loughborough trip was to get working people out of the city pubs.
It was such a success that Cook negotiated deals with several railway companies for cheap group bookings. Soon he was advertising and selling trips in the English Midlands and in Scotland, and within a few years was also organizing trips to mainland Europe.
Travel in the early days of package tours was not as easy as today. When a party of 70 tourists headed for Rome in the early 1860's, it took nine stagecoaches, 432 horses, 108 men and numerous bullocks to get them over the St Gotthard Pass. Cook himself could only speak English. "Where are the ladies who know French and German?" he used to ask his tourists when he got into difficulties; "Forward please, and say what this man is jabbering about!"
What with terrible weather, illness, collapsing tents and falls from horses, Cook's first Middle East tour was not the happiest of trips. And although only one traveller actually died, it seems that many of the others thought he was the lucky one.
Despite the problems, Thomas Cook hoped his tours would promote international peace and understanding. His son John, however, was a hard-headed businessman who did not believe in cheap tickets for Baptists, and was quite happy to arrange trips to horse races, and even to a guillotining. He gradually turned his father's company into a profitable and efficient commercial organization.
Thomas Cook died on July 18, 1892 and the business passed into John's hands. One hundred years later, Thomas Cook & Son became part of the German TUI travel group.

Step 11 A + B Pronunciation

In July eighteen forty-one, Thomas Cook offered a day trip by rail from Leicester to Loughborough for one shilling (five pence in today's money). A hundred and fifty years later, the company he created advertised a day trip by Concorde to Lapland for one thousand five hundred and ninety-five pounds.

Step 11 D Pronunciation

The man who started it all was born on November the twenty-second, eighteen hundred and eight in Derbyshire, England. He left school at the age of ten and worked in various jobs until eighteen twenty-eight, when he became a Baptist missionary. He was a teetotaller and the aim of the Loughborough trip was to get working people out of the city pubs.

PREVIEW D

Step 3

1. airport / station
2. car / bike
3. hotel / camping
4. living room / bedroom
5. TV / radio
6. toothbrush / hairbrush
7. future / past
8. children / parents

UNIT 13

Step 2 A

1. I bought this sweatshirt yesterday and when I got home I discovered this hole under the arm, you see? If you've got another one, I'd like to change it.
2. I don't think this camera is working right. Can you check it for me, please?
3. I haven't got enough cash to pay for all this. Will you take a eurocheque?
4. I'm looking for a pair of walking shoes. What's a size 39 in English sizes?

5. Excuse me, can you help me? I'm interested in a radio alarm clock. Can you tell me something about these? Is there one you'd specially recommend?
6. These grapefruit I bought this morning are all rotten inside. I'd like my money back.
7. Excuse me, have you got any smaller bottles of this shampoo? I don't need this much.

Step 6 B

Too much

Sweets wrapped in paper, in packets and jars,
Three dozen different chocolate bars;
I can't count the types of biscuit and cake –
It's so hard to choose I'm starting to shake.

There's too much, just too much of all this here stuff,
An awful lot less would be more than enough.
(It's all sugar, isn't it? It all rots your teeth.)

Cheddar or Stilton, Chester or Brie?
How shall I choose? Which cheese shall it be?
Thirty fruit yoghurts in small or large pots –
Trying to pick one brings me out in spots.

There's too much, just too much of all this here stuff,
An awful lot less would be more than enough.
(It's all animal fat, only good for a heart attack!)

Big packets, small packets, jumbos and babies;
Cornflake variety really amazes!
Ninety-five p or two pounds ten:
How many grams in each packet again?
Eight types of milk and six sorts of cream –
Which should I take? I silently scream.

There's too much, just too much of all this here stuff,
An awful lot less would be more than enough.
(Who needs breakfast? Just give me coffee, no milk!)

With so many choices I really can't think,
I feel like relaxing at home with a drink;
Just what I need for some peace of mind,
But under the DRINKS sign what do I find?
(The usual situation, of course!)

Sherry, martini, madeira, port – cheers!
Kiwi-fruit cocktails and eighty-five beers;
Whisky and brandy and vodka and gin –
Total confusion's the state that I'm in.
Red wine or white wine, medium dry, sweet?
Please, someone, choose for me – I'm dead on my feet!

Because, let me tell you –
There's too much, just too much of all this here stuff,
An awful lot less would be more than enough.
(It's all too much for me, anyway!)

Step 7 A

Here are some of the special offers we would like to draw your attention to today.

In our photoshop today only: buy two films and get one free. Three films for the price of two in our photoshop on the first floor.

In our sports department on the second floor you will find a wide range of top-class running shoes at super-reduced prices.

Join our holiday competition and win a free holiday. Forms from our travel agency on the ground floor.

A pound off this week's top ten CD's in the music department on the ground floor, and big reductions on computer games, also on the ground floor.

In our kitchen department on the second floor you can watch a demonstration of cooking with an electric wok. While you're there, don't forget to try out our new range of dining room chairs in the furniture department.

If you're feeling hungry, today's special in the basement restaurant is vegetarian lasagne. Or choose some marvellous French cheeses and patés from our French food corner in the food department in the basement.

Step 8 B + C

❐ I've been talking to Peter Willems, the manager of a large department store, and I asked him how stores like his are planned.

❐ Er, Peter, let's start with a brand-new, empty store. What would you put where?

○ Well, the first thing I would need to know, if it's a store with more than one entrance, is which is going to be the main entrance? And my main entrance is going to be on the busiest street.

❐ Because that's where the most people are.

○ That's right. And it's the space near the main entrance which is the best space in the shop from the store's point of view. For some reason, the majority of customers who go into a department store turn left rather than right, so the most valuable space of all is the space near the main entrance towards the left of the shop. And that's where you put what you most want to sell.

❐ Any idea why people go to the left?

○ I don't think anybody knows, really. But it's a fact of life for department stores.

❐ Interesting. So in this valuable space at the front of the shop, you put what you can sell fastest.

○ Well, it's not that simple. You sell food quickly, but food doesn't make much money, so what you actually want in the best space are things that sell quickly but which also give you a good profit.
❏ Like?
○ Like cosmetics, perfume, toothpaste, that kind of thing. Women's tights, men's socks. These are all everyday things which people need to buy regularly, and they're things that people will buy when they see them. Like chocolate, sweets and so on, and of course your special offers. So if somebody sees a nice pullover, perhaps they didn't come out that day intending to buy a pullover, but it's a nice pullover and a good price, and so they buy it. Ladies' clothes, blouses and so on, also tend to be near the front, or if it's a shop on several floors, women's clothes are nearer the entrance than men's, often on the first floor, and the men on the second.
❏ That's the front of the shop, so what about the rest of it?
○ Generally, the further back you go in the shop, or the higher up you go, the more you will find the kind of articles that last longer, and that people don't buy so often. Electrical goods, say. Or if a department store still sells furniture, you'll often find it on the top floor. People don't buy fridges or furniture on impulse, just because they happen to see something they like. You see, there are always more people on the ground floor, and always more people nearer the entrance. And where the people are, that's where you show the goods you want to sell. Within the shop, of course, there are ways of getting the customers to go where you want them to go, for example you can make the …

Step 11 B Pronunciation

1. I'm looking for a pair of sandals.
2. I'd ask for the manager.
3. This is a bit too big for me.
4. They'd probably give you a funny look.
5. Have you sent a fax recently?
6. Can you recommend a good hairdresser?

UNIT 14

Step 4 B

The most important thing we've learned,
So far as children are concerned,
Is never, never, never let
Them near your television set –
Or better still, just don't install
The idiotic thing at all.
In almost every house we've been
We've watched them gaping at the screen.
They sit and stare and stare and sit
Until they're hypnotized by it.
Oh yes, we know it keeps them still,
They don't climb out the window sill,
They never fight or kick or punch,
They leave you free to cook the lunch
And wash the dishes in the sink –
But did you ever stop to think,
To wonder just exactly what
This does to your beloved tot?

Step 5 A

As you listen to the music, imagine a scene.
Where is it? On a beach? By a river?
What time of day is it?
Do you see any colours? Any objects? Are they near or far?
Is the mood of the scene happy? Sad? Peaceful?
What's happening?
Are there any people in the scene? What are they doing?
Who are they? What do they look like?
Are they talking? What about?
Why are they there? Where are they going?
What do you know about them?
Keep listening, and when the music finishes, describe what you saw to a partner.

Step 6 A

Three pieces of music

Step 7 B

1. I live on the third floor and I play the clarinet. I listen to jazz and blues on my cassette recorder every evening. I just love the blues.
2. I live on the second floor. I prefer classical music, and I've got a lot of classical CD's. I also like playing the guitar.
3. I live on the first floor and I play the violin. I've got lots of LP's and I particularly like folk music.
4. I live on the ground floor and I like pop music. My hobbies are playing the piano and listening to the radio.

Step 10 A + B Pronunciation

1. We're going to start with the news at six o'clock.
2. Taxis are convenient but not very cheap.
3. Would you rather watch a programme about social problems, European history or animals?

4. What were the main stories in today's paper?
5. Can you check it for me, please?

Unit 15

Step 1 B

1. I think it's EI, but Mary says it's IE and Peter's not sure. He thinks it might even be EA, so I'm going to have to look it up in the dictionary.
2. Oh! I didn't understand a word of all that. Could you just ask him again what time the coach is picking us up and where we have to be?
3. At the beginning it was all great fun and it wasn't very difficult, it was just nice to be able to say anything at all – but after a while you realize that you have to put in some work. A couple of hours a week really isn't enough. And then of course you start to think, "Well, can I really afford the time?"
4. I have to deal with customers from different countries and there's just no way I could work here without it. I have to be able to speak it.
5. People were really nice and friendly. I know everybody says it, but it's true. And they didn't mind saying things again if I didn't understand. They were always very patient; it was nice to talk to them. After a while I stopped worrying about mistakes and just talked.
6. The grammar they do is far too complicated for me, but that doesn't bother me, really. I can actually say more than they can. Checking their vocabulary's quite good fun – we have competitions, and it helps me to remember words.
7. It's the most difficult thing for me, especially all the different accents you hear. The problem is you can't see the person you're talking to, and it's difficult to know if they've really understood what you say. You have to concentrate very hard.

Step 2 A

1. △ ... and what time does it arrive?
   ○ Well, ten past twelve, I think.
   △ Did you say ten past twelve?
   ○ That's right.
   △ Oh, dear. That's too late, I'm afraid. Isn't there an earlier one you can take?
   ○ Sorry? What was that again?
   △ I said, isn't there an earlier one? Ten past twelve's too late. We have to be there at 2.30 and it's a three-hour drive from the airport.
   ○ Oh, well, I'll have to change the booking. I'm sure there's one that gets in at about eight thirty.
   △ I'm afraid I didn't get that.
   ○ Half past eight; I think there's one that gets in about half past eight.
   △ Fine. You'd better take that one then.

2. ❐ ... I see, well in that case I'd like to leave a message for her.
   ▽ Of course, go ahead.
   ❐ It's about the chairs we ordered a week ago, on the twenty-fifth. The order number's TA38574.
   ▽ Can you repeat that, please?
   ❐ Of course, TA38574.
   ▽ TA38574. And what's the problem?
   ❐ Well, we'd like to change the order if that's possible. Perhaps she could ring me tomorrow and we can talk about it. It's 5674451.
   ▽ Could you say that a bit more slowly, please? What was your number again?
   ❐ 5674451.

Step 5 A + B

1. ○ Where were you last night? I waited for you for over an hour!
   ❐ Oh, dear. Well, er, let me think. Er, well, you see, what happened was, er, I, er ...
2. ○ I think Frank Sinatra's absolutely brilliant, don't you? Just fantastic!
   ❐ Well, er, I don't know really. I mean, er, it depends, doesn't it?
3. ○ How did you vote at the last election?
   ❐ That's an interesting question. What do you think?
4. ○ How much do you earn in your new job?
   ❐ I beg your pardon?
   ○ I was wondering how much you earn in your new job.
   ❐ Oh, er, it's difficult to say.

Step 6 B

My head is the apple without any core
My mind is the house without any door
My heart is the palace wherein she may be
And she may unlock it without any key.

Werkübersicht BRIDGES 2

Classroom Book	Klett-Nr. 501420
2 Cassetten zum Classroom Book	Klett-Nr. 501421
2 CDs zum Classroom Book	Klett-Nr. 501425
Practice Book	Klett-Nr. 501422
1 Cassette zum Practice Book	Klett-Nr. 501424
1 CD zum Practice Book	Klett-Nr. 501426
Learner's Pack	
mit 3 Cassetten (501421 + 501424)	Klett-Nr. 501404
mit 3 CDs (501425 + 501426)	Klett-Nr. 501405
Teacher's Book	Klett-Nr. 501423
Teacher's Pack	
mit Teacher's Book (501423) und 3 Cassetten (501421 + 501424)	Klett-Nr. 501406
mit Teacher's Book (501423) und 3 CDs (501425 + 501426)	Klett-Nr. 501408

BRIDGES 2 Wettbewerb

Für die Autor/innen und die Redaktion wäre es sehr interessant zu sehen, was Sie im Verlauf der Arbeit mit **BRIDGES 2** geschrieben, gezeichnet und gestaltet haben. Wir möchten Sie deshalb einladen, ein Exemplar Ihrer Kurszeitschrift oder das Ergebnis eines anderen Kursprojekts an uns zu senden:

Ernst Klett Verlag für Wissen und Bildung GmbH
Redaktion Weiterbildung Englisch
Postfach 10 60 16
70049 Stuttgart

Einmal im Jahr vergeben wir für die beste Einsendung einer Kursgruppe einen Preis!

QUELLENNACHWEIS

Bilder und Cartoons

S. 13: © 1994 KFS/Distr. BULLS; S. 20: (l.) Topham Picturepoint, Edenbridge, Kent; (M.) R. Sebert, Augsburg; (r.) Brenda Boulton, Minehead; S. 23: The Royal Photographic Society, Bath, Adolf Morath: G.B. Shaw; S. 26: aus "Miss Manners", Fireside plc, New York 1983; S. 27: © 1994 KFS/Distr. BULLS; S. 28: (1) York Pullman Ltd., York; (3 + 7 + 9) Britische Zentrale für Fremdenverkehr, Frankfurt; (5) Edinburgh School of English, Edinburgh; S. 30: (l.) Institut für Auslandsbeziehungen, Stuttgart; (M.) Centre for Alternative Technology, Machynlleth; (u.) Walterscheid GmbH, Lohmar; S. 37: © 1994 KFS/Distr. BULLS; S. 38: (l. + r.M.) Nokia GmbH, Düsseldorf; (M.) Braun AG, Kronberg/Taunus; (r.o. + r.u.) Bauknecht Hausgeräte GmbH, Stuttgart; (u.) © Mark Grant/Knight Features reproduced by permission; S. 39: E. Vorrath-Wiesenthal, Böblingen; S. 43: Copyright PUNCH/Lüning, Lübeck; S. 47: © 1994 KFS/Distr. BULLS; S. 48: © 1994 KFS/Distr. BULLS; S. 53: C. Birkhold, Schwieberdingen; S. 55: Carlton Tourism Promotions, Auckland; S. 59: (A) C. Birkhold, Schwieberdingen; (B) Klett-Archiv; (C) C. Sawyer, Crawley, Sussex; (D) Brenda Boulton, Minehead; S. 61: © 1994 KFS/Distr. BULLS; S. 62/3: (1 + 2 + 4 + 5) Klett-Archiv; (3 + 6) Topham Picturepoint, Edenbridge, Kent; S. 66: (A) J. Allan Cash, London; (B) Topham Picturepoint, Edenbridge, Kent; (C) Denis Thorpe/The Guardian; S. 68: (1) used with the permission of General Mills, Inc.; (2) Rosamond Richardson: "Sainsbury Cookbook, Vegetarian Meals", photograph by Laurie Evans, published by Martin Books; (3) Elizabeth Ayrton & Theo Fitzgibbon: "Traditional British Cooking" published by Octopus Books; (4) Dharamjit Singh: "Indian Cookery", photograph by Robert Golden, published by Penguin Books Ltd; S. 72: (a – e + g – h) Klett-Archiv; (f) Christine Easterbrook, Sindelfingen; S. 73: reproduced by permission of Newspaper Enterprise Association, Inc.; S. 74: Hugo Dixon; S. 78: (1) Dr. G. Mungai-Maier, Stuttgart; (2 + 3) J. Allan Cash, London; S. 81: © 1994 KFS/Distr. BULLS; S. 83: (1) R. und S. Ersing, Stuttgart; (2 + 3) C. Sawyer, Crawley, Sussex; S. 92: © Schirmer/Mosel Verlag, München; S. 93: © 1955 United Feature Syndicate, Inc.; S. 94: Ulrike Preuss, London; S. 95: © 1994 KFS/Distr. BULLS; S. 96: Brenda Boulton, Minehead; S. 97: Copyright PUNCH/Lüning, Lübeck; S. 100: (l., M., r.) C. Sawyer, Crawley, Sussex; S. 102: Mary Evans Picture Library; S. 108: Beaminster Chamber of Trade; S. 115: Carlton Tourism Promotions, Auckland; S. 120: Private Eye Productions Ltd., London; S. 122: © 1994 KFS/Distr. BULLS; S. 129: Deutsche Bahnen, Mainz.

Texte

S. 37: Source: Reader's Digest Eurodata Survey, 1990; S. 39: © The Sunday Telegraph Ltd./Alan Scott Publishers Ltd., 1985; S. 43: Wendy Cope: "Serious Concerns" published by Faber and Faber Ltd.; S. 55: L.L. Szkutnik, Warschau; S. 56: Stephen Pile: "Return of Heroic Failures" published by Martin Secker & Warburg; S. 72: Louise Hudson: "Men, who needs them" from Lions Teen Tracks, published by Harper Collins Ltd.; S. 74: Wendy Cope: "Serious Concerns" published by Faber and Faber Ltd.; S. 76: © Vicky Feaver 1981: "Coat from Close Relatives" published by Martin Secker & Warburg; S. 89: L.L. Szkutnik, Warschau; S. 91: © The Telegraph plc., London, 1985; S. 92: © The Sunday Telegraph Ltd., London/Alan Sutton Publishing Ltd., 1985; S. 99: with the kind permission of the British Railways Board; S. 104: The Automobile Association, Basingstoke, Hampshire; S. 120: Roald Dahl: "Charlie and the Chocolate Factory", Penguin Books Ltd.; S. 124: From the title "CHILDREN'S LETTERS TO GOD", reprinted by permission from Workman Publishing, Inc. New York, NY USA.

In einigen Fällen ist es uns trotz intensiver Bemühungen nicht gelungen, die Rechte-Inhaber zu ermitteln. Wir bitten diese, sich mit dem Verlag in Verbindung zu setzen.

Wortschatz systematisch erweitern und wiederholen

Der Thematische Grund- und Aufbauwortschatz von Klett bietet methodisch und lernpsychologisch die besten Voraussetzungen für besonders effizientes, motiviertes Lernen.

Das Wichtigste im Überblick:
- Thematisch und nach Bedeutung geordneter Lernwortschatz mit Satzbeispielen und gebräuchlichen Wendungen
- Jedes Thema in Grundwortschatz und Aufbauwortschatz unterteilt
- 5.786 Worteinträge
- Aktueller Stand
- Praktische Lerntips
- Umweltfreundliche Ausstattung

Von Gernot Häublein und
Recs Jenkins
384 Seiten
Klettnummer **519551**

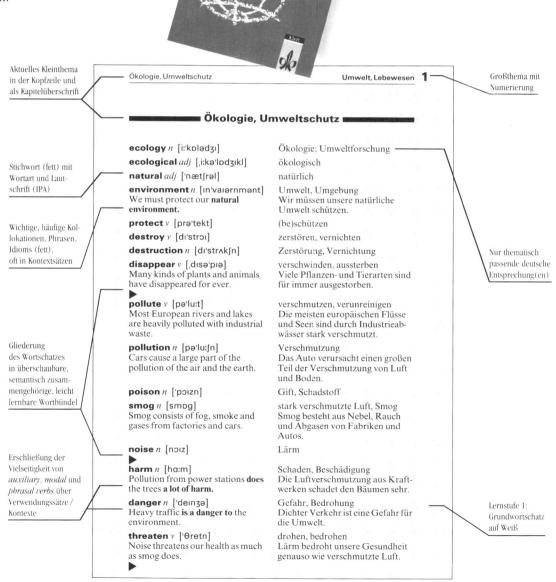

Aktuelles Kleinthema in der Kopfzeile und als Kapitelüberschrift

Ökologie, Umweltschutz — Umwelt, Lebewesen **1**

Großthema mit Numerierung

Ökologie, Umweltschutz

Stichwort (fett) mit Wortart und Lautschrift (IPA)

ecology *n* [iːˈkɒlədʒɪ] — Ökologie; Umweltforschung
ecological *adj* [ˌiːkəˈlɒdʒɪkl] — ökologisch
natural *adj* [ˈnætʃrəl] — natürlich
environment *n* [ɪnˈvaɪərnmənt] — Umwelt, Umgebung
We must protect our **natural environment**. — Wir müssen unsere natürliche Umwelt schützen.

Wichtige, häufige Kollokationen, Phrasen, Idioms (fett), oft in Kontextsätzen

protect *v* [prəˈtekt] — (be)schützen
destroy *v* [dɪˈstrɔɪ] — zerstören, vernichten
destruction *n* [dɪˈstrʌkʃn] — Zerstörung, Vernichtung
disappear *v* [ˌdɪsəˈpɪə] — verschwinden, aussterben
Many kinds of plants and animals have disappeared for ever. — Viele Pflanzen- und Tierarten sind für immer ausgestorben.

Nur thematisch passende deutsche Entsprechung(en)

▶
pollute *v* [pəˈluːt] — verschmutzen, verunreinigen
Most European rivers and lakes are heavily polluted with industrial waste. — Die meisten europäischen Flüsse und Seen sind durch Industrieabwässer stark verschmutzt.

Gliederung des Wortschatzes in überschaubare, semantisch zusammengehörige, leicht lernbare Wortbündel

pollution *n* [pəˈluːʃn] — Verschmutzung
Cars cause a large part of the pollution of the air and the earth. — Das Auto verursacht einen großen Teil der Verschmutzung von Luft und Boden.

poison *n* [ˈpɔɪzn] — Gift, Schadstoff
smog *n* [smɒg] — stark verschmutzte Luft, Smog
Smog consists of fog, smoke and gases from factories and cars. — Smog besteht aus Nebel, Rauch und Abgasen von Fabriken und Autos.

noise *n* [nɔɪz] — Lärm

Erschließung der Vielseitigkeit von *auxiliary*, *modal* und *phrasal verbs* über Verwendungssätze / Kontexte

▶
harm *n* [hɑːm] — Schaden, Beschädigung
Pollution from power stations **does the trees a lot of harm.** — Die Luftverschmutzung aus Kraftwerken schadet den Bäumen sehr.
danger *n* [ˈdeɪnʒə] — Gefahr, Bedrohung
Heavy traffic **is a danger to** the environment. — Dichter Verkehr ist eine Gefahr für die Umwelt.
threaten *v* [ˈθretn] — drohen, bedrohen
Noise threatens our health as much as smog does. — Lärm bedroht unsere Gesundheit genauso wie verschmutzte Luft.
▶

Lernstufe 1: Grundwortschatz auf Weiß

Grammatik systematisch erweitern und wiederholen

In der **Englischen Grammatik im Griff** werden die wichtigen grammatischen Themen knapp und übersichtlich dargestellt.

Das Wichtigste im Überblick:
- übersichtliche Tabellen der grundlegenden Formen
- Erklärungen zu den wesentlichen Schwierigkeiten
- Übungen mit Lösungen

142 Seiten, ISBN 3-12-560956-9

some, any

I bought **some** bananas. – *Ich habe ein paar Bananen gekauft.*
Anybody upstairs can help you. – *Jeder da oben kann Dir helfen.*
She did**n't** say **anything**. – *Sie sagte nichts.*

I like **some** fruit.

I do**n't** like **some** fruit.

I like **any** fruit.

I do**n't** like **any** fruit.

Some bezeichnet nicht alle/s, sondern nur einen Teil.

Any bezeichnet alle/s, **not any** keine/s.

any

She does**n't** drink **any** alcohol, not even beer. There are**n't any** shops near our flat.	»keinerlei«
You can take **any** bus from the station. When can you come round? – **Any** day next week. I like **any** kind of cheese.	»alle« (welche/r/s, ist nicht wichtig)
Did you take **any** photographs? Have you **any** small change, please?	»irgendwelche/s« bei offenen Fragen